Paradise Remembered

by

Ursula Vaughan Williams

(Edited by Roger Buckley
with the assistance of Joyce Kennedy)

Albion Music Ltd

First edition 2002

ISBN Number: 0-9528706-3-0

Published by Albion Music Ltd, a division of The Ralph
Vaughan Williams Society
(Registered charity number 1017175)

Printed in England by Basingstoke Press

<u>Contents</u>

Publisher's Note   i

Editor's Introduction   ii

1.   Early Life   1

2.   Michael   30

3.   On the Road Again   53

4.   War and Sorrow   80

5.   John's Death   122

6.   Peace   139

7.   Ralph, Marriage and Happiness   158

8.   Aftermath   197

      Photographs between pages 138 and 139

      Index   225

Publisher's Note

When the Ralph Vaughan Williams Society published *The Collected Poems of Ursula Vaughan Williams* in 1996, we were delighted to bring back into circulation poetry of originality and beauty. Ursula had begun writing poetry at the age of ten and her sense of atmosphere, vivid descriptive power and eye for detail also distinguishes her autobiography, *Paradise Remembered*. It is a remarkable story with, at its heart, her enduring relationship with Ralph Vaughan Williams. Their collaboration was a success, both personally – they married in 1953 – and artistically. For this reason, the RVW Society is honoured to be able to publish Ursula's autobiography. It provides unique insights into one of the most important relationships in RVW's life, one that was vital to the composer's astonishing creativity in the last decades of his long life. This book, moreover, demonstrates Ursula's remarkable achievements in her own right.

The RVW Society and its publishing subsidiary, Albion Music Ltd., would like to record a special thanks to Joyce Kennedy for her help with proof reading and with the index. In addition, we are particularly grateful to Ursula Vaughan Williams for making available to us her extensive collection of photographs and for providing permission to reproduce a number of these in this book. All photographs, to the best of our knowledge, are the copyright of Ursula Vaughan Williams. Finally, we are grateful to Simon Bunyan and all those at Basingstoke Press who have worked so hard to publish this book speedily and professionally.

Stephen Connock MBE
Chairman
The Ralph Vaughan Williams Society

February 2002

Editor's Introduction

Ursula Vaughan Williams wrote the greater part of her autobiography in the late 1970s. Although she contemplated publication at that time, the project remained on her files. In 1999, while I was compiling a catalogue of her numerous collaborations with composers of songs, oratorios and operas, Ursula showed me the manuscript and agreed with my suggestion that it be prepared for publication. Many agreeable meetings followed, during which Ursula's vision of the work became clear. She decided to leave its scope largely unchanged, and not to attempt to bring her story fully up to date.

It is a pleasure to acknowledge the great help that I received from Eva Hornstein, Michael Kennedy and, in particular, Joyce Kennedy, who also compiled the index.

Many of the situations described in the later part of this book will be familiar to readers of Ursula's celebrated *R.V.W. – A Biography of Ralph Vaughan Williams*. However, the tone is here more personal, and what emerges is a clear and accurate picture of a woman whose dedication to two husbands, the second of whom was a great composer, did not obscure her own exceptional accomplishments as a writer and poet.

In her late poem *Remembering Paradise*, Ursula defines that ideal place as being:

> *'where friends, word-charmed, delight each other*
> *with wit, with kindness and with dancing grace.'*

This work is the embodiment of such civilised harmony; in these pages we can perceive and celebrate Ursula's own special 'dancing grace'.

Roger Buckley

Chapter 1: Early Life

I was conceived in Venice and born in Malta at the Auberge de France, a house near the battlements of Valletta where the French knights had lived until 1798. I was able to start my life at such a romantic address because my maternal grandfather, Arthur Penton, was GOC Malta and my father, Robert Ferguson Lock, then a gunner captain, was his ADC. My parents had a small house nearby, in Windmill Street (then Molino à Vento, named as were all the streets in Valletta, in Italian). My mother returned to the more comfortable and better staffed house for my birth. I was my parents' first child and a very great disappointment, for they, or at any rate my mother, had hoped for a son. However my grandparents were delighted with me and I was looked after by a gentle and loving Maltese peasant nurse, Carmela, nourished on the milk of a little donkey, clothed in fine Indian muslin dresses, and generally made much of. I cut my first tooth at Verdala Palace where we were all staying on a visit to the Governor whose time, in those days, was divided between his palaces of Verdala, St. Anton and Valletta.

I spent the first year of my life in the delightful Mediterranean climate. I learned to see where blue sea, rose-oleanders, orange trees and noble architecture were the everyday scenery; I learned to hear where the daily sounds were bells, fireworks, the sound of hooves as ponies trotted to and fro drawing either the little canopied carriages in which everyone travelled, or country carts, and the pattering and bleating of flocks of goats as they were driven through the streets to be milked on doorsteps of the poorer citizens. Before memory started to catalogue and name these pleasures my grandfather was posted to Devonport and there, in 1912, we all settled into Government House. Carmela was left behind and a young Norland nanny, Noonie, took charge of me and of spacious nursery quarters with a view over Plymouth Sound. Here my conscious, as well as my social, life began.

My grandfather was to me a lively and friendly figure. He and my grandmother had married young, when he was a gunner subaltern serving in India where she had come as a girl of seventeen, with her slightly older sister, straight from Cheltenham Ladies' College and the firm rule of Miss Buss and Miss Beale, to look after their father who was a judge. His wife looked after the girls when their father was unable to go out with them. She and my grandfather met at a dance, at many dances; white gloves, fans, frangipani, waltzes and finally kisses, led to marriage. It was an unsuitable marriage. My grandfather was cheerful, selfish, unintellectual, extravagant, fond of parties and ladies. My grandmother was deeply unselfish, shy, religious and would have liked a great deal more education than she had had, exiled as she had been from her parents' life in India and looked after by guardians. How she had ever managed to get to a proper school for even a short while I do not know. However, she enjoyed India, where at some point early in her marriage she was the only woman riding with the Regiment during some border incident on the Afghan frontier and had to journey back to civilization looked after by a small detachment of soldiers while my grandfather attended to warfare.

He must have been a good officer for, by the time I remember him, he had had interesting jobs, including a command in New Zealand, which my mother, their only child, had found delightful. But she and Grannie did not stay there long, for my grandfather became involved in a tremendous love affair and, on the pretext of seeing to their daughter's education, Grannie swept her off to school in Brussels, where they stayed for several years, till both my grandfather's love affair and his New Zealand job had come to an end. The episode was forgiven and after various postings they went to Edinburgh where my father, then a subaltern, was stationed. He was the fourth son of a major in the East Yorkshire Regiment who had retired early because of deafness and a broken knee cap. His family was of Scottish and English descent – a remote forefather, John Lok, as the name was spelt till the eighteenth century, had been a sort of King's messenger in the fourteenth century. There were Ferguson relations who had been bankers to Catherine the Great – a much-painted Admiral of the White, in Nelson's time - one of whose seven sons was my great-grandfather. My father's father died soon after my parents' marriage; his widow, Grannie Lock, an Anglo-Irish woman who, as I was to discover, was as good at being a grandmother as her opposite number, Grannie Penton.

At the time of my parents' meeting my father had already been stationed in India and in Mauritius. He was a good-looking young man. I was told by one of her friends that my mother had fallen in love with him very rapidly, had organised his appointment as ADC when my grandfather went to Malta and had, by dint of getting engaged to another ADC, Wilfrid Lindsell, roused him to competition and finally to a proposal. For a few dizzy days she supported two secret engagements, and finally abandoned Wilfrid for Bob. They married in May 1910, spent their honeymoon in Venice, and returned to Malta where I was born on 15th March the following year.

Of course I was unaware of all these histories and dramas in the comfort of my nursery at Devonport. Here I had a very enjoyable time; half the house was some sort of military headquarters, filled with young officers who had tea in Grannie's drawing room every day where, as was the custom of the time, I was sent down dressed in white to spend an hour or so of social life each day, which I enjoyed enormously. All these captains and subalterns paid me great attention, drank small cups of tea from my rose-patterned dolls' tea set, and generally pampered and amused me. I do not remember my parents at all at this time. My grandparents and Noonie and the young men were the characters in my life.

During the early summer of 1914 my parents had taken a little house, Tamarisk Cottage, at Mawgan Porth in Cornwall. I remember that well, the front garden with round pebbles instead of grass, bushes of purple Hebe, with leaves fascinatingly folded in pairs, as clever as Chinese boxes or Russian dolls, diminishing as one unfolded them; the wide sandy beach, and pools where I bathed in innocent nudity; and the coastguard who lived in the only other cottage and kept pigs. When clothed I wore linen suits that had been outgrown by a cousin, Stephen Vernon, and the coastguard thought that I was a boy.

The Government House years were the best part of my childhood; I remember much about them. Tall daffodils, and later cushions of lady's slipper in the garden; hay parties, parties on grandfather's official launch, watching and listening to the band playing outside the house on Sunday mornings, are all recorded by snapshots, but the memories of scent and touch are still vivid, though probably reinforced by those fading pictures.

My brother was born on 7th August 1914. I don't remember having any particular feelings about this event for more interesting things were happening, such as being taken down to the basement to see where we should go when zeppelin raids started – a stimulating idea as the cellars were mysterious and there was a stove sprouting with flames, which I was told provided our hot water. A few days later Noonie and I were leaning out of the nursery windows waving bath towels in salute as the troopships left full of young soldiers going to the war.

My father had a very bad riding accident, in which he was cut, bruised, and concussed. The house was full of whispers and rumours about his health. When John, my infant brother, came to share my nursery, the tea parties ended. There were fewer young officers to amuse me – though at Christmas that year the remaining ones gave me clockwork toys which I was allowed to look at as they raced them up and down the ballroom floor on Boxing Day morning, where yesterday's Christmas tree, having yielded up its presents, burnt out its candles, stood forlornly in the morning light.

Soon after this my father was posted to other places, and the peripatetic life began as my mother, with Noonie in charge of John and me, followed in his wake from furnished rooms to furnished house. Sutton Veny on Salisbury Plain, Ripon, Woolwich: each has some small memory attached.

Later my father served in France, was severely wounded, losing an eye, then spending many weeks in the Herbert Hospital on the Embankment in London. After this his work led him into the technical side of military life, but first he convalesced at Camberley. I remember winter there, pine trees and ice-covered pools among the dead bracken, purple tweed winter coats with velvet collars for John and me, and going to kindergarten. That was a horrid experience, for I went filled with excitement and without foreboding. There was a boy called Billy, son of friends of friends of my parents from Devonport days. His nanny and mine used to go for boring daily walks together, each pushing a younger child in a pram, and Billy and I walked and talked together. So naturally enough, on the first morning of term I sat down at an empty desk beside him. At eleven o'clock glasses of milk were distributed, and while I was wondering if the beastly stuff had to be drunk, a small pink-and-blonde child called Angela came up to me and threw her milk all over me. I don't think she said a word, but I knew then that she was Billy's last term's love, and in a flash I understood all about triangles and jealousies. It may have relieved her feelings, but it did neither of us any good with the faithless Billy, for he took up, almost at once, with a girl who had a fairy-cycle[1].

---

[1] A child's bicycle

Camberley was where I was suddenly enchanted by rhyme, and I used to go round muttering long strings of words that rhymed, a habit that maddened my elders when they overheard my incantations. This helped to pass the time when my walks were no longer accompanied by Billy.

There is one other, and a very different memory of Camberley, or at least of a dream I had, the first vivid and coherent and memorable dream of my life. I seemed to be awake, lying on top of the world, leaning on a parapet of earth and looking into an immense depth of space, and night, blue and surrounding, where many other globes, light or fire-coloured, were circling below, around, and above. It was silent, mysterious and amazing, but not at all frightening. When, as a fourteen-year-old, I read 'I saw eternity the other night' I knew exactly what the poet Henry Vaughan[2] meant.

Whenever my parents were involved in a move, which was sometimes as often as once or twice a year, we were dispatched to stay with one of our grandmothers. Being very fond of both I remember well leaving one to stay with the other, crying in homesick despair for the one I'd just parted from in the arms of the one with whom I'd arrived. This anguish was soon assuaged, and was taken in good part by both, knowing that my tribute of tears would be paid – in reverse – next time round.

I had a very happy time having measles with Grannie Penton in lodgings in Brighton – not such fun for her, as she had to queue for coal for the bedroom fires, but she read to me, endlessly, and for me 'The Assyrian came down like a wolf on the fold'[3] is for ever associated with a Red Indian head-dress I'd been given, and a little dead fish, silvery pink like the winter light over the sea, lying on the shingle beach as I walked there, chanting the newly-learned words. Grannie Penton taught me to read. I used to follow her round

---

[2] Henry Vaughan (1622-1695), metaphysical poet
[3] Lord Byron (1788-1824), *The Destruction of Senaccherib*

imploring her to finish a story some of which she'd already read to me. One day she said briskly, "If you could read you would not have to wait for me." In a very few days I'd managed the last stage between short words and long sentences, so the world was mine. There were lots of books at Grannie Lock's house; she had moved from Devon, and with her daughter, my aunt, now lived at Easebourne, near Midhurst. This was a blissful place to stay. There I read historical romances left over from my father's and uncle's childhood, my aunt's copies of books by Mrs. Ewing[4], Mrs. Molesworth[5] and Miss Yonge[6], and of course *Black Beauty*[7] over which I cried a great deal, as well as *The Story of a Red Deer*[8] which made me absolutely against hunting of all kinds, as I have remained for life. The house itself – rather a dull and solid red brick house of no great age – was filled with treasures, each having a story. Great-great-grandfather's portrait as a young sailor, and one of him painted in full fig when he was an admiral, another relation as a supporting character at a noble death – was it Lord Howe? – was it the glorious first of June? Ships in full sail, miniatures of the Isle of Wight relations and pastels of some of those killed in the Indian Mutiny, great aunt Isabel's pictures of Ceylon, framed in bird's-eye maple, and her ivory workbox lined with sandalwood, so that every reel of silk or cotton smelled delicious. I had this workbox; it was a link with all my visits to Midhurst and their many pleasures. But alas, no one is sewing well now, so I have given it to the clothes museum in Bath. Grannie Lock was a superb needle-woman; she taught me to enjoy sewing. I did cross-stitch and made brilliantly coloured pin-cushions and other such things for Christmas presents from delectable scraps of silk, saffron or shocking pink or lilac, the remains of her ball dresses worn long ago in Ireland. Now a widow, she dressed in

---

[4] Juliana Ewing (1841-85): writer of books for children
[5] Mary Molesworth (1839-1921): novelist and writer of stories for children
[6] Charlotte Yonge (1823-1901): writer of fiction and of books for children
[7] The best-known work of Anna Sewell (1820-78), novelist
[8] By J.W. Fortescue (1859-1933)

black, but she wore everything with a certain dash and the taffeta dresses she put on for dinner rustled delightfully. She had very white hair and blue eyes; nothing ever ruffled her. It was calm in her house, and everything I did or wanted had her approval. The words 'naughty, disobedient, unhelpful' and 'you are old enough to know better' that were my dole at home (though never John's) were unspoken and unthought. Though her garden was small it was full of flowers. She believed that gardens grew best for those who gave flowers away – bunches of roses and dark velvet pansies were given to neighbours and friends. Whenever she travelled, Grannie Lock would scatter seeds of forget-me-not or wallflowers from the window of the train hoping they would flower suitably on the railway banks.

Both Grannie and my aunt were passionate archers, and I loved going to the Archery Club meetings at Cowdray. We used to go to Cowdray ruins most days anyhow, for our walks, to scramble about the broken stairs and look through the empty windows, imagining a life of splendour and courtly pleasure. At least I did. I was always pining for a grown-up life, and I remember well walking slowly down Grannie's very ordinary staircase, murmuring "the princess came down the marble stairs, attended by peacocks."[9]

In the autumns of the war years we used to go into Cowdray Park to collect horse chestnuts. They were, mysteriously, useful for munitions we were told, and it was our patriotic duty to find as many as we could. This was no hardship, and the thick green and spiny husks splitting open to show the glowing chestnuts, shiny from their creamy cases, were another delight for eyes and hands, a sport almost as enjoyable as searching for mushrooms or picking blackberries – free for the finding and treasure for the finder.

---

[9] UVW remembers saying this, but not hearing it; so it is probably original

As the family moved so often, we made no friends. We had a few cousins; they and children of my parents' army friends were our world of contemporaries, and not always congenial. At Midhurst there was the doctor's nephew, Yoppy, the Easebourne vicarage boys, who were alarming, and two girls whose father was vicar of Midhurst. Their mother gave us little tiny ginger nuts to eat in a wigwam under the rhododendrons in their garden. Hiawatha was a hero to me then, one of Grannie Penton's contributions to my reading, and the Brighton feathers were worn with even more conviction in Barbara and Bunty's garden.

Some time in the later part of the war, my father was stationed at the arsenal in Leeds, Noonie had left to get married and I had to do proper lessons with a governess. In the summer after our first Leeds winter my grandparents, the Pentons, took a house near Skipton. There was a stream in the garden, and we used to go for marvellous walks, or for picnics driving for some miles in a pony trap; the verges of those dusty lanes were full of blue cranesbill and meadowsweet. Sometimes, greatest pleasure of all, Grannie would call me at six and we'd go mushrooming together, barefoot in the wet grass. I noticed with surprise that she had very pretty feet.

My grandfather was a splendid ally if I really wanted anything. Once, it was to wear a new dress, not the white silk smocks that were my usual tea-time adornment, but a dashing sky-blue linen creation with pockets. I explained to him that Miss Suttle, our governess, said: "my white would do..." We worked through all the white smocks pretty briskly, for each time I was put into a fresh one he threw his walking stick into the stream and implored me to go into the water and retrieve it. I feel for Miss Suttle now, for I'm sure she'd never met such wickedness in a man before, but then it was a happy triumph as, in the dress I loved and in which I felt most worldly, I went to greet Grannie Lock and my aunt who arrived to stay with us.

Back in Leeds there were lessons, a Yorkshire cook who baked tiny cottage loaves for the nursery, and my first experience of music lessons. I loathed the piano, couldn't learn my notes, and could see no sense in the horrible sounds I made. It had no relation to the military bands, or to the sound of pipes I'd heard when some Scots regiment marched by at Sutton Veny, so I didn't and couldn't imagine any pleasure emerging from wasted hours, when I might have been reading. However I was delivered from this, for the following spring I went to Somerset with Grannie Penton to stay with her younger sister Mary and brother-in-law Richard, near Taunton[10]. The plan was for me to go to Cornwall to stay with Mrs Hicks, a good friend of my parents and the mother, now widowed, of some of my Government House playmates. She can't have been quite as terrifying as I thought her on the platform at Taunton, where I was to join her and Bill, my contemporary, the youngest of her sons. I'd never been away alone before. I screamed and clung to Grannie, lay on the platform yelling, and finally bit the station master when he tried to bundle me into the train. The great steam engine panted, puffed and left, taking Mrs Hicks and Bill towards St Columb Halt. Grannie and I, in tears of shame, remorse and despair went back to Bicknoller for a few more days, and then to Cornwall together. Finally she left me to do lessons with Bill, by then content to be in a house I came to love. I had been there before, when I was a four-year-old, and I remembered the deep-banked lanes thick with flowers at my low eye level. I suppose I was a naturally observant child, for I had learned the names and habits of flowers even then. I could never understand why the grown-ups hated crowing cocks. It was a sound that delighted and charmed me, a heraldic and fire-coloured signal from another civilization it seemed to me, lying in bed with the first glimmer of morning coming through the curtains. I liked waking early for there

---

[10] At Bicknoller, on the edge of the Quantock Hills

were all the Andrew Lang[11] Coloured Fairy Books in the house which I read with eager pleasure. I possessed *The Orange Fairy Book* myself, the rest were all new to me, full of stories of princes and princesses, talking beasts, adventures and magic from all over the world.

I had a lovely summer in Cornwall. Mrs Hicks enjoyed my visit less than I enjoyed being there. I let the hot water run away washing dolls' clothes, lost the dogs down rabbit holes, changed my clothes as many times a day as I had dresses, with the abandon of unsuppressed vanity. Bill and I fought over the watering cans for the privilege of watering the garden. I liked asparagus which came from that large and cherished garden and most of all I liked going to the sea. The great pale beaches, the caves, sinister and cold, and the rock pools with fringes of green seaweed, all remembered from other summers, were both familiar and strange. Later in the summer Grannie and Grandfather, my parents, John, and a new governess, Miss Hellon, arrived and we all stayed in a furnished house at Watergate Bay and spent each day on the beach. That summer's poet was Stevenson[12]:

Now that you have spelt your lesson lay it down and go and play

seeking shells and seaweed on the sands of Monterey,

watching all the mighty whalebones, lying buried by the breeze,

tiny sandy-pipers, and huge Pacific seas.

---

[11] Andrew Lang (1844-1912): poet, scholar and man of letters. He published twelve fairy-tale books, identified by the colours in their titles, between 1889 and 1910

[12] Robert Louis Stevenson (1850-94): novelist, poet, playwright, essayist, travel-writer and writer of children's literature

There were, of course, no mighty whalebones, but there were huge seas, hot days, cool days, long evenings, flower books that told me how the monks used to make an ointment from Eyebright to help bad sight – I brewed it, with lard, and by courtesy of the cook, for Grannie, who was always losing her glasses. She said that she had tried, but it didn't do her any good. There were single dark pink roses in the garden, pale pink shells on the beach, if one was lucky enough to find them. A cousin and her son, John's age, came to stay, a great unsuccess all round as the two boys, both about four, frequently fought and hit each other with their spades, but I kept clear of this warfare. My mother was pregnant. I thought she looked terrible and didn't know why she'd got so fat. No-one thought of telling me. Church-going started to be a problem that summer. It made Sundays horrible, for it meant a hat with an elastic, gloves, and a wasted morning sitting through interminable stuff. How I loathed 'the glorious company of the Apostles' each week; no matter how lovely a day was, no beach till the afternoon. It was both boredom and frustration and, like music lessons, it never 'took'. We used to go to church at Easebourne, but only to children's services, where we were indulged by being asked questions, so, being a non-singer but a talker, there were opportunities for invention and flights of fancy which made it more bearable, and some competition too, with the Vicarage boys. No consolation of this kind enlivened Cornish Sundays.

The Hicks boys came over to Watergate sometimes; the two elder ones were already at prep school, rather grand and aloof. They had been somewhere the last day of the holidays, and I had already gone to bed, hair done up in its knobbly bundles of curl-rags, a nightly and inescapable torture, when I was fetched. The eldest boy, another John, had flatteringly insisted that he must say goodbye to me. To my intense surprise and joy, he kissed me solemnly on the forehead. I sailed back to bed, proud and serious, feeling that life was beginning in earnest.

My sister, Rosemary, was born on November 5th 1919. John and I were at Easebourne again, out of the way for this event. I don't remember being pleased by the news and indeed it only added complications to life – a small baby was even less use as a companion than a small and illiterate brother. However, we struggled on, or at least that was how it seemed to me. Very soon after Rosemary was born we moved from a rented house at Bexley Heath to the only house my parents ever bought, the Red House at Blackheath. Father was working at Woolwich so we were near enough for him to get there by bicycle.

It was a long, low, early Georgian house with a covered verandah all along the south side, a big garden, an orchard, and a cedar tree. Mysterious brick pillars with tall wrought-iron gates stood in the garden leading from nowhere to nowhere. There was a white japonica as well as a coral one, an early white single rose, a crab-apple tree, a fig tree. There were cellars where once, we were told, there'd been a secret passage. John used the cellars a great deal. He was thin as an eel, and if there was something he didn't want to do, people he didn't want to see, he would lift the iron lid of the coal chute by the front door and drop through it and lie concealed and unreachable on top of the piles of coal, for no-one wanted to climb over that to get him out. He emerged when he felt it expedient, black faced, smelling of coal, unrepentant and unpunished.

There were a lot of pleasures in the years we lived there. The best of all was a dog. He belonged to someone who was going to have him put down. My parents heard of this and said they'd have him. My mother loved dogs; she'd missed having one since her marriage, now it looked as if we were settled for a long time so she was delighted. Bruce was a young, wildly intelligent, gentle near-Labrador. We all loved him and he made our daily walks in Greenwich Park infinitely more amusing; when we went rowing in miniature boats on one of the ponds on the Heath, he ran round the edge barking in an encouraging way. He developed a great fondness for our cat, Elizabeth, and used to fetch her at night to share his bed. Bruce was, all his life, wonderful as a comforter; when I was unhappy he would sit very close and allow himself to be cried on. I never allowed anyone other than Bruce to see me cry, for it was a matter of pride to hide tears for injustice, loneliness and inadequacy, so I cried in the lavatory, safely locked in, or in bed, or on Bruce's warm and kindly shoulder, and when I emerged from any of these sessions with despair I could be in command of both my voice and my behaviour.

My unhappiness was mixed with a strong sense of injustice, for I never could do well in my mother's eyes, whereas whatever John did was unquestionably right. He and I aggravated each other. I never wanted to 'run about and play' so I was always in some sort of trouble. I never felt particularly liked, let alone loved, by anyone but my grandparents at that time. While we lived at the Red House Grannie Lock died. I was taken to see her about a week before, an uncomfortable and unnatural visit to that friendly house at Easebourne where she was propped up in bed. I felt that I was meant to say something special, but what? and how? When my father told me early one morning soon after that she had died I remember thinking, 'I ought to cry'. But I had no desire to cry and it all seemed very remote. My grandfather Penton died later the same year. I was sent to stay with friends at the seaside and I came home unaware of the immense change his death had made to Grannie's life, though I realized that she now had more time to spend with me and rejoiced for that.

We had two more governesses at the Red House. A bony one with frizzy red hair who was no fun at all was succeeded by the nicest we ever had – Mademoiselle – who came daily by bus from London. She was fat and plain, always dressed in brown. She had had a life of much romantic sorrow. She had been the only daughter of a rich man, well educated, happy and secure. Then, within a month, her much loved fiancé was drowned in a sailing accident, her father's business failed owing to a dishonourable partner's wickedness, so he shot himself, then her mother died of a broken heart, and something calamitous also happened to her only brother. So, from having everything, she found herself solitary and penniless. Although she did not look like the heroine of a tragedy, she brought a firm courage to life, her French was beautiful and, besides lessons, we had delicious tea times with her, when she told stories of her other pupils or, after tea, she would stay for an hour helping us to make Christmas presents and paper chains or, in summer, to press flowers or to draw them. She read to us and taught me poems, La Fontaine, of course, and the sad little poem on Monsieur du Perier's daughter, *'Comme une rose elle à vecu l'espace d'un matin'* – words she spoke with much feeling, thinking perhaps of her handsome lost fiancé.

Even better, we read Racine together, and I thundered through such speeches as:
*'C'estait pendant l'horreur d'une profonde nuit
Ma mère Jezabel devant moi c'est montrée
Comme au jour de sa mort, pompeusement parée ...'*

This was grown-up life indeed, the grand drama for which I thirsted.

We lived at Blackheath for about three years. Besides my grandfather's death and Grannie Lock's death, I was dramatically near death myself. Always a great one for catching colds, one winter I had an abscess in my ear. For three weeks of alarming pain Grannie valiantly shared sleepless nights, reading Walter Scott aloud. She enjoyed the novels as much as I did, which helped me to sustain violent and prolonged misery. She took me to Broadstairs to convalesce, which I enjoyed, though how poor Grannie spent her evenings in 'rooms' there, I can't imagine; probably letter-writing, for she was always a splendid correspondent. However, when we went home I had ear-ache again, was rushed to a specialist, and the next day a trestle table appeared and I was operated on at home for a mastoid. I remember the horrible, stifling sensation of the chloroform mask, and my last waking thought as I finally succumbed to its power was that I had kicked someone really hard. When I returned to consciousness I was pampered and admired, and felt none too ill until the first dressing was done. The pure clear pain of that dressing was the discovery of a new dimension.

That summer, because I was not allowed to get my head under water, and must never in life dive, we stayed at a country village near Seaton; we went to all the places of my father's boyhood. Musbury[13] where his parents had lived was near, and all the village rejoiced to see 'Master Bobby' and told us stories of fearful things he'd done as a boy. He disclaimed most of them, but it certainly showed him to us in a new light. His brothers, whom my mother tended to patronize by using the prefix 'poor', were by now scattered.

'Poor' Fred, a major in the East Yorkshire Regiment, had led a jolly bachelor life in Beverley enjoying race-going, dinners in the Mess and, undoubtedly, ill-chosen mistresses (one cropped up much later on) until deafness caused him to retire; and Grannie Lock's death made finding a home for Lily, the only sister, a family concern. Stupidly she and he consented to share a house; it had very little advantage for either. Lily was ill-educated – being, as she was, the only girl, no-one had bothered, but she had a lively disposition, adored parties, and should have married one of the young men with whom she had spent her youth dancing or playing tennis at month-long house parties with cousins in Ireland. But, in true Victorian style, she had had a driving accident, and spent the rest of her long life being considered delicate. I don't think she was at all, but in some mysterious way the fun stopped, and she was always at home, though occasionally she escaped to Italy or France for a few weeks in the winter. She was a darling, and full of wonderful stories of

---

[13] A village between Seaton and Axminster in Devon

strange and eccentric relations, and all sorts of goings-on in the past.

'Poor' Perceval had been in the Navy, then left to settle in Canada, to marry a Canadian girl, and to die young. His widow and two daughters lived in Vancouver. When his widow 'Poor' Muriel died the girls were brought up by her parents, and very nice they were.

'Poor' Walter farmed in Ireland, and his wife Mary, a tough little woman, was alleged to have gone out in her night-dress to shoot rebels, successfully, they said. They had one son, Peter, who like the Canadian girls had the family face, a strong likeness to our grandmother.

'Poor' Henry had been a Marine and had died on board HMS Bulwark long ago when she blew up in harbour.

The villagers in Musbury had loved Grannie Lock. They still spoke of her in such a way that it was clear that she had been the authority to whom everyone turned in times of crisis. Fifty years after she had left Musbury the grand-daughters of village girls who had worked for her at Mountfield were sending bunches of primroses to my aunt for Easter, and two or three of them came to her funeral and told me what their grandmothers had told them of 'the old days'.

We spent one summer holiday at Selsey, but that summer we never had a tide low enough to find the remains of the forest that once grew where the beach ends in sea, nor did we go out in a boat to look for the drowned monastery from which the Saxon carvings in Chichester Cathedral had come. But the main part of life was at Blackheath. Dancing classes were in London, the journey on the 53 bus was a weekly term-time pleasure taking me to bob about, bare footed in a yellow tunic.

There were excursions to the London Museum with an old friend of my father's, Colonel Shakespeare, who devoted himself to my pleasure, showing me the lively proofs of history – little scenes of London as it had been, the necklaces found hidden that had belonged to some Tudor girl, chains of tiny flowers made of enamel and pearl, as well as furniture, china, glass, teaching me to observe the links between things and people, between then and now. These excursions ended with tea at his flat, and then being put on the bus for home. They stirred my imagination, taught me the pleasure of museums, and showed me how delightful it was to be taken about by someone who appeared to enjoy talking to me, answering questions, feeding curiosity with information.

As a girl my mother had been a regular visitor to Sir Frank Benson's Shakespeare seasons at Stratford-upon-Avon. She probably went to the Old Vic fairly regularly, and once my brother and I were taken to *Henry V*. I don't remember who was in the play, but it was pure delight and glory, much more exciting than the usual Christmas treat of *Where the Rainbow Ends*. *Peter Pan* had been tried too, but I didn't like it.

In 1923 my father was posted to Malta. The Red House was sold, Bruce our dog went to live with friends, furniture was packed, and we embarked at Southampton in an ancient troopship, Hecuba. John and I shared a cabin with our latest governess, Miss Horsfall, a sad, unloved and elderly woman who was as seasick as I was, until we reached Gibraltar. After that we all enjoyed the silky pale calm of the Mediterranean. We reached Malta and came into the Grand Harbour on Easter morning. Huge battlements of golden stone towered above us, excitement prevailed. Before long we disembarked and drove by wagonette to Tigné barracks. Our quarter was a new house with only a road between us and a steep path leading down to the bathing club and the sea. The water was deep and absolutely clear, fringed with greeny-gold bushy seaweed that furled and unfurled in the gentle movement of the water.

Malta was full of quiet and secret villages. Women still wore the faldetta, a black cloak that fell from a curved stiffened top that covered the head and was clutched at the waist or hip; it flowed and its blackness framed the pretty young faces, or the wise-looking old ones. The older women were all dressed in black, the younger ones in cotton, grown, dyed and spun on the island in sea colours or stripes of white and the magenta pink of sainfoin. There were unfamiliar wild flowers, dark blue pimpernel and fringes of lemon yellow oxalis grew below all walls. Women still drove flocks of goats through the streets, and milked them into jugs on doorsteps. All the traffic was horse or donkey drawn, carrozzi and things known as country carts, something like a five-bar gate on high wheels, that carried produce and people from place to place. The harbour traffic was done by djhaisa, boats with gondola-like prow and stern, painted in brilliant colours, each with an eye on the prow, rowed by a man standing to handle two oars. Colours, sounds, and smells were brilliant, loud and pungent. The days were differently shaped, too. Lessons were early, about half-past eleven we went to bathe. There were lots of army families and some naval families there; the wives sat about and gossiped between swimming; the children were in and out of the water, mostly in, till lunch time. Then the same pattern after siestas, till the grown-ups went home to dress for dinner parties and the children to go to bed. Because we lived so close to the sea I was able to go back for a last swim at dusk. My siblings John and Rosemary had to go to their beds, but I escaped, and would swim out to the raft, the island fading from the orchid colour it became at sunset, to pearly grey, the sea a paler grey, with faint pink and gold dapplings. Lying on the raft, almost eye-level with the water, turned away from the land, I had often the whole Mediterranean to myself. Sometimes the two Maltese boys who worked at the Club would bathe at this time, and practise diving; both were beautiful divers and their concentration on perfection seemed a miracle of fearlessness.

There was one other pastime, one that I was expected to hail with joy, and that was riding. We were taken down to the Marsa race course. I was scared out of my wits as the pony I rode went faster and faster. I held on to the saddle, couldn't manage the reins, and generally made a fool of myself and did not dare to say I found it horrible. It wasn't so bad when I graduated to our old grey horse who also pulled the wagonette for, accompanied by a groom, I went for what could be described as long walks on horseback. There was no open country and nothing more than an occasional trot was expected of me, so I could go through villages and along the narrow roads westward that were never out of sight of the sea with its little cross-sailed flights of Gozo boats that looked like butterflies.

There were other diversions: dancing classes, which were rather pleasant, an awful few months in the Girl Guides which was an incomprehensible way of wasting time. Who, in their senses, would try to light a fire with two matches when a boxful was available, do first aid, or play idiotic team games or worst of all, wear uniform? I loathed the whole thing and soon managed to get myself dismissed for dishonourable conduct, which was less dreadful than it sounds – going to the meetings by cab, sixpence worth of pocket money, or failing to remember to wear a tie.

The most exciting places in Malta were the Hypogeum and the temples by the sea, Hagiar Qim and Mnaidra. They had not been tidied up for tourists then. We could see the carved stones almost buried in wild asphodel, scramble about between the standing stones, finding the smaller semi-circular enclosures, grassy floored with perhaps a goat or two tethered there. Hagiar Qim is the higher one, Mnaidra is close to the sea, looking south towards Africa, a quiet, smaller, Stonehenge, a temple for the gods whose needs and offerings were forgotten, but where there was still some brooding power. The Hypogeum is a strange underground place, to which one went lighted by a flaring torch carried by a guide; there were piles of bones, lying in darkly hollowed pits in the rock. One of the braver children scooped up a handful of them and kept them in a jam jar at her bedside. She was the hero to my princess in a play that one of the mothers wrote for us to act during the following winter. I discovered later that the writer was a great-great-great-niece of Jane Austen's – small, nut brown, with dark eyes and great liveliness, she adapted the story of 'the princess who couldn't laugh' for us and wrote in lots of small parts, so that when the autumn brought bathing to an end the children were kept busy with rehearsals. The play was done in our drawing-room; a cousin in the Navy had sent ship's carpenters who rigged up a stage and lighting for us. Cousins in the Navy were a great asset and we were asked to children's parties on ships and sometimes, in a grown-up way, out to lunch. Grannie came out for Christmas, and the comfort of having her there was extreme. By this time Miss Horsfall had left. She was a dismal governess and was succeeded by visiting teachers. A delightful French woman who had escaped from the Russian Revolution with the family she had long lived with in Russia taught us French, an Italian gave lessons to my mother and me, while her sister strove in vain to make me like the schoolroom piano. Best of all, my cousin Veronica du Boulay, to whom I had been bridesmaid, came to live in Malta where her husband's ship was stationed. Every week she spent at least one morning telling me about pictures and about painters. I think these lessons were called Art Appreciation. They were enjoyable and exciting, and gave me the beginning of a pleasure that has been increasing ever since.

To fill in the one serious educational gap, my father decided that he would teach me arithmetic. He devised sums based on snails climbing walls and slipping back, and other such pleasant matters, but I could not master the principles involved. It was a dismal failure, and even father, who was a patient man, grew exasperated. Our sessions always ended in my tears. Once he went so far as to throw a chair at me. It missed, probably intentionally, but after that, by mutual consent, there was no more arithmetic. The word innumerate had not then entered our vocabularies. I was very glad when I first heard it, for it was one I can claim as a definition of my state. Since growing up, I have never suffered the slightest discomfort from not being able to use arithmetic. On the first of January I found my first wild narcissus; soon the rocky ground was covered with miniature iris and low-growing flowers of pink and blue and yellow. In Miss Hughes-Hallett's garden between her low house and the sea there was a bed of the darkest blue hyacinths. Winter storms, long ridges of waves sweeping over the bathing club rocks, subsided. We looked forward to more swimming, but our Malta year came to a sudden close as my father was posted to Woolwich to be Secretary of the Ordnance Committee. He left us to pack and follow. It was dreadful to leave, but sadness was mitigated by a promise of a visit to Rome. Grannie, still with us, shared my excitement as, spared a troopship's misery, we went by night ferry to Syracuse and by train through Sicily, flowering even more magically than Malta, to cross at Messina to begin the longer train journey northwards.

We stayed in Rome for a week. Grannie suffered from other people's garlic-eating so she carried eau de Cologne – soaked handkerchiefs behind which she took refuge in trams or buses. She and I went to the Colosseum, to the Appian Way, to the Forum and to Castel St. Angelo, and to Hadrian's Villa, carpeted with blue windflowers. I didn't like St Peter's, but the Sistine Chapel was up to all the expectations that Veronica had awakened with her picture books and discussions. It was a very well-spent week for both Grannie and me. The rest of the outfit, my mother, our pretty Maltese maid, Connie, John and Rosemary, had also been to the Colosseum and St. Peter's and Hadrian's Villa, otherwise it was the Pincio gardens for them and, I think, rather a lot of boredom.

We spent Easter in Brussels and then, after a very rough crossing, arrived in England. We lived for a few months in a furnished flat at the Cromwell Road end of Addison Road; a sad place after Malta. I was sent to Norland Place School, about a mile away. Each morning I started too late and had to run, until I discovered that some girls came in to the Assembly after prayers. I joined them, rather to their surprise. This also puzzled the authorities as I was not thought to be Jewish and so allowed to miss prayers, but nothing was ever said about it. I found it a great convenience.

Owing to my entire lack of Latin, and my dreadful mathematics, I didn't do well. But there was one woman, Miss Flavel, who taught ancient history and all things were worth enduring for her lessons. Suddenly it was observable that facts of history, of literature, of art, related to each other. Those days with Colonel Shakespeare at the London Museum, the extraordinary section about ancient Egypt, pictures of the mummies, and the hawk-headed gods – classical myths, in the back of my Bible, which I much preferred to the actual scriptures – were each a part of the world she taught us about. If only all teaching were like hers I felt I could have learned everything, even Latin grammar, with ease.

It was the summer term and we had to play cricket. We were taken to and fro by bus; I found myself sitting next to a child called Veronica Wedgwood. She was the same age as I was, but in a higher form. We talked about Shakespeare, literature and the Gods of Olympus. It was all very stimulating, the only thing that made this extraordinary game bearable. No-one told me the rules, not what to do, only where to stand, in some far-off place. I looked at the sky and the trees, and was very surprised when a ball hit my hand. I went to the games mistress and asked if I need come to cricket as it seemed a waste of time and dangerous. This was not well received and I had to continue to attend. However, I suffered no injury at any other session, and there were the conversations with Veronica on the bus journeys to look forward to. During one of them she mentioned that a composer called Ralph Vaughan Williams was her cousin. The name caught my fancy, for one of our many governesses had had, once, a pupil called Ralph. He seemed to have been a tiresome paragon of learning and virtue, but even so I thought then that his was a most romantic name. Both she and Veronica pronounced it properly, without sounding the 'l'. I was not at all sure what a composer did.

After the summer holidays, spent that year at Painswick in Gloucestershire where Grannie had taken a house and settled, we moved to Woolwich Arsenal where we lived in an eighteenth century house in Dial Square. Our furniture had come back from Malta, we had exchanged Blackheath and Greenwich Park for the riverside marshes and the river itself. It wasn't at all a bad place to live. After working hours when all the people employed in the Arsenal had streamed out past our house, there was empty quiet, and we could go to the riverside and down towards Plumstead marshes; there were lots of wild flowers, and long stretches of nothing much where Bruce took the exercise a large dog needs; he had been restored to us by the friends who had looked after him while we were abroad. Now he too had working hours, for he attached himself to the police at the Arsenal gate and kept unauthorised dogs from entering. These self-appointed duties went to his head, and when we stayed with Grannie at Painswick he continued to keep a sharp eye on local dogs, and indeed it was said that all the small white dogs in Painswick had paws in slings or were on crutches during Bruce's visits to Gloucestershire. There was a place that John and I used to take him for walks, by a stream in the valley between Painswick and Bull's Cross. We took a ball to throw across the stream to make him jump over to fetch it. It was a game he enjoyed. One day the ball fell into a mass of marsh plants growing round a willow enclosed by a sunken wall two or three feet deep. We'd never climbed down into this place because it looked so muddy, but of course we went to get the ball. Bruce refused to join us, and as soon as we'd got in, both John and I were seized with an absolute terror, and scrambled out and ran away as far as we had breath to run. There was a mill the other side of the lane that led downhill from the village and I heard later that a miller who lived there once had murdered his wife. It must have been in that place, so stricken and fearful an atmosphere remained. Long afterwards, when I was extraordinarily happy, I was being driven down that lane. I stopped the driver to go to see if I could find the place for I felt that no lingering horror could withstand my power at that moment. But the course of the stream had changed, the old willow tree had gone, and it was no longer the place I remembered with so much fear.

Once we moved to Woolwich I could no longer be a day girl at the Norland School. My first boarding school was at Bussage[14] in Gloucestershire; one of the two head-mistresses was the niece of the great Miss Beale of Cheltenham Ladies' College, who had been Grannie's headmistress. She looked like a little shrew-mouse and taught Latin. Her partner, Miss Johnston, was large, fierce, and against swearing. She was also against my being hopeless at arithmetic, so I was put in the bottom form where I added up little squares of figures, crying with hopeless rage when the answer was different each time. Each time I added, the figures took me longer to do. The other lessons were rather boring too. Then there was netball, icy cold walks before breakfast, and a weekly ration of about four inches of candle to be the going-to-bed and getting-up light. The chilly spring term ended early with an outbreak of mumps. The next term wasn't so bad as the weather made our early morning walks quite pleasant. There were no summer games as far as I remember. We did have a paper chase one Saturday but, averse to exertion, I sat under a may tree until the others returned, then joined in, in an appropriately modest place, at the end of the string of hot and exhausted runners.

My family had decided that none of us was musical, though my father's mother and my mother's father had been happy performers of drawing-room songs. My father said that he knew only the tunes of the Regimental Slow March, *God Save the King,* and *Onward, Christian Soldiers* and I had never sung a note in my life. At Bussage a master came to teach the whole school – there were about forty of us – to sing. I managed to disguise my inability by opening and shutting my mouth, until one day when having handed out a song called *Linden Lea*, he walked between each row of girls

---

[14] A few miles east of Stroud

listening carefully. I rather liked the poem, and there was
Veronica's cousin's name on the music – but I couldn't croak
anything that was remotely like the tune the others managed so
easily. "You", said the music master, "need not come to the rest of
the singing classes."

We were all found guilty when Miss Johnston summoned the
middle-age-group, fourteen to fifteen year olds, to ask if we had
ever blasphemed. Confused, we all confessed to damn and blasts,
and were punished as well as being consigned to predestined hell-
fire, did we not mend our ways. I was glad to leave that school. I
heard no more about it until years later when I was told that in her
great old age Miss Johnston staged a full-dress rehearsal for her
funeral, with pall-bearers and mourners – which she, at least,
enjoyed. Floral tributes were also exacted.

My next school was run by a clutch of three headmistresses who
were sisters: Miss de la Mare who ran the house; Miss Guilbert de
la Mare and her inseparable peke, Toto, who took prayers and who
taught arithmetic and French grammar; and Miss Kathy de la Mare
who taught scripture. St Margaret's was one of the many
Folkestone schools. There I made some pleasant friends and moved
through three years with them, in the same form. Only nine of us
from start to finish, so we all knew each other well, battling through
our Junior and Senior Oxford Examinations: Joan, pale, pretty,
who married young; Pamela, the cleverest of us all who owned
delectable things like emerald green shoes; Doreen, a sympathetic
games captain who always put me to play opposite Patty at awful
lacrosse because we were both so bad at games (she forbade us to
join in as we always got it wrong, so we spent our time on the
games fields in conversation, which we both enjoyed). Sybil was
tall with a roman nose, good at mathematics. Eleanor, another day
girl, who seemed to move in a secret world, so uncommunicative
was she. Freda and Winifred were my closest friends. Freda wore
glasses with thick lenses which made her eyes seem even larger
than they were naturally, candid, kind, industrious, and usually

homesick. Winifred had the only really attractive mother, red-haired, blue-eyed and beautifully dressed. Winifred had not inherited these dramatic good looks but had an easy charm which, allied to the fact that it was supposed that her father was killed in the war – actually her mother had divorced him and had married again and was obviously in love with her second husband – gave her a sort of incalculable advantage over the rest of us whose parents seemed to have no romantic charm. Freda lived at Eltham, so she was also a holiday friend, and Winifred was my companion in explorations of literature and romance as well as, for a few fearful weeks, religion, when we were in training for confirmation. Miss Guilbert would summon the little group of pilgrims-to-holiness to her bedroom, a shaded green light making us all look like hobgoblins as we crouched around the gas fire, Toto snorting horribly in the background. The local vicar was a fervent and popular preacher; his sermons were very, very long and we had to go to both morning and evening services. On the eve of the confirmation this vicar called to interview each candidate alone. "Now", said Patty, "he'll tell us what happened between the Virgin Mary and the Holy Ghost." Nothing was said on this enthralling subject, but we were each given small illuminated copies of the Communion Service. Winifred and I, who slept in the same four-bedded room, had been plunged in the Christian Year and Thomas à Kempis, reading to each other those sultry works. However, when it came to the ceremony itself, "I'm using talcum powder on my face, it's not so deceitful as real powder," said Winifred, boldly advancing to meet the Holy Ghost pale as a lily, dusted with Yardley's. I thought that she was probably right. We had lots of make-up bought for us by the day girls – but following this example of virtue I too became a white faced wraith, using heavily scented Du Barry's Golden Dawn. No Holy Ghost touched us with a silver feather or a tongue of fire, and it was all very disappointing. We went to communion, and still no exaltation; sweet wine, which was horrid, church three times instead of twice on Sundays made passionate atheists of Winifred, Patty and me – a sinister bond, one that made my life difficult at home in the holidays. As well as trying to avoid going to communion without too much trouble from the family, there was the trouble of trying to avoid the Garrison riding school. This, fortunately, was a Christmas holiday diversion only, well-intended by my parents for John and me so that we might learn to have good seats and to jump. The cavernous riding school, the horses, brown, chestnut and bay, the other children, all agog with pleasure, and the sergeant instructor, filled me with terror. When it came to jumping I decided I couldn't bear it. Stupidly, cowardly, deceitfully, I invented headaches, tried to sprain my ankle, anything rather than confess the truth, that I was miserable so far away from the ground. I don't suppose they'd have been distressed, nor do I think it would have crossed their minds that any child of theirs could be terrified by such – to them – pleasurable exercise. I lied my way through the Monday and Thursday mornings far more successfully than through Sundays.

I didn't like school, the bells that chopped life into sections, the cold bedrooms and, though I didn't recognise it then, the lack of intellectual excitement in most lessons. However history and literature were tolerably well taught, French grammar and arithmetic were emotional and exhortative experiences with Miss Guilbert. I had some extra history lessons when the rest of the form had singing, work outside our exam syllabus that was for pleasure.

Then there were lectures – sometimes concerts, to which the older girls went, mostly at the theatre. I liked the ones that were real lectures. I didn't understand the chamber concerts – a sad waste of Thibaud, Cortot and Casals, which now I regret. One of the younger-than-I girls had a father who had been on the Irvine and Mallory Everest expedition[15] and talked about it and showed us slides of the great views from unimaginable heights of rock and snow which had frightening splendour and woke imagination and inspired poems.

---

[15] 1924

There were summer outings to Dymchurch where the sands were all ours and Romney Marsh shimmered in June heat, to St. Margaret's Bay, to Canterbury. Walks sometimes instead of games, when we would go along the road below the Leas, close to the sea – excitingly wild if there was a storm, for waves broke over the road and over us. In lessons we acted our way through *A Midsummer Night's Dream* for our Junior Oxford exam., *Julius Caesar* for Senior Oxford. Helena and Cassius were my parts – both characters I appreciated being involved with. We had a small library. I read both *Tess of the d'Urbervilles* and *Jude the Obscure*[16] one summer, as well as Arthur Waley's translations of Chinese poems. These helped me through an oral French exam, for the examiner's great interest in Chinese literature led him to discuss the difference in English and French translations. Having discovered that I knew Waley's *170 Chinese Poems* and had heard of Judith Gautier's *Livre de Jade*, he gave me very high marks as well as an unexpectedly enjoyable exam. This was in my last term at school, nobody minded any more if we were using make-up, talking after the bedroom lights were out or committing minor misdeeds. The oddest omission, looking back on it, was that none of the staff stopped us when, following the example of one of the girls whose father was a jockey – or did he run a stable? anyway, something horsey at Chantilly – we said both 'bugger' and 'fuck' very often, and soon all of us did – thinking them useful alternatives to 'damn' and 'blast'. I suppose they were all ignorant of such words and their meaning in those innocent days. Luckily for me, my brother advised me not to say them when my father was about – my mother certainly did not know them, for I had used them in her presence without reproof, before I knew they should be avoided.

---

[16] Both by Thomas Hardy (1840-1928), novelist and poet

Chapter 2: Michael

Leaving school was a great relief, a feeling that now life would begin. By this time my father had left Woolwich to become Commandant of the Chemical Warfare Experimental Station at Porton. The retiring first holder of that office must have lived somewhere else, for we came into an absolutely new quarter. It was a square, ugly red-brick house, two storeys high with some small attic rooms above, built on a hillside curve, with the road into the camp below and the main line railway from Waterloo to the West about fifty yards away in a deep cutting. The sappers had made no provision for a garden, but had made an extension of the road that ran between a row of twelve or so bungalows, the officers' married quarters known as Harmony Row, to make a semicircle round the north of our house to the front door. There was also a free-standing brick garage built on the side of this drive. The house stood on chalk; a thin layer of soil netted with couch grass and bindweed was poor material for garden-making and so was the windswept site. However my parents were determined to have a garden. A boundary was planted with quick-growing macrocarpa and any able-bodied visitor was press-ganged into work with pick and shovel to dig out rather simply-shaped trenches which my mother's eye saw as rosebeds. That garden, predictably, was never a success in our time. What it may have become later I do not know, for the macrocarpa has grown tall enough to hide both house and garden. That dark fringe is all that can now be seen from a train. It was during that first summer that I went one day with my parents to lunch with a retired friend of my father's, Colonel Marriot-Smith, who lived just outside Dorchester. When we arrived I discovered that his was the nearest house to Max Gate, and that he knew Hardy quite well. He offered to take me in to see him after lunch. It was an exciting thought, but I was sensible enough to realise that it would be an intrusion. What could I say or do to make it worth-while to interrupt whatever he was doing? – so I refused the chance, and regretted having done so, though it seemed magical enough to be so close and to see a landscape he saw each day.

I was invited, as I had been the year before, to stay at St. Columb. Mrs. Hicks was no longer the frightening creature she had seemed to me as a child, and I loved her house. There was no electricity, so one still went to bed by candlelight. The garden was full of late summer flowers, there were bowls of sweet peas between the candelabra on the dining-room table, raspberries and cream every day, and nothing for the young to do but amuse themselves. Both Roddy and Bill were at home, both had motorbikes on which they tore down winding lanes to the sea or to tennis parties. I travelled on Roddy's pillion, Mrs. Hicks in Bill's side-car for these jaunts. There were all good tennis players, I a bad one, which was a pity, but even this did not blunt my pleasure. We went for walks on the cliffs, most days we bathed, sometimes at Watergate or Porth, sometimes further afield at Treyarnon or Mother Ivey's Bay, still with almost empty beaches. Sitting on the cliffs above Constantine I asked about rocks out at sea. Roddy said they were called Quies – so many ships had come to grief on their jagged points, so many sailors gone to their deaths in the waves that broke on them in storms.

I was sad when my fortnight was over and I went back to Salisbury Plain. Porton was a lonely place for me. The inhabitants of the other officers' quarters were youngish married couples, the only girl of my age was the eldest daugher of one of the scientific staff, an extremely pretty girl called Winkie who lived with her family in a beautiful manor house in the valley below our house. We were barely acquainted with each other before I was sent to Brussels 'to be finished'. I had wanted to go with my school friend, Winifred, to the University at Tours, but my mother, who had been at school there herself, insisted on Brussels. My father took me over after Christmas and left me with Mademoiselle van Oye.

She was a stately woman with a crumpled face which lit to charm when she smiled. She had lived long in Russia as a governess to noble families and indeed there was an air about her of faded eighteenth-century splendour. She had a small, tall house, a dining-room and salon on the ground floor, and rooms for eight girls. When I arrived there was one other English girl, Angela, a cool blonde with beautifully waved hair, Sonja, a dark lively Dutch girl who had brought tubes of cheese from home, which looked as if she was spreading toothpaste on her breakfast bread and butter; two tall Norwegians, one engaged to be married, two Finns, one, Eri, who looked like a boy dressed in a very tough way, with heavy shoes, mackintosh and beret as her outdoor clothes who was, in consequence of her appearance, always being turned out of ladies' lavatories, and a very sophisticated young art student, Stella, born in Russia, registered Brazilian, whose parents lived in Shanghai.

I was furnished with new clothes, including my first black evening dress, a rustly taffeta affair, a cause of great satisfaction even though it was made by the village dressmaker. Not so satisfactory was the fact that, against all my pleas, I was sent with three pairs of woollen combinations as winter underwear. These horrors I threw away the first week I was away and spent almost all my first month's pocket money on two pairs of cotton cami-knickers which were chilly but very pretty.

It was, after all my protests, quite a pleasant time. We read French literature and I became deeply excited by Baudelaire and Verlaine. We were taken to the opera, I heard *Manon* and *Lakmé*, and the whole of *The Ring*. We went to plays, I began to enjoy Flemish painting, particularly Breughel and Bosch. We went to stay at Spa for a chilly Easter holiday where there were walks in the pinewoods; I found a copy of Elinor Glyn's *Three Weeks*[17] in the house which I read with enjoyment.

Back in Brussels for the summer we settled down to mild dressmaking, helping in the kitchen one or two mornings a week to learn a little about cooking. We had delicious food and began to learn about the pleasures of alcohol. Having discovered that liqueurs were cheap, we would invite each other to bedroom parties – "bring your tooth-glass" – to drink Cointreau. The Scandinavians provided biscuits and piccalilli to go with it, the more conventional of us offered little buns. Some time in June we spent a few days in Bruges. The lime trees were in flower, reflected greenly in the canals. We looked at pictures there and at Ghent, then a few days later I left Brussels and went home. I had been to the hairdresser for the first time in my life, so I arrived feeling sophisticated, with wavy hair, a passion for French poetry and desire for a life of conversation and worldly pleasures to begin.

Porton was no place for this. The downs were isolating and Salisbury, eight miles away, was not in those days a lively town. For my father it was an absorbingly interesting job. He had a staff of all ranks of army, a few naval and air force officers and many scientists under his command. The work was secret, so the many labs behind the living quarters were out of bounds, as was the whole large enclosure of ranges around. Red flags were hoisted when there was to be firing, otherwise we who lived there could walk or ride over the downs. We had two horses, my father's charger, Jude, a big chestnut, and an elderly bay called Podge who had, it was alleged, once eaten a bucket full of Irish stew when taking part in manoeuvres. This must have done him good, for old as he was, rising thirty it was said, he was a skittish and frivolous character. My mother, who rode side-saddle, would take him out,

---

[17] Elinor Glyn (1864-1943) published 21 romantic novels which were noted for their treatment of women's sexual feelings. *Three Weeks* (1907) contains erotic scenes played out on a tiger skin

with my father riding Jude, as often as they could. For these two we had a groom, a gypsy-looking gunner, whose wife was a village girl. I got to know him well for he had to go with me when I was sent out to ride, usually on a pretty grey mare belonging to the station. She was supposed to be gentle and easy-going, but the minute I was on her back she showed a lively spirit. She, like all the other horses I met in my riding days, knew that I was totally in her power. Even Podge ran away with me, all through the camp. I felt desperate by the time I managed to steer him into a big coalyard where many willing soldiers, on their way to lunch in Mess or quarters, surrounded me and helped me to dismount. I was without Farringdon, the groom, that day. He told me stories when we were out together, of his life and travels. He'd been in the army for years and had had many adventures. He swore that the worst blind he'd ever had was on his mother-in-law's parsnip wine which had caused him to lie in a ditch all night. Having experienced Arak and other exotic drinks he was horrified to think that a mere country brew could lay him out.

I disliked riding more and more. Walking was all right, trotting bearable, but the good canters and gallops that were supposed to be so exciting were terror to me. I used to give myself little nips of father's whisky before going out to ride, and when ever I had to go alone, I knew I'd be in for a John Gilpin episode. So, when my parents offered me a proper riding habit for a birthday present I plucked up courage enough to say I'd rather give up riding. After that I had a much happier relationship with the horses; when not on their backs I found them friendly and kindly creatures.

We lived in great comfort, with a cook, daughter of a gamekeeper from Winterslow; her cousin, a dark, creamy-skinned beauty whose face I see whenever I think of Tess of the d'Urbervilles, was the house parlour-maid, and both slept in attic bedrooms. As extra help, an older woman, came in from a village near. Her husband was a shepherd, a man of great stillness with blue eyes, eyes that had a look that sailors' eyes have, more used to distance than to foreground. Whenever he came to the house he'd bring his dog and they would sit together by the range while the girls gave him a cup of tea. Our dog, Bruce, would go to sit at his feet gazing at him with awe and reverence – traits he showed at no other time and for no other person. He was nice to the sheepdog, too. Between them, these people gave us an easy life.

Sometimes we had rather grand scientists to stay for various secret work. The one we all loved was Professor Barcroft, a man who had risked his life in gas chambers (those words did not mean then what they came to mean later) testing the effect of a gas on the human frame after it had proved fatal to animals, to prove his opinion that this particular gas was not worth manufacturing as a commodity for war. He gave my mother a copy of Hazlitt's *Winterslow*[18], and I became aware that our local pub had been a haunt of that dark spirit.

We had dinner parties, usually for eight people. The food was good. I doubt if the drink was interesting. My mother arranged flowers with originality and pleasure but she did not enjoy her guests and I don't think the guests ever enjoyed the parties for they tended to leave fairly early. My father may have had good half hours with the men over port; we, in the drawing room, were dull enough over coffee. I remember once a couple who had been to the Italian Exhibition at Burlington House and excited pleasure I found in talking with them about the pictures which I had seen, then conversation being cut off, somehow, by my mother. It was not permitted to enjoy conversation, or perhaps for me to do so.

Another dinner party I remember very vividly was at the G.O.C.'s house at Salisbury. Naturally, I was not usually asked out to grand dinners, but this time it was I, not my parents, who was invited. My

---

[18] William Hazlitt (1778-1830), essayist, journalist and critic; his son selected the 17 assorted essays that make up *Winterslow*, which was published in 1906

father drove me there. My mother had told me that we should go in arm-in-arm, I with the youngest A.D.C. I could not believe that such customs still prevailed, but it was so. As soon as we were seated the young man on my right dutifully turned to me.

"Do you hunt?" he asked. "No," I answered. "I hate blood sports." "Oh!" he said. I was outraged that he should take it as probable that I should engage in such horrors. The young man on the left, having finished his soup, asked, "Get much hackin'?" "I like horses," I said, "but I hate riding; I find it alarming to be so far from the ground."

He was obviously shocked. I thought, "Why should they have it all their way?" We had got to the fish. "Do you," I said to my right-hand neighbour, "like symbolist poetry?" (I was having the nearest I could get to a decadent life, but the furthest manifestation available was having bunches of nettles to decorate my bedroom.) By the pheasant – or was it guineafowl? – I was a failure, there was no point of contact in the world. However after dinner all went better. When the ladies went upstairs my hostess, Lady Montgomery-Massingberd, talked to me, asked me what I liked, talked about plays and music and I felt at ease and chattered away. I discovered that she had been a member of a well-known group of amateur singers before she was married and still played the violin. A composer, Ralph Vaughan Williams, was a life-long friend. I remembered her kindness on that evening vividly, and reminded her of it, long, long after, when I was her hostess. "Oh yes," she said, "it's always necessary to take care of the youngest or least important person at a party."

When the men joined us I was alarmed to hear that we were to play cards for money. My evening bag contained a clean handkerchief and a very small Tangee lipstick. To my further dismay the General, Sir Archie, asked me to play with him: he too believed in taking care of the youngest guest. By now I was more at ease and I said that I was afraid he'd have to pay my gambling debts. I have always failed at cards and I lost him ninepence. My father collected me – he came in about half past ten to have a drink. When, as we drove home, he asked me if I'd enjoyed myself I said that I had. But I was convinced that I had failed pretty dismally as a social being.

There were dances sometimes. The camp dances were not very exciting, though cheered-up by having one or two cousins to stay as partners to take to the rout. One, on my father's side, was a superb dancer; the other, on my mother's side, a fascinating talker, not so good as a dancer; but it was in either case pleasant to have someone of my own age to stay in the house, even for a couple of days.

Days were very much longer then, for with no work, no duties, no rides, they had no shape except as long stretches of time between meals. Sometimes I went for walks with Winkie, the beautiful blonde, and her huge Great Dane, or, if we could raise the money, to the cinema in Salisbury. Once, when her parents were away, I stayed to keep her company in their old and spooky manor-house. We had been to see *Dracula* and we came back to the dark house. The Great Dane seemed to observe things we could not see. We terrified ourselves with ghost stories until we were so tired we had to go to bed. Far too nervous to sleep alone, Winkie said that we must sleep in her parents' bed so, in that none-too-large double bed Winkie and I and the Great Dane slept and woke and shuddered and longed for day. Being the only girls of the same age, Winkie and I were thrown together by the isolation in which we lived rather than by similarity of interests. Those we did share were for dancing, for clothes, and for improving our looks. We spent gloomy and idiotic afternoons patting our chins – where they might, we feared, become double – with springy shoe-trees bound round with cold-water-soaked cotton wool. We were both without any regular allowance or source of income, so we were not often able to buy things or go on jaunts. My desire was always for London, plays, new books, and of course, new clothes; Winkie's, even more clearly, for Romance. The camp dances didn't provide much scope for either of us. The occasional more lively ones at places such as Bulford were much better in prospect than realisation. We drifted along, waiting for life to begin to be exciting.

Three years isn't a very long time, but those years at Porton seemed interminable. In the summer we spent days at the sea, New Milton and Milford were the nearest places, and the roads were empty enough for the drive not to be too tiring, for both my parents drove. Little by little John and I were discovering the pleasure of each other's company. The gap of three and half years was ceasing to be a chasm. One summer, when he was old enough to drive, we amused ourselves by inventing a couple who would be returning from India and who wanted to buy a house in Wiltshire. They became real to us as we looked at house after house on their behalf. We saw some lovely ones, some awful ones, and found it an easy amusement. One year Porton went mad on the game of Murder, and there were parties, with supper picnics either in the New Forest or in a nearby valley. We made huge bonfires and played the sinister game in the woods just beyond the range of those friendly flames. There were fallen trees to trip one, branches to clutch, and somewhere a murderer's hand to touch and to strangle. Later, picnicking by the fire, the scene was changed again by moonlight between the bastions of trees. This sport was a good cover for various love affairs that were in progress.

I had no love affair in progress or in prospect and no friends particularly, except Winkie. The camp M.O. and his wife were the only couple who read much and whenever they had their book of the month they lent it to me. Otherwise I was soaked in poetry, literally so, for after dinner, when they had finished their coffee, my parents tended to go to sleep in their armchairs. I would leave the drawing room and take *A Shropshire Lad*[19], or the Oxford Book[20],

---

[19] The best-known work (1896) of A. E. Housman (1859-1936), poet and scholar
[20] *The Oxford Book of English Verse*

or Verlaine, while I had a long sad bath. Sometimes I wrote melancholy verse in my bedroom, sometimes I sat and cried with boredom or frustration. I didn't know what I wanted to do, nor was there any money available for further education. John was still at Cheltenham, Rosemary had a daily governess, I had had my education. The only suggestion my parents ever made was that I should become a masseuse – I suppose they meant physiotherapist – as it would be useful in the next war. I was horrified by the prospect, and refused to consider such an idea. There seemed nothing at all I could do to earn a living to escape from home. I might have gone to live at Painswick with Grannie, but her life was even more quiet, I thought, and I stuck around, a most unamiable, uneasy third adult at home. I must have been a great trial to my parents, for I sat about reading, changing books at Smith's as often as there was a shopping trip to Salisbury, and being as horrible as I could about hunting which they loved, and of course of which I disapproved, refusing, whenever possible, to go to church where my father read the lessons. It was a natural thing for them and my doubts, dislikes and refusals filled my mother with dismay. "I have failed!" she would say dramatically, when I said that I could see no reason to do something which I did not believe in. When I said that she was not responsible for me she was hurt and offended.

A new interest came when I discovered that one of the scientists, Dr. Stone, was an amateur archaeologist with some reputation, who sometimes needed an extra pair of hands. Porton had great advantages for him for the ranges were undisturbed territory. Air photography was beginning to be used to help archaeologists, with pictures taken at early morning and at evening when shadows were longest, when old earthworks, invisible to someone walking over the ground, were plainly seen and a guide could be established for digging. Dr Stone had done work on Woodhenge, and he was occupied mostly at weekends, digging Beaker period settlements and flint mines. Rabbits knew the flint mine sites, and found it easy burrowing, another help to humans in search of the past. These were sunny days, with the bleached grass, the tiny blue and purple flowers of milkwort, or the geometrical designs of the heads of pink centaury and scented thymes peeled back to the squared sides of the ancient diggings, where we followed looking for what the original miners had left of trace or artefact. To my inexperienced eyes, the antler they had used as a pick leant against the wall of the dug-out pit as if it had just been left there while the owner went to lunch. There was a feeling of immediate contact with a remote time which was both illuminating and alarming. I had the feeling that the whole of the plain, with its ancient trackways and burial grounds, where for miles nothing taller than juniper bushes grew, was used up and finished with. This seemed particularly so at night, when walking up the hill from Winkie's house in darkness or moonlight was frightening. I observed that horses stared at things I could not see. Winkie's sister's pony, alone in their orchard at night, was a great starer. I had to pass him as I too walked in fear and dread and dared not look behind. Strangely enough, the camp was haunted. Three of the officers' quarters in Harmony Row shared a ghost, a short figure in white that came through closed doors and was seen frequently by successive inhabitants. The aerial photographs showed that these houses were all built on one of the many ancient trackways that converged at Stonehenge.

All our visitors had to be taken sight-seeing and Stonehenge was one of the obvious places to go. I came to know it very well in all seasons. It was most spectacular and frightening in snow and moonlight. By day it was in sight of Larkhill Camp, of traffic passing on main roads, and there were sometimes other people there. Once I went with three other people to the Midsummer sunrise. We went about midnight, expecting lonely mystery. However, charabancs full of people were there, a bicycling club, scouts, a preacher, a black and white minstrel party, hot-dog stalls, and rows of cars. We settled down to doze and woke when the sky was light, about five. The two of us in the back seat had cramp. Indeed, I was woken by my companion rubbing my ankle and saying in a despairing voice, "I've no feeling in my legs!" The other two started sneezing directly we got out of the car into the chilly air. As the morning grew lighter a procession of druids emerged from temporary lavatories beyond the stones looking remarkably odd with ordinary shoes beneath their sheeting. It was damp and disappointing; we went away disillusioned to an early breakfast.

The other sightseeing places were Avebury, Salisbury and Winchester Cathedrals and Romsey Abbey. We knew them all well. One cousin who came to stay and was taken round all these places was about my age, the sister of the one who was a superlative dancer. She was a pretty creature and much more sophisticated than I was. She asked me if I shut my eyes when I kissed. I was flattered by the question, but I hated to say that no-one had kissed me, so I prevaricated. It wasn't quite true that I had never been kissed, but I could not admit to my two mild adventures. One concerned a friend of my father's who looked gloriously like a pirate king. He had kissed me behind the conservatory when we'd all been over to lunch with him and his wife. The other one was the fat and charming brother of my mother's old school friends, Betty and Georgie and Zara. I used to stay in London sometimes with the unmarried one, Georgie, and her mother. Georgie, like her sisters, had always shown a marvellous kindness to me, and we chattered away about books and plays and life with, on my side, no feeling of a generation gap. Once when I was staying, her brother had taken me to the Tate. He steered me into the Watts room, full of pink aspiring nudes, to kiss me with great assiduity. I knew that these adventures of a fifteen year old were not what Beryl meant, and I felt my lack of experience acutely. The local young men were the subalterns. Porton was not like the other camps where there were lots of such young officers. Of ours, one was in love with the young and beautiful wife of a sapper major, one was the devoted swain of a girl with golden eyes who lived at one of the neighbouring farms. He was an amiable rather colourless lad who could not dance and talk. If one was dancing with him he pushed one round rather like a wheelbarrow and then stopped dead to answer a question or to say something. We knew the son of the pirate king who was at that time one of the young officers' course at Bulford, or Larkhill, who came over to see us sometimes and brought friends occasionally, and there were others, sons of my father's contemporaries who were sometimes about, but none of them was for me an object of romance, nor was I for them.

I had grown up without any interest in, or knowledge of, politics. Until I went to school I had not met any children whose parents were not in one of the services and there were no discussions of current events at home. My own reading of newspapers was confined to the book and theatre pages, my knowledge of the world was drawn from novels and from history. History lay in the past and though I had heard a great deal about 'The War' as it used to be called, I found it boring unless it was seen through the eyes of poets. Rupert Brooke had given way to Sassoon and Owen[21] by now, and it began to be very difficult for me to accept the accepted outlook of my parents. Pride in the Service, the Regiment, duty, whatever it was, seemed as hard to believe in as Christianity of which the Army was, to them, some sort of sub-section. I understood, I thought I understood, courage, honour, looking after the horses and the men (the wives and families were the officers' wives' responsibility) but when it came to the use of poison gas in warfare I was jerked broad awake. One evening my father rehearsed a lecture he was to give the next day, which filled me with misery and dismay. It took me a long time to realise that for the professional soldiers there were technical problems, of gunnery, of the use of weapons, and that was their business. If there were wars they would use their knowledge and skill to the utmost. Gentle people like Professor Barcroft and my archaeologist friend were occupied with the means of death, and I was living on father's

---

[21] Rupert Brooke (1887-1915), Siegfried Sassoon (1886-1967), Wilfred Owen (1893-1918): poets of World War 1

army pay which belonged to this preparation for annihilation. It was as black a shadow over life as the boredom of daily life. I did nothing about either. This was partly owing to having no money at all, partly to a complete lack of self-confidence. There was no one with whom I could talk about my problems so they remained as my constant companions.

Pleasant things did happen. One was a sudden and last minute invitation to a May Week Ball. The son of one of my father's friends was on a young officers' course, and the brother of the girl to whom he was engaged had invited them to his college ball. The second girl of the party could not go – so would I? It was lucky that I had a dress in which I had confidence and that there was time to stop in London to buy new shoes – buttercup yellow moiré with high heels – so I felt properly dressed for an evening in the magical world of Cole Porter tunes, late darkness and early light, madrigal singing on the water and breakfast in evening dress.

I wore the yellow shoes and the same chiffon dress at another dance that summer, at Bulford. I spent a lot of time sitting out in the garden with a tall man, rather older than most of the subalterns I'd met. He talked a lot about India, and obviously liked sitting out better than he liked dancing though he did dance quite well – so I had a very agreeable evening. Somehow we never caught each other's names. Nor did we meet again for some months.

The other event of that year was having a poem printed in a magazine called *The Decachord*. It arrived by the early afternoon post, and seeing myself in print for the first time I was beside myself with pleasure. I rushed to show it to my mother. For some reason we were without a housemaid for the moment: she barely looked at my name in print but said, "Very fine. Have you hoovered your bedroom?"

When I'd just come home from Brussels, Georgie Clopstoun stayed with us, and at her suggestion and with her encouragement I had written to J. C. Squire to ask if I might send him some of my work for criticism. He suggested that I should send some to a critic on the staff of the *London Mercury* which he edited. He will charge you a fee, he said. But Mr. Twitchett's letter – the smallest writing I'd ever seen – was reassuring. He wrote that he was sure I'd understand that critics had to protect themselves from idle scribblers and it ended, "it will be a pleasure to tear your work to pieces." This correspondence was fitful; it started in November 1929, my first winter at Porton when I was eighteen, but I did not get my first criticisms until June 1930 and that letter was manna indeed. He wrote:

"(1)   Your sense of words is much above average.

(2)   You will write poetry if you keep at it, but there's nothing in the batch you sent me which I should care to print were I an editor. All the same, you might try some of it on, say, the *Observer*, who get many worse poems sent them, I should say ...
Will you send me your other stuff?"....

His wife, he said, who was a better critic, would take charge of them and see that they were attended to within a week.

I didn't try the *Observer*, but I sent the other fruits of solitude to the Twitchetts and their letters to me about my work were warmly encouraging, a comforting life-line from another and more desirable world.

My other attempt to make life more interesting involved going to Bournemouth by bus every fortnight to have lessons from a woman who taught speech and drama. As well, Grannie gave me a present of a fortnight at a queer place, Citizen House, at Bath, for a summer school of drama. We rehearsed all day and every evening for the final weekend performances of *The Trojan Women*[22], in which I was Pallas Athene and a member of the barefoot, green-tunicked chorus as well as taking part in some Tennysonian one-act blank verse caper, in which to my surprise I was cast as Beauty. Among the people I met there were Imogen Holst, who was in charge of the music, and a girl called Mary who was having a sad time, fruitlessly in love. She came to stay with us for Christmas. We kept in touch for some years but met rarely for geographical reasons. Later she became a writer and achieved enormous success as Mary Renault.

During the next few months, some time in 1930, a new subaltern arrived at Porton. He was older than the others and much more interesting. He was an amateur artist, a naturalist, and impressed the camp by the absolute accuracy of his gun team. There was great excitement one morning when they shot the distant flagstaff, which was the marker for their practice, in half with the first shot. We got to know each other slowly; it was quite a long time before we realised that we were the couple who had spent so much time talking in the dark garden at the Bulford dance. He had a string of names, John Michael James Forrester Wood. His army nickname, from his time in India, was Lackri[23], but he offered me a choice of the others. Michael suited him, I thought, so that was my choice. He was a good naturalist, indeed he had intended to go into the Forestry Service. The war started while he was at Cheltenham, so he had gone into the army in time to spend the last few months of the war in France. He was tall, dark haired with grey eyes and beautiful hands, a delightful addition to Porton. He joined the camp amateur dramatic society which was diverting and occupying during fairly long rehearsal periods, producing plays of a rather boring kind, mostly detective stories. There was no theatre, but we used a big room in the camp office block. There was practically no room behind the stage so we had to dress in offices in another wing

---

[22] By Euripides (480-406BC), Greek tragic playwright. UVW later speaks of Gilbert Murray's translation
[23] The translation, he said, was 'stick' (UVW)

and either stand pressed between the wall of the building and the flats from the start of the act, or wait in the dressing rooms then nip across a patch of grass, up step ladders and through a window to the appointed door in the scenery. In one play I was involved in a love scene which should have been interrupted by my outraged stage-father, but he did not arrive on his cue. My stage-lover and I were left on the sofa to improvise for what seemed hours. I remember hissing "Kiss me, can't you" to the poor young man who was dismally shy. Eventually we were locked in a pretty convincing embrace, cheered loudly by the audience. It was our first night – troops night (sergeants and families came on the second night and officers on the last). They found it greatly diverting. I've rarely been more glad to see anyone than I was when my outraged parent arrived, having been fetched from his dressing room by Michael who was prompting the play.

Michael contrived some excellent scenery for me when I made a cut version, fairies and mechanicals, of *A Midsummer Night's Dream* for the camp children. They were a mixed bunch from fourteen-year-old boys to three- and four-year-old fairies. Rosemary, now twelve, a tough and horsey child, wished to play Bottom, and there was an obvious Puck, a daughter of one of the sergeants, a quicksilver elver of a girl who might have been a changeling. The changeling child himself was the bad child of the camp; aged four he had a most inventive brain and caused infinite trouble. One of his favourite pastimes had been to break the fire alarm. He did it several times before the crime was traced to him. When asked WHY? he answered simply, "I like to see the men run." He asked his mother for a mug of water to put flowers in one day. She was surprised by this gentle request and wisely investigated further. "It's for a funeral," he said. He'd buried his small sister as there was no dead bird or mouse at hand. Luckily, she was found while still alive. Eventually Billy's fantastic invention got beyond his parents' control and his father asked the Adjutant for help. This splendid Irishman, Vic Hallinan, brought Billy along to my father's office for a defaulters' parade – it was an extra parade, no other sinners were arraigned with him. Between them Vic and my father thought out some telling doom which subdued Billy for a few weeks. He caused havoc at rehearsals, but the other children were able to cope because they were enjoying themselves rehearsing and didn't want interruption. At the performance my father sat in the cramped backstage and controlled the unruly – I was busy getting everyone on and off the stage and prompting. So I was very grateful for his help and co-operation. We had good audiences partly because the parents of all the performers came to both shows, partly because Porton was an isolated place and any entertainment was welcome.

Soon after this Michael's father died. When he returned from a short spell of leave to be at home for the funeral, his mother came to stay in Salisbury. He brought her to tea with us. She arrived rather grandly in a big car with a chauffeur. She was small and plump with bright brown eyes, like a squirrel, and tiny hands. She wore a large Duchess-of-Devonshire-hat and I liked her immediately. She started by being very shy, but soon she and my father chattered away. Her own father had been in the Indian Army which provided some common ground. Conventionally well-dressed, she was a most unconventional woman. "Would you mind," she said to my mother, "if I took out my teeth? They are new and painful and I do want some of that lovely bread and butter." It was splendid, we all laughed and, the teeth removed by a discreet and modest sleight of hand, she settled down to a good tea and racy anecdotes about her journey from Wales. There was some question about her car, the make or the age, the sort of ordinary things car owners ask each other, to which she answered, "I suppose it was extravagant to buy it, but one must have a *little* pleasure in one's life." When I knew her better I learned to be nervous of these words – they meant that she'd spent more money than she could afford. Then it seemed an original way of reacting to becoming a widow.

My parents gave a small dinner party for my twenty-first birthday in March 1932. I chose the Hallinans, another couple and Michael for our guests. It was a quiet celebration, but I had a new dress of a worldly kind which was a success, one of the dresses that always made me feel happy to wear, so I always had a happy evening when I wore it. Soon after this Michael and I were in a play together which we did in Salisbury instead of the camp. This involved a good deal of being given lifts to rehearsals, dinners at The Haunch of Venison, where I had earlier learned to like beer as it was the cheapest thing to drink when taken out by impecunious young men, and lifts home again. Michael, as mess secretary, kept calling to bring my mother presents of special kippers he had discovered, special coffee he was trying, and with other frivolous excuses. At the same time our cook, who was my contemporary, had a suitor, a gunner who was the camp postman. He delivered letters at curious times, so that we sometimes had as many as four or five posts a day. These two sets of attentiveness excited no particular suspicion in my parents' minds. Michael took me out for a long trip to Glastonbury and Wells, both places I had never seen. I did not say much to him about the surprising idea that had come from my speech and drama teacher at Bournemouth who had asked me if I would like to go to the Old Vic audition for students. It was an improbable idea; I accepted with excitement and fear. I spent all my spare time declaiming one of the gloomier speeches from Gilbert Murray's translation of *The Trojan Women* to our horses, who didn't react much, before the day on which I went, shaking in every limb, into the stage door at the Vic. It was extraordinary, draughty, grubby, unalive. There were other young people waiting. I talked to a boy who was as nervous as I. "I'm doing 'for God's sake let us sit upon the ground'," he said, "so shall I sit upon the ground?". When it was my turn I went to the front of the stage, the lights glared, I could see the group in the stalls in outline, Miss

Baylis[24], Harcourt Williams, one or two others. I poured out the wrath and grief of Hecuba to the best of my ability. They stopped me half way through, which was dismaying. Once in the stalls being cross-questioned I made them laugh, and went away feeling much happier.

I had inherited fifty pounds from my godfather on my twenty-first birthday so I knew that the fees for a season's training could be paid if I was lucky enough to be accepted. Then there was a dance in Salisbury, after which Michael declared his affections, a day in the New Forest, all bluebells and cuckoos on which I declared mine, and a day later a letter from the Old Vic saying that rehearsals would start in August. August! It seemed an impossible tangle, for a few days. Of course we thought that we could get married at once, then after the summer I could go to the Vic while Michael worked through the year for his promotion exams which would take all the time when he was not on duty – inevitably his evenings and weekends would be committed to paper work rather than to me. These plans were brought low at once. During some casual conversation I had said once "When I'm married I'll never eat stale bread, only new crust or toast" – my mother had said furiously "and who do you think will ever marry you?" I had no idea who would in those far off, seventeen-year-old days, but her reaction to this engagement was strange. She was first angry, then tearful and finally hysterical, insisting that we must be engaged for at least two years. Father remained as aloof as he could, and I felt both hurt and shamed by their behaviour at what should have been at least a cheerful occasion. Certainly Michael was eleven years older than I was, but officers could not marry before they were thirty if they wanted to have the army's marriage allowances, so that seemed a poor objection. He was eminently eligible, intelligent, delightful and good looking, so the objection was inexplicable. Gradually the engagement was accepted and we had to meet each other's

---

[24] Lilian Baylis (1874-1937): celebrated theatre, opera and ballet manager; best known for her work at the Old Vic and at Sadler's Wells Theatre

relations. Grannie, I think, had been frightened that I was marrying to escape from home, but she liked Michael and felt reassured. He and my aunt took to each other and my friends seemed pleased about this development in my life. I liked Michael's mother very much and already I was soon calling her Mabel as her sons did. She said that she had always wanted a daughter and that now there'd be someone to frivol with.

Michael had no great liking for the Army, but as he had had to join it (he had been in the last few weeks of the 1914-18 war) he stayed on. With two brothers both intending to become doctors, as their father had been, the elder of them then about to go to Cambridge, he felt that his parents could not afford to let him be retrained for a profession he'd have preferred, so he remained in the army. He'd spent years in India where he'd had the misfortune to have a Colonel who'd insisted that he should play polo. He hadn't the money to replace a pony that died, so he had borrowed from an Indian money-lender to get the new pony on which this unreasonable man insisted. He didn't even like polo, but he was under pressure and bought another creature, which came to some fearful end. This left him in debt so he resigned from every club and gave up all social life to save to repay both debt and interest. Work done, he resorted to solitude, to natural history and to painting the flowers and butterflies of the district. For leave he walked, taking his bearer with him, and went to Kashmir and up to the edges of Tibet. He learned to behave in the proper tribal ways, and disguised as his bearer's servant he made a map of some of the Tibetan border. Another Colonel discovered his financial plight, arranged to pay off the money-lender and for Michael to pay him small monthly instalments until the debt, cleared of the appalling interest the money-lender had required, was settled. He returned to normal life, to join clubs and go to dances and Government House parties. This period of loneliness had done both good and harm. He had learned two or three Indian languages really well and he could write a beautiful flowing oriental script. He had become a good draughtsman and his butterfly drawings were to be published as illustrations to a natural history but, unlucky as ever, they were stolen, and so that source of income and recognition failed him. On the debit side he had become withdrawn and learned to be self-sufficient. I did not realise the implications of this, for it seemed to me that we should liberate each other and enjoy ourselves sharing all the pleasures of the world. That these would turn out to be dissimilar pleasures never crossed my mind. Beguiled by romantic fulfilment one is truly gullible, for whatever the loved one does appears to be a marvellous discovery of something new in oneself – and both of us were in this dazzled state. The summer was ours. We went as a party to the Gunner Ball at Woolwich, my parents in one car with my cousin Vera – 'Poor Percy's' elder daughter – over from Vancouver for the summer, and another subaltern newly arrived at Porton, as her partner. Michael and I had been in London for the night, staying at a hotel with Mabel who incited me to have my horrible bun of hair cut off. I had a wonderful evening, wearing my birthday dress, a green orchid and my curls from an expensive morning with a hairdresser.

At the end of June Michael and I set off, for his leave, to stay with his uncle at Bettws-y-Coed, and then to go on to the Lake District where Mabel had taken rooms for the summer. By careful arrangement of dates we had planned to spend a night on the way to Uncle Frank's and another between Wales and the Lakes. We had managed a good deal of dalliance at Porton, but this freedom together had another quality though it was still an adventure heightened by the chance of meeting anyone we knew, a pretty unlikely contingency in mid-Shropshire. We managed, we thought, a cool performance as a long married couple at dinner in the hotel and I remembered to take off my Woolworth wedding ring before we arrived to stay with Michael's uncle.

Michael's parents had gone to live at Bettws when his father retired, to be near to him, as well as to the hotel they had bought – a gravely mistaken venture. Neither of them knew anything about running a hotel – Mabel's idea was to equip it with fine linen sheets and all other luxuries. They employed managers who either knew as little as they did or else were rogues, and as all of a lifetime's savings were involved the place was a financial disaster. However, during a spell of leave from India Michael had enjoyed staying in his parents' house and fishing in the Conway. It was after an evening's fishing that he'd seen a ghost.

Walking home late in the June twilight, he saw a woman about twenty yards ahead of him dressed in the oddest clothes. A bit old-fashioned even for *here*, he thought. She turned off the road and when he came to the place where she'd left it he looked, casually, to see where she'd gone. There was a tall, stone gateway – but it was blocked up with big square stones. Directly he got home he asked about the place and the woman. "Oh yes, she's often seen," the cook said. "She was the housekeeper there and he murdered her."

After Wales we went on to Hawkshead where Mabel had taken rooms in a cottage belonging to a carpenter who worked for Beatrix Potter – we saw her once, a stocky figure in a coat and skirt and felt hat. Much of the landscape, glades full of foxgloves, streams and fields were familiar from her picture books. It was a good holiday for us, full of pleasures. There were a few more weeks at Porton, then I left for London, a tiny room in a hotel in Earls Court, for which Grannie angelically paid, and life at the Old Vic while Michael settled down to a dreary syllabus of work for his promotion exam.

Chapter 3: On the Road Again

The Old Vic rehearsals started in August. I fell into the pattern of life very easily. For the first weeks the evenings were free so I met everyone I knew to go to films or plays. When the season started in September the evenings were, of course, occupied in the theatre. There were eight girl students, and the same number of young men. Our dressing-rooms were small, cold and stone-floored with basins, cold water only, a shelf and mirrors, unshaded centre lights, hooks for clothes, bentwood chairs and no more. It was an interesting season with Peggy Ashcroft, Roger Livesey, Malcolm Keen, Morland Graham, Alastair Sim and, among the younger actors, William Fox, Marius Goring and Anthony Quayle.

The first production was Shaw's *Caesar and Cleopatra* and, as Egyptians, we were all darkest brown, arms, legs, necks and shoulders. After the first night nearly everyone turned up in polo-necked jerseys and washing was minimal. We the girl students, all palace slaves, were at one moment chased, squealing, across the stage by Roman soldiery. They were realistically rough in this scene and one of us, though luckily not on the first night, Mary Norris, who was very short-sighted, went too far east in her attempts to escape and the curtain, falling on her flight, swept off her black Egyptian curls and left her clawing at the velvet folds crying plaintively "let me in, let me in". We had that year *As You Like It*, *The Winter's Tale*, *She Stoops to Conquer*, *Cymbeline*, *Macbeth*, *The Tempest*, and *Romeo and Juliet*, with Peggy Ashcroft and Marius Goring as the doomed pair, both touchingly young. My favourite of all was *Cymbeline*, in which we were involved as court ladies and later as soldiers. I had a grey velvet dress for the first act, so I forgave the pain of a too-tight helmet which I wore as a legionary, blacking out my front teeth, deciding to be an aged Roman to avoid the more realistic bits of battle. Morland Graham was a wonderful old Belisarius; from him in that part, in his relationship with the King's lost sons, as in his Old Adam in *As You Like It*, and as Perdita's adoptive father in *The Winter's Tale*, I learned that one of the greatest and most touching things in all Shakespeare's plays is the affection that reaches across divisions of age and station. He was a noble Duncan, too. The other actor in the company whose work was a delight in every part he played was Roger Livesey. Pisanio, Macduff, Old Capulet – these were all whole and real people.

One of the many duties that befell us as students was that of prompting, a ghastly responsibility and one that led me into a moment of extreme horror. I had chosen for my stint *Romeo and Juliet* and *Macbeth*. We had an appalling time with *Macbeth*. Malcolm Keen fell and hurt his back, so Marius Goring and Alastair Sim in turn succeeded him in the part. With Alastair Sim it was nearly a comedy. Finally John Laurie came in to finish the run and his dark and passionate hero-villain with a Scots accent was a most exciting experience. It was, though, in every way a hellish three weeks for the prompter. Was a pause really a pause or a loss of word? I watched over each Macbeth when not on stage as one of Lady Macbeth's retinue, or a horrified Thane-ess at the banquet, or making eldritch screams in the corridor behind the stage ('wail of women from without' is the stage direction, but passing Thanes would use us for spear-practice so the screams were pretty authentic). The England scene with Macduff and Malcolm was as safe as houses, I believed, and had one night fallen into a daydream when I was horrified to hear Malcolm say, "Don't go, Macduff, I've got something to tell you – I mean – I must say something, Macduff, so please stay ..." and so on. I had no idea where they'd got to and had to leave it to the nobly sorrowing Roger Livesey to manage the prompt himself. It was a lesson reminding me to concentrate. That production was the work of Teddy Craig, Gordon Craig's son, and it was visually very exciting, with real torches and the Thanes dressed barbarically – actually in hessian, which it had been the duty of the students to paint in wild green patterns of terracotta and green, a nice messy occupation which we had enjoyed doing in the draughty rehearsal room. The trouble was that once encased in their breeches, tunics and leggings the Thanes found the hessian was like hair-shirts and they itched most uncomfortably and became very cross in consequence.

Miss Baylis was remarkably nice to the students. Once or twice, between matinées and evening performances, she came and sat in the dressing-room I shared with two others; she told us wild stories of her life in South Africa when she was a girl and of how she'd loved a curate with hair on his chest. She had a party for all of us, opera, ballet and Shakespeare companies, at her house near the Oval, and how we all got into it I cannot think. It gave point to the story that having been to tea at Buckingham Palace someone asked her if she'd enjoyed herself. "Well," she said, a little sadly, "they only gave me buns like I give the students." She used to sit in her box – it's no longer there – on the prompt side, curtains drawn, at some rehearsals as well as at performances, and if anything went wrong the curtains would be twitched aside and a note made. In Hermione's trial at which we were muttering away, on Hermione's side of course, one of us got so carried away that her voice rose above all the rest – "It's a bloody shame," she cried – and the action almost stopped.

Some time during the winter we started using the new Sadler's Wells. We alternated with the ballet company and on Monday mornings some of each company would have forgotten where we were supposed to be and would arrive at the wrong theatre for rehearsal. Sadler's Wells was wonderful for us, big dressing rooms with hot water and, instead of the usual lunch in the bar, a ham roll and a cup of coffee, there was a Lyons[25] where bacon and egg and chips was only one and six[26], a treat for the days on which allowances started. Also, there was Collins Music Hall, to which

---

[25] Lyons: a chain of tea-shops or 'corner-houses' (restaurants and cafés)
[26] $7\frac{1}{2}$p

we went sometimes if our play ended early. On Mondays there was no performance for us, but there was for the Ballet Company and we could go to see them, free. One night I went to the Vic when the ballet was a new one and saw *Job*. Normally I didn't notice music, being interested in what was happening on the stage, but *Job*, with Gwen Raverat's[27] designs taken from Blake's illustrations, absolutely bowled me over. Dolin was Satan, and various dancers I'd met between rehearsals in one or other of the theatres were changed to these familiar creatures of Blake's imagination, sons and daughters, comforters or seraphs, the whole thing was an extraordinary, exciting, moving and shattering experience quite unlike anything else I'd ever seen or heard. Marjorie Stewart, one of the other Shakespeare company students had been a dancer, and had been, the year before, Mrs Job in the Camargo Society's first performances. I remembered the composer's name – the Vaughan Williams, who was Veronica Wedgwood's cousin, whose *Linden Lea* had caused me to be expelled from singing class at Bursage. Even so, I never enquired about other works of his, though I saw *Job* every time I could.

We had classes, rather irregularly, in dancing, in acting scenes from plays; otherwise we attended or took part in all rehearsals and did odd jobs – prompting and helping with less important clothes. The prettiest clothes that season were made by the Motleys[28] who were just starting their career, and who dressed *The Merchant of Venice*. No student parts in that, except as a riot of masquers – three minutes on stage about 8 pm – so such a weekend as this left was worth going home for or, better still, meeting Michael in London. We dined sometimes at the Trocadero or the Criterion and stayed in an attic at the King's Cross Hotel. But these treats were seldom, for he was working for his promotion exam and saving money for our future.

---

[27] Gwen Raverat: A Darwin cousin, engraver and artist
[28] 'Motleys': generic name for theatre designers. 'Designs by Motley' was a familiar credit in theatre programmes.

Mary Norris, one of the students rather younger than I, became a great friend. She had never intended to be a drama student but wanted to study production. She was a strange, original creature with a sharp sense of the ridiculous; she had second sight, a dangerous talent which she concealed most of the time, then. Her father used to bring her washing from home. They lived at Eastbourne but his business brought him to London each week, which was convenient for her and very lucky for some of her friends – I was one – for he'd take us out and give us good solid lunches. We were all getting thin on the usual one-ham-roll regime. I had fifteen and sixpence[29] left of my weekly pound, after paying for my tube train ticket from Earls Court, and out of that I bought shampoos and stockings, paid for cobbler and cleaner, and went to at least one matinee a week. Michael had given me a library subscription at Harrods, so as I was able to read new books all the tube journeys passed in a flash – and we needed few clothes. I think I had one corduroy suit, one skirt and two jerseys, which carried me through seven months – and two dresses for going out to lunch or tea on Sundays, or to the Players Theatre, or Theatre in the Round which was very much the fashion and considered new and wonderful. One of my companions for some of these treats and pleasures was the girl to whom an old friend, my father's godson, Pat, had become engaged before he left for India. She was teaching in a south London school and we were both planning that old-fashioned pleasure, trousseaux for our weddings, which were both to be in May.

During the winter my father's command at Porton came to an end and he returned to Woolwich as President of the Ordinance Committee. This time it was not to live in Woolwich, but in London. The family established itself in a large flat on the first floor of one of the Victorian houses in Emperor's Gate, near Gloucester Road. John was at the Royal Military Academy at

---

[29] 77$\frac{1}{2}$p

Woolwich, Rosemary went to a nearby day school and I left the independence of my Earls Court hotel to return to the family. My mother was near various old friends and Harrods delivered hot croissants early in the morning for our breakfasts.

It was a tiring life for my father who had to make the journey to Woolwich; it took about two hours each end of a long and responsible working day. But it was a pleasant flat and the rooms in the front, facing on to a triangular garden, were quiet enough. Rosemary and I had bedrooms at one end, at the back, where we heard the trains and at the other end of the flat down three stairs, there was a kitchen and a bedroom for the maid. I remember fighting a great battle for her. She was, perhaps, twenty-three, and had to be in by ten on her days out which seemed to me totally unjust when I could be out as late as I chose, as long as I stuck to my old plan of saying I'd be much later than I intended to be, and then saying, round-eyed, "Well, I didn't expect to be in till two – and I was in *bed* by then." Extraordinary reasoning, but it worked for me, and I won her freedom too, till midnight.

Michael was worrying about his mother who was in financial troubles. The hotel at Bettws-y-Coed had not been sold and wicked managers seemed to succeed each other with great rapidity. Mabel and Christopher, Michael's younger brother who was still a medical student, were living at Little Missenden, while Rodney, his other brother, who had just taken his FRCS exam, was in Moorfields Eye Hospital. He had lost the sight of one eye when hit by a cricket ball at his prep school; now his good eye had to be operated on. For three weeks he did not know if he would be able to see, let alone work as a surgeon. During this time he showed the most calm courage. In the end all was well, and he was able to work but it had been a fearful few weeks for him. Meanwhile Michael's savings had to be spent on getting Mabel out of difficulties, and it looked for a time as if he might have to keep her rather than me. However, the hotel was sold, and soon after an Easter weekend, which we spent at Chichester with my aunt and uncle, the season came to an end as well as Michael's promotion exam which of course he passed very well.

It had become clear to me that my life wasn't going to permit a career on the stage and that anyway I didn't seem to have much talent for acting, so I didn't look for work or busy myself about the future. It had been an interlude, a marvellous eight months that showed me the pleasures of an urban occupation and congenial company. If I hadn't committed my future I might have made some effort to find some sort of work in London – or, if my parents hadn't come to London, I might have tried to stay there. I do not know, but I think that by then, having become involved in Michael's life so deeply, having watched Rodney's recovery, and Mabel's financial problems, and Michael's own endeavours with his tough programme of work, there was no way in which I could abandon him. Nor did I want to, though I thought about it, but I did wish he had some other profession for I was beginning to dread going back to army life from which it had been so lovely to escape. I asked him if he would think of leaving – but he was sure that our lives could be different; there were weekends, after all, and surely two people could make life congenial for each other whatever the daily necessities of their circumstances. I wanted to be convinced. Affection, sensuality and hope were there in equal proportion and the doubts about where we should be, cut-off perhaps, as I had felt at Porton, from the things I most enjoyed, were blocked by his certainties. And there was always the chance that we might be posted to India – a chance of travel and seeing the world I longed for.

I had a gap of about three weeks between the end of the Vic season and getting married. Most of it seemed to be spent at the dentist and the dressmakers. My father said that I should be handed over sound in wind and limb, so two wisdom teeth went and various stoppings were done in this cause. I refused to be married in the local church as it was nasty Victorian Gothic and, as we were cried down on our wish for a quick, quiet wedding, I chose St. Clement Danes. Wren I felt I must have, and London that was London. Ours was much like all weddings at that time – it happened at the miserable hour of two-thirty as no-one was allowed to be married after three; some relic of Georgian rakehelly drunkenness that presupposed no groom would be sober later in the day. All the women wore long dresses, as for a garden party, most of the men morning coats so they looked festive. As my father and I were driving to the church we got involved in a traffic block just outside St. Michael's, Chester Square. An awning was up and a red carpet down, and an usher waiting by the curb saw all the veiling and stepped forward to open the car door. For a split second I wondered what would happen if I sailed up the wrong aisle ... But the car moved on to St. Clement's, Michael, church bells, and all those mad and awful promises.

After the reception, kissing aunts and cousins and old friends and everyone else, being photographed and having failed to drink as much champagne as we needed, we drove away to spend the night in London. We sat in the bar of the Kensington Palace Hotel and after several dry martinis began to feel human again and very hungry.

Next day we were amused to find our photographs in some of the daily papers. We lunched with my parents to collect luggage and Michael's car. My mother seemed surprised that I was still alive and apparently none the worse for marriage. We set off westwards for anywhere we liked the look of, intending to get to Cornwall at some point. It was magical weather, the may trees in heavy blossom, buttercups, campion, bluebells and young leaves unfurling still freshly green. The most delightful thing that happened to us was when we stayed at Clovelly at the little hotel on the quayside. About six in the morning the chambermaid banged on our door. "Get up, get up and come out to see it!" she cried. We scrambled into dressing-gowns and went out on to the jetty to see whatever "it" was. In the morning mist one of the grain ships, with all her sails set, was moving slowly up the Channel. The cliffs were a mass of flowers, red may, white may and purple rhododendrons, faintly veiled in dewy cloudiness. Everything was pearly and very still, the ripples on the beach made the faintest murmur, the water was almost still below the jetty, and the great ship moved in silent splendour.

We stayed for most of the rest of the time in Cornwall. It was new country to Michael, and we walked on sands or cliffs and bathed from the then secret and empty beach at Mother Ivey's Bay. It was all peaceful, pastoral and flowery. When we went back to Porton it was for his last two months of service there. We lived in the Station Hotel, kept by a most extraordinary couple. She was a Welsh woman, he a tough little man who had been valet to the King of Siam. They were marvellous hosts to us, warmly hospitable – rather too hospitable, we thought, when we found a dish of twelve eggs with bacon to match for our first breakfast. Michael managed four eggs, I two, but this was not up to what was expected of us. They did revise their estimate of capacity but it was against their generous hearts. Nor did they like it when we invited friends to dinner and then, naturally, protested when we found no difference in our weekly account in consequence. "If you don't like the way the place is run, you can leave," they said. Eventually we reached some compromise and were allowed to pay for our guests. Mr Short had wonderful stories of his life with the King, letters to show us, proudly, which started "Dear Walter" and ended "with love from Rama". He had a gold watch set with rubies given him by the Czar and all sorts of other tokens of 'esteem and affection' from assorted Royalties. I had one problem with Mrs Short. She would not let me wear green, and I had green dresses; it was difficult to manage, but I had to whisk out covered by a macintosh if I wore them. She'd had a daughter who died, who would have been my age, and she had worn green. "Unlucky, unlucky," she would say sadly, remembering the dead girl.

Winkie had married while I was at the Vic and had gone to live in Venezuela and I found to my surprise that I missed her gossip and frivolity enormously. Mary Norris stayed with us, and I was glad of her company. Michael was out all day and I found the hours long, with nothing to do but read or go for walks. After the pleasures of London, life on Salisbury Plain was as depressing as it had been before. I had supposed that being married would make everything different, but the geographical limitations and the financial ones remained exactly as before, and I began to wonder to what my life was committed and to feel frustrated.

However, the gunnery staff course started, and we left Porton for Blackheath. It was ten years since I'd gone from there to Malta, but it was still familiar territory. The Red House had been pulled down and an ugly block of flats replaced it, but the shops in the village were the same and so was Greenwich Park and the view from the top of the hill over the river and the city, where the church spires and the dome of St Paul's varied the skyline with their finely-drawn outlines above the bluish blur of the crowded houses.

We lived in a small private hotel; two or three other Gunnery Staff Course couples were lodging there, the men going over to Woolwich for their work leaving the women with nothing to do unless they could invent amusement and employment for each day. Life in a double bed-sit with no duties, no work and infinite leisure had very little to offer, I found. In spite of the amount of cramming that had to be done, Michael managed to spend at least one, sometimes two, evenings at the Art School. He had become interested in etching, and went to learn the technique and to use the press. It was a lifeline for him and I hoped that perhaps, in time, he could be persuaded to leave the army and work at some kind of drawing or painting and find a way to earn a living in a more congenial way, for he had great talent as a draughtsman.

On the non-art school evenings we sat in our room by the gas fire and Michael did his extensive homework while I read and fretted for a livelier life. After Christmas we moved on to Biggin Hill, then a very small place, and found rooms in a chilly bungalow with a landlady whose cooking left much to be desired. I suppose that was another month or two, for we spent the summer at Shoeburyness, once again in rooms. By now the people on the course all knew each other well and I found some congenial wives, all more or less bored with the conditions in which we lived and longing for the course to be over.

We went to the Woolwich Ball again that summer, with a young party; John, now in his last term as a cadet, and Mary Norris, came with us. I wore my wedding dress, sleeves replaced by plaited shoulder straps which were not lined, so they stretched and my dress became more and more Restorationally low. Eventually I had to borrow a trail or two of smilax[30] from the supper table to fill the gap between immodesty and exposure – it tickled, but was quite a successful decoration. That was one of the summer highlights for me.

There were more amusements at Shoebury. It was part of the world I did not know at all, with mud flats, marshes much loved by birds, and though I found bird-watching a bore, there were some wide views with sea lights. Once I saw the gun carriage go out to reclaim a spent shell, white horse silhouetted against a dark thundery sky. In the summer evenings it was possible to go exploring after Michael's day's work. We discovered Canewdon church. The church warden let us in and told us that the tower was built by Henry V's orders as he returned to England after Agincourt, sailing up the Blackwater Estuary, and this was a form

---

[30] 'Green leaves – quite decent' (UVW)

of thanksgiving. At that time Michael was studying lettering and calligraphy and this churchwarden showed us the church charters and documents and allowed him to borrow some of the early ones to copy and to study, which seems extraordinary now but which we found delightful but unsurprising.

I used to go into Southend sometimes, to buy carnations. They were grown locally and for a shilling I could get a big bunch, dark and bright and scented, which cheered up our rooms. I made one expedition there on Bank Holiday Monday and it seemed proper, as we were thereabouts, to enter Southend by tram on such a day. It was exactly as expected, hot and tired and sticky families, rock, winkles, candy-floss, cross children and a smell of low-tide mud and beer.

The gunnery staff course rolled on and ended. Michael was posted to Biggin Hill when it was over. It would be a three-year job, so we found rooms and started house-hunting. The house nearest to the camp that was to let was an ugly 1920-ish place, but I knew when we first looked at it that there we should live. I'd seen it before, when we'd found it empty and picnicked on the doorstep on one winter drive from Woolwich Arsensal, picking holly for Christmas. The charm of the place was in its wild garden, the rooms were fairly big, and there were long views southwards over the valley. The house stood on a loop-road west of the main Westerham Hill road. It took a long time to get the lease fixed and to move in. Meanwhile John had been posted to India, and just before he left my parents had a party for him. He had been assembling kit. My mother bought a gross of tubes of Kolynos (toothpaste) for him. It was, I can see now, a gesture of anguish and protection; at the time it seemed wildly silly, and John irritatingly made a snake of the yellow packets right though the flat and round the drawing room. When we got to his last day at home, and the party, he had a rash, which we supposed, after all the other farewell parties he'd been to, was alcoholic. After he left, almost everyone who'd been there developed German measles. He was out of reach of recriminations. Living as we were, in a guest house, I found it infuriating to be isolated in our bedroom so as not to spread infection. It was cold weather so I huddled in bed, sitting wrapped in my winter coat while I made curtains, till the bed was full of pins.

Eventually we got our house and Grannie, who had gone to live with friends in Painswick so had given up her house, provided us with furniture. I had never liked domesticity but after a year of lodgings I was ready to find pleasure in housekeeping. At first it was very difficult and the last week of the month we subsisted largely on herrings and baked apples. We had a living-in maid, a cook-general as they were called, and with her a trail of dramas; she sent for the police when there was a thunderstorm and she was alone in the house because she was frightened. She later introduced her husband and child to the house, and while we were away at practice camp he tried to murder her. However, she was a good cook and her eccentricities were mostly engaging.

We were tremendously lucky in our neighbours the Coopers. Francis, like his father Paul Cooper, who had died recently, was a gold and silversmith. Mrs Cooper and her younger daughter Ursula were weavers and both made beautiful materials, particularly silks, and the elder daughter Kanty, was the most adventurous creature I have ever known. She and I met when she came back from a holiday in Spain and we spent much time together, going for explorations and jaunts in her Baby Austin car. She'd bought it for three pounds so it was neither new nor utterly reliable; once both its headlights fell off in busy traffic near Marble Arch, but in general it did well. She took me to see the ruined hunting-lodge deep in woods which Ann Boleyn and Henry VIII were said to have used as a meeting place – then secret and hard to find, but now the woods are cut and all the magic has gone from the small squat building.

Michael bought a second-hand etching press and set it up in the glass porch of the house – when they came to dinner the Colonel's wife thought it was a mangle – and worked on various plates from sketches he made. In fact he never lacked for interest or something to do. I spent most of most days alone, except for our maid or times with Kanty or occasionally with Mary Norris who lived at Sevenoaks with her parents. I was bored with myself, and when Michael came home I wanted to be amused and entertained. I approved his drawing and etching wholeheartedly, but it left a gap where companionship might have been. I realised more and more certainly that I hated country life and solitude and I missed the sense of things happening that my time at the Vic had provided. On the other hand it was marvellous not to live in rooms any more.

Another pleasure was space. We'd had over a year since we were married of living in one, occasionally two, rooms. Now we unpacked our wedding presents and what books we had and we did not have to share the meagre accommodation of one lodging-house wardrobe. These were in any case mostly needed by Michael as he had to have so many different kinds of uniform. Khaki jackets, breeches, slacks, blues, full dress mess kit, Sam Browne, sword, boots and shoes and boots for evening and a boot jack as well as dinner jacket and tails and mufti. It was quite an extraordinary outfit but one that was so familiar, I never questioned it. The only thing that all the women hated was the barbaric habit of wearing spurs at all times. There were even small 'dress spurs' worn with mess kit for dances. Sometimes they were allowed to be removed at midnight, but a lot of damage to the hems of dresses could be done in the couple of hours before that.

At last we could spread ourselves, but not for long. We took possession of our house in March; by June we were preparing to leave for Practice Camp in Somerset, where Michael was to be one of the instructors teaching territorials anti-aircraft gunnery. We let the house and packed up the car and set off westwards.

The practice camp was between Williton and Watchett on the Bristol Channel. I suppose there was very little shipping using the Channel, for the R.A.F. flew up and down, up and down, towing a sleeve as target, and shells must have fallen into the water. The territorials were in camp. I don't know where the regulars were – camping too perhaps. Those of and above the rank of Lieutenant Colonel lived in the Egremont Hotel in Williton, those below, in the Railway Hotel. I think we had the better deal. The Railway Hotel was a very old pub – it had been the Lamb before the little Taunton-to-Minehead line was built – solid, old-fashioned and with wonderful food, the very best English cooking. It was run by a delightful couple, Mr and Mrs England, and Mrs England's mother was the talented cook. The only trouble was that there were such a lot of us. Seven bedrooms, seven couples and six dogs. There was no garden and only one sitting-room so once again we were cramped and congested, but by now I had become a very good packer and very tidy. My great aunt and her husband lived at Bicknoller so I used to go over to see them often. There were quite a lot of pleasant walks, and that first summer quite a lot of books in the village post-office library that I hadn't read, and one congenial wife among the other six in the pub, with whom I went for walks. She had to walk, anyway, as she was one of the dog owners. At weekends Michael and I went to Exmoor or to the sea or generally exploring. There were three summers there, and the memory of them runs together – one year there was a fair on the quay at Watchett; riding on the roundabout the horses and dragons swung out over the dark waters at high tide in the harbour. One year we went to look for monastic fishponds at Nether Storey and found ourselves in the farm yard behind the beautiful house with the gazebo. The owners asked us to tea and showed us the cloister – where of course Cromwell had stabled his horses – and we left with the present of a flower from their magnolia, a bowl of scented petals which brought back unexpected memories of Devonport and the magnolia whose flowers opened the nursery window. Then there was Cleeve Abbey, red Somerset-stone ruins among walnut trees, where the curator, who was born in the village and had the striking name of Cleeva Clapp, kept talking about The Disillusion of the Monasteries, which seemed a fair description and one I have liked to use since.

Michael and I had one holiday abroad. He had sold a stamp collection for forty pounds and we went to Provence. The third-class tickets were five pounds each, return, from Victoria to Marseille. We spent a night in Paris – my first visit – as close as possible to the Gare de Lyon, dined out modestly, and went to the local music hall. Then at eight next morning we started on the miraculous journey to the South. We shared a carriage with a waiter and his wife going to Mâcon, and two Maltese sailors. We had all bought long crusty rolls with ham in them for our lunches. They tried to teach us to drink, pouring wine from the bottle into our mouths. The train bucked and raced, so the result was messy but hilarious.

We were going to Avignon to start with, and we were glad of our plan to travel by day so that we could look out of the train windows and see France, a land neither of us knew. After Lyon, as the landscape became familiar from pictures, the world of Van Gogh and Cézanne, tiled roofs, bamboo windbreaks, cypresses, it became almost unbearably exciting. We reached Avignon as the February dusk was changing to dark, and saw a fair with flaring acetylene lamps above the stalls where dark-faced soldiers strolled in long cloaks. The air was soft, smelling of oranges and garlic and narcissus, the south and spring.

The next day we went to the Palace of the Popes and with half a dozen other tourists were shown round by a guide who proudly loved the place. He took us to the two painted rooms, one decorated with tapestry-like frescoes of sports and pastimes of the Seasons; the other was more formally painted but in its window embrasure were frescoes of maize plants on which perched and pecked little bright marauding birds. He spoke of fading colours – saying that we might be the last generation to see the blue skies of the medieval world before they flaked away, and last, as we thanked him, he recommended with emphatic authority, Chateauneuf du Pape – "soleil au coeur", he said.

Avignon was a delight, the broken bridge, the distant walls of Villeneuve les Avignon on the far bank, the streets which I explored as Michael spent a day drawing. In the gardens a peacock was displaying, rattling the quills of his fan as he stepped and bowed to the modest peahens.

We had planned to do all our journeys by bus, which was a very good idea. At Uzès we found a hotel full of people 'demonstrating Persil'. One was put to sleep in a bath and a room with three double beds was made over to us – not fair, but accepted gratefully if a little nervously, but no other travellers came to share it.

Finding that we were interested in food, we were given marvellous dishes, wines from the neighbourhood and our washing done, all for four-and-six[31] a night. Near there, we discovered the Château d'Argillières, a square grey turreted house with curving colonnaded wings. It was in some dilapidation with tufts of wild violets cascading from the balconies. While Michael drew the little pavilion at the end of one of the wings I wandered in the shrubbery of myrtle and box behind the house, and sat on a stone bench thinking of the four old sisters who had been the last owners before the house was taken over by peasants. I could imagine ball dresses and satin slippers, lace scarves and yellowing gloves piled in the cupboards as they grew older and older, remembering their own young days and the story we'd been told of their ancestors, for it was said that the house had been built for a Queen by her lover

---

[31] $22^1/_2$p

while her husband was at the Crusades. Probably it was an imprecise story, but the house looked as if it must have been true.

As I sat wrapped in romantic daydreams I heard a patter of hooves, and a little brown goat with golden eyes came to me and put its head in my lap. Instead of the golden collar it should have had, it wore one of hinged box-wood; it may have belonged more to Pan than to the Courts of Love. That world waited for us further east, at Beaucaire with its memories of Aucassin and Nicolette, at Arles, and at Les Baux – at that time still more ruined than repaired, wild and strange and desolate except on Sundays. Then the people from Tarascon and around came to lunch at La Reine Jeanne, where we stayed, and walked on the battlements. One of the local shepherds made a good addition to his livelihood by going round beneath the ramparts on Mondays to collect and sell hats that had blown off the sightseer's heads. Another shepherd had trained flies, which he kept in a match box, to find truffles. An old woman came to talk to me where I sat idling on a rock among the lavender and rosemary scrub. "Look," she cried passionately, "what they did to our city in the war!" The ruins, cut jaggedly into the pale sky, still hurt her. "The war?" I asked. The war, to me, then, meant 1914-18. "See," she said, pointing, "that's where Richelieu put his guns." Standing there in her dark dress and shawl she could have belonged to any age – to the time of the landing of the three Maries, to the reign of Queen Jeanne, to Richelieu's wars, to Mistral's[32] *Miréio*. Lines from that poem were everywhere, even on plaques in railway stations.

The proprietor of the hotel was a young half-American, half-French javelin thrower, who had played football for Belgium and thrown javelins for France in the Olympic Games but had been disqualified for this double allegiance. He was married to a Provençale who cooked like an angel, but as he didn't want her to become fat, he

---

[32] Frédéric Mistral (1830-1914): poet and founder of the Provençal renaissance movement; awarded the Nobel Prize for Literature in 1904

told us, he made her get up early and do exercises while he lay in bed reading the instructions from a magazine called *Votre Beauté*. He told us stories of the lock of golden hair found in a grave, now in the museum at Arles; of how his father-in-law had asked a village carpenter to mend a fence, and when the man didn't turn up on the day arranged, nor the next nor the next, he came to look for him and found him with some wild-eyed men sitting arguing at a café table, where they'd been for three days. "And what was the argument about?" he asked. "The distance of the sun from the moon."

There was a little farmhouse in the valley, a terraced first floor above a stable, vines and a few olive trees. "If you'd like it," the owner said, "we'd put in electricity for you." The price was eighty pounds, but we hadn't any capital, eighteen or eighty or eight hundred pounds were the same impossibility. But for this lack of money the valley might have been spared one of the most expensive hotels in France and we might have lived quietly above the Val d'Enfer at Mas Beaumanière.

Somewhere, in some village, I went to the hairdresser, planning to be ready to catch the eleven o'clock bus. But the hairdresser was so excited by having hair that was not black to play with that Michael, who'd put our luggage on to the bus for Cassis, came to say that we'd miss it unless I was ready at once. The hairdresser was firm: I should not go till he was satisfied. So he sent a message to the bus driver and the bus was kept waiting for another twenty minutes. When the moment came, the hairdresser led me proudly to the bus and everyone got out and walked around me and congratulated the artist. Michael had used the time to sketch, so he hadn't minded either, and we had a conversational drive to the coast. We were asked to which hotel we were going; our choice was criticised and we were recommended to another, and by common consent of the passengers we were driven to the door and introduced to the proprietor. It was just right – red tiled floors, white walls, jars stuffed with bunches of wild narcissus in the dining room. After fifteen years' separation I saw the Mediterranean at last. The haunting memory of Malta was assuaged by pale rocks growing with golden ferny seaweed, and the blueness of the spring sea.

One day a fisherman took us out. He was gathering sea-urchins with a long-handled prong, looking for them through his glass-bottomed bucket. I had a try, and nearly fell in when I attempted to manoeuvre the weapon that he used so easily. I'd never actually seen what under the water looks like before. It is quite magically unreal when looked at from above the water-surface, but seen without the dazzle and refraction I found I felt as vertiginous as I should have done standing on the edge of even such a modest height as the boat was above the sea-bed. The urchins, like sweet chestnuts in their husks, golden green and golden brown, were still alive, their spines moving desperately, but he took two and cracked them open, one each. I looked at Michael. He liked oysters, I didn't. "Like vodka," he hissed, and shutting my eyes I gulped the poor thing down from the half shell. It seemed unrefusable, as it was a gift, but I refused any more.

The hotel became full of Spaniards who had come over the border escaping from the Civil War, listening to news bulletins leaning close to a crackling wireless. These were the first refugees I'd ever seen, and as a thoroughly a-political person I began to see the terrible implication of Causes in human casualty.

When we got back to Westerham from soft weather and sunny days, there were inches of snow and we both had flu. The lease of The Homestead had come to an end so we spent a few weeks in a furnished flat in Westerham. It was small and ugly, but it filled in the gap before we went off for the summer to Practice Camp. That year Michael was sent to Manorbier instead of Watchett, so we drove up to Tenby at Easter to find somewhere to stay. There was a vicarage converted to a guest house in the village where we took a large bedroom and, as we were going to be staying for two months or more, they let us have what had been the pantry as a sitting-room as well.

When we drove up in June the wild flowers were astonishing, masses of wild roses, much darker than any I had seen before, columbines, as well as the usual hedge and field flowers, and even the ivy-leafed toadflax on the walls had an exotic purple and yellow flower instead of the usual pale mauve.

It is a beautiful coast, rather like North Cornwall but much less populated, and there were beaches we found to which we walked through fields and usually had entirely to ourselves. Michael's immediate superior, a little senior in age as well as in rank, Jocelyn Pollock and his wife Ann lived in a bungalow near our old vicarage. Ann, who was a most elegant beauty, had been before her marriage one of Mr Cochran's Young Ladies[33]. We found each other immensely congenial. We were the only wives without children, so we had an abundance of leisure: we spent a lot of time together sewing, gossiping, sitting on the beach when it was hot, or in her bungalow when it wasn't. As we were both very fair-skinned we never went brown, and both our husbands sunburned beautifully, so, believing an advertisement, we bought a bottle of a mixture guaranteed to turn pale flesh golden and spent a busy morning in her bathroom applying the contents of the bottle. There was just enough to do our legs, and we hoped for a glamorous result. What happened was that the stuff took very well and by lunch-time our legs were a reddish-mahogany. An afternoon session with soap, water, cold cream, pumice stone had no effect at all, and by bedtime each of us was found out, red-indian to our thigh tops. The laughter that ensued was all very well, no one minds being an entertainment, but for the next two weeks we were taken bathing to the remotest beaches where no-one else would see our shame, and how thankful

---

[33] Sir Charles Cochran (1872-1951): theatrical producer. The Young Ladies were chorus girls in his inter-war revues

we were when at last the dye faded or wore off and our pale legs were restored to match the rest of us.

We had some good expeditions, to St David's, to all sorts of castles and little towns, and often we'd go for an hour in the evening to watch puffins come back to the same high islanded rocks. The local word for puffins is Eligug, and it was this odd name that made us first go there. 'Eligug stacks' was an intriguing thing to see on the map. The rocks were nearly as high as the neighbouring cliffs and not far from them, but surrounded by deep water so the birds were safe from everything but overcrowding. We would sit and watch them coming in to roost. It was easy for the early arrivals, the later ones crowded on and the birds already there shuffled about to make room, but when the latest of all arrived the rock was so full that as they landed on one edge the same number of birds fell off on the far side and had to circle round and push their way on somewhere else. It was a never-failing amusement as the birds' faces and movements were so expressive -- rage, disgust, triumph, self-satisfaction were clear to see.

These diversions were well enough in their way, but by the end of the summer I was heartily tired of Manorbier. I hoped that Michael's next job might be at the War Office. But no, his next posting was to the Isle of Wight. We took the remains of a lease, from the man he succeeded, of half of a very pleasant house at the Springvale end of Seaview. It had long been divided: the other half belonged to three elderly sisters, Mary, Mercy, and Kitty. Before we'd been there long their brother Jack came to live with them. They were splendid neighbours, particularly Mercy, who was stocky, tough and adventurous. She swore that she had sailed to Australia 'before the mast', disguised as a sailor. Mary and Kitty were gentle and more self-effacing, though Kitty's gardening was eccentric but ardent. Jack was by his own account an adventurer, telling stories of his life in the Army, the Navy and the Foreign Legion. His sisters admired him and enjoyed, as much as he did, the idea that he was a reprobate. The Island was rather a dull finale for such an exciting life, but he nourished his decline with memories and with stories that may or may not have been his own experiences originally but had become his own by then. 'Remembering with advantages' was his pleasure.

Other neighbours were the Vernon Harcourts, living in a big house with a huge garden; they were acquaintances at first, but we got to know them well later on. Then I had cousins at Bembridge. They lived by the sea, no longer in the Priory, the house which had belonged to my father's family and which I had visited as a child when the last descendant of our great-great-great-grandfather still lived there. There was a ghost story belonging to the house.

A girl, who died when she was seventeen, had been painted by Gainsborough wearing a blue dress. She owned a little white dog whose stuffed body, in a glass case, was kept till the house was sold after Cousin Laura's death, with all the odds and ends that no-one had inherited. The house was bought by a rich American who converted powder closets to lavatories and made all sorts of changes that my family found distasteful although it was no longer any concern of theirs. When the Americans moved in they were disturbed by a voice calling for a dog. No-one ever told me the dog's name, but I later learned it was Pip. At last, exasperated by this, on the advice of one of the retired servants, they were forced to look for the little glass case with the mothy dog inside it and buy it back from a junk shop. The case was fixed in an unobtrusive place above a flight of back stairs, and there it was and probably is still, though the Priory now belongs to the W.E.A.[34] Once her dog was back in the house the girl ceased to call for it. Though her portrait was left to some other descendants who lived in the West Country, my Cousin Jack, a contemporary of my father's, said that he had often seen the girl wandering by the sea-shore.

---

[34] Workers' Education Association

Another pleasure of the Priory was a camellia tree – the biggest camellia I have ever seen, with white flowers. Jack's daughter, Sheila, and I used to go into the garden sometimes, the house being unused by the W.E.A. in winter and once, in February, we helped ourselves to branches of flowers, walking carefully to avoid crushing clumps of iris stylosa that crowded round the bole. I walked back to Springvale with my bunch, through the after-tea twilight, and saw for the first and only time in my life, the ragged flaming banners of Northern Lights streaming above the Solent.

Spring starts early in the Island. Primroses are to be found in sheltered places early in January, and violets soon follow. When the cowslips start on Reculver Down they are the best I have ever found, sturdy and brilliant.

One early spring day Michael and I were walking on a common near Brading on short, rabbit-bitten turf; there were a lot of birds about and we weren't talking. Suddenly beyond a gorse bush we came upon a weasel standing, or rather capering on its hind legs, waving its front paws, dancing as if for pleasure or celebration until, with a final jump, it landed on all four feet and streamed away into a bush. It was a new light on weasels which I'd always supposed villainous and charmless.

There was a road between our small garden and the sea wall. In summer evenings we used to take a tray of coffee or tea out and sit with it between us, looking over the beach to the mainland. At high tide reflected sea-light made patterns on our bedroom ceiling. When there were storms, waves broke over the road, over the garden: sometimes the windows would be covered with streaks of salt. One winter day I saw a draggled bird wandering about on the sands. It was there the next day so I went to investigate and found it was a fairly big creature, covered in oil. It let me pick it up and I took it home and put it in a box while I rang the R.S.P.C.A. to ask what I should do.

"Feed it with raw fish and clean it with butter," they said. Luckily there was some fish in the larder, but at first it refused to eat. The poor creature had been trying to clean itself and felt sick with the taste of oil. It was something about which we knew nothing then, not, as now, a sadly familiar story. It was exhausted, it let me butter it, I cleaned it bit by bit, and talked to it as I did so. At the end of the first session it was obviously feeling better, stretched its wings and finally tried a bit of raw fish, and then went to sleep. Next day I buttered it again, and it began to look more like a bird. Michael identified it as a razorbill. There was still a lot of matting of the feathers and, I thought, too much butter, so I got a bowl of warm water and Lux and spreading our newspapers, put it into the improvised bath. Eventually I had to tie its head up in a handkerchief to stop it from biting me as I washed under its wings where it seemed hopelessly ticklish. There was a great deal of kicking and splashing and muttering, but after two changes of water I'd got almost all the horrible dark oil off.

We were both exhausted. I was soaked, and the bird clean. I dried him carefully – by now he was perfectly content to be handled, and he started to fluff out his feathers and to preen. I gave him more fish and put him back in the box full of crumpled newspapers which was all I could offer as accommodation and went up to sit with Michael, who was in bed with 'flu.

Next day I had a fine-looking bird. He must have worked hard at his appearance and I fed him again and decided that he should go back to sea. The tide was going out, and I took him down to the beach and launched him. He sat on the water, and I thought that was the end of our relationship. However, as I watched, I saw that he was in difficulty – he seemed to be sinking, and he turned towards the land and gave me a look of total despair. I rushed after him. He hadn't gone far, and I was less than waist deep when I reached him. He was almost drowned. I tucked him into my jacket, waded out, and ran home. Michael, who had been watching from upstairs, had come down with a towel, which I think was intended for me. We dried our bird, though he was apparently dead, and with an anthropomorphic first-aid reaction gave him half a teaspoonful of brandy. It had an astonishing effect. He stood up on the table, raised one foot in a slow high-kick and looked at it for a few seconds, then he spoke, a loud "crork" and he keeled over and started to snore. We rolled him up in a dry towel and put him in a chair with a hot-water bottle of warm water and left him to sleep it off. I changed and went to the fishmonger. Michael telephoned to the R.S.P.C.A. who said that he obviously had lost his natural oil with the tar, and wouldn't be seaworthy till after his next moult, so we had a house guest. We had the great luxury of a married couple living in the house – Gunner Wood was Michael's batman and he had married a cook, a very good cook, but of uncertain temper, so I had to be a little careful about not upsetting her. However, when we all four discussed the matter of an unhousetrained seabird living-in, it was she who suggested that we should take up the carpet in the smaller of our spare rooms and put down newspaper. This we did and there Cuthbert had his headquarters. Mostly though, when we were in, he had the freedom of the house. I took him to the beach once a day, at low tide, to wash in a sea pool and take a stroll on the sand. Sometimes he would flap away towards the sea, and wait for me and when I'd almost reached him, double back towards the sea wall, and obviously enjoy this version of hide and seek. When eventually he got bored with his game he'd wait for me, or come to meet me, so that I could carry him up the steps and over the road.

Otherwise he much enjoyed sitting under the hall radiator, or by the fire, or on my knee, holding one of my fingers in his beak with great gentleness. Everyone in the house was fond of him, and I took him down to the fishmongers, wrapped in a red cotton pocket handkerchief, to choose his own fish. The fishmonger called him 'Mrs Wood's duck'.

The story ended sadly. We had to go to Williton once more, and we couldn't leave him or take him with us, so we gave him to the Zoo on the understanding that when we returned to the Island we could reclaim him. The Zoo were very pleased to have him as the bird department had never heard of a razorbill surviving in captivity; we'd had him for five months, so he was to be televised. But he died in a few days. Whether he pined for the seaside and his daily jaunt to the beach, or whether he missed domestic life I cannot tell. I felt responsible for his death, and regretted the freedom to which I had hoped he might in time return.

Chapter 4: War and Sorrow

My parents still had their flat in London and I would sometimes stay there for a few days. While we were still at Westerham I had written a scenario for a ballet, and because I had been so overwhelmed by *Job* I wanted to send it to the composer of this work.

I thought about it, put it off, wondered what to do, and generally dithered. But by this time I had had quite a few poems printed in the *Observer* and in other places. I had compiled several programmes for the BBC so I felt a little more assured as a writer. Finally I sent my letter, 'Dear Sir', my script on Margaret and Clerk Saunders[35], to Ralph Vaughan Williams care of the Royal College of Music.

A few days later I had a 'Dear Madam' letter, saying that it might do as a mime and that it had been sent to the Director of the English Folk Dance and Song Society for his consideration and advice. A letter from Douglas Kennedy, the Director, followed almost at once asking me to come to see him at Cecil Sharp House.

I went, to find an immensely sympathetic man, with a collection of many versions of the ballad spread on his table. He was easy to talk to, and quick to understand my ideas. For the next few months he wrote to Ralph, Ralph's answers were relayed to me, and mine to him. It was all most unsatisfactory though Douglas was kindness itself, and when in desperation I suggested, "All right then, if he won't have Margaret, what about Spenser's[36] *Epithalamion*?" he supported the idea. By this time I'd a little more idea what the English Folk Dance and Song Society was all about, and Douglas invited us to the Christmas Ball at Cecil Sharp House. I love

---

[35] A folk ballad
[36] Edmund Spenser (?1552-99): poet

dancing and I was introduced to some of the simpler dances. Maid in the Moon, I remember and some of the 'longways, for as many as will'. Michael didn't venture much, but it was good to have his support on such still alien ground.

Meanwhile the three-cornered correspondence went on, until in exasperation I said to Douglas, "Do tell the man to ask me out to lunch." The message was given, and when I was in London at the end of March 1938 the lunch date was arranged. A few days before the meeting, at home in the Island, I wrote a poem that seemed quite extraordinary to me, and which I did not understand. It was one of those few that was complete, and came from an unknown part of brain or thought at dictation speed, one of the experiences that seemed to have no relation to anything already known, but which was prophetic:

> Flesh to this meeting moves,
> aware and sensual,
> threading between casual
> moments and things, to loves
> predestined by some choice
> made with both mind and voice
> but blindly...
>
> Mind, like a bird in air
> or comet, scars with flight
> the distance, in delight
> to find such freedom there,
> but will not stare behind
> to trace the path we find
> blindly.
>
> *'I am two fools I know*
> *for loving, and for saying so ...'*

When Ralph Vaughan Williams collected me from my parents' flat I was charmed and surprised to see that the hat he carried was a green pork-pie, a kind I'd only seen worn by cavalry subalterns, and not the horrible bowler which I expected someone of his age to own. I was impressed, too, by someone who kept a taxi waiting. When we were in the taxi voice, eyes, hands were somehow familiar, so that I felt that I was meeting again someone I had known before, and this recognition was the same for him.

Though he wrote me a long letter about the projected masque and sent me the two Bullen anthologies, we did not meet again till May, when I was in London gadding with my brother who was on leave from India. Ralph and I lunched together and went to the British Museum. Walking through the Abyssinian galleries among huge man-headed bulls, he asked me if I was a Christian and seemed relieved when I said that I was not.

Next time we met I was staying in Winifred's flat, one room in Lamb's Conduit Street which she'd lent me for a few days. Ralph took me to dinner at Pagani's and to the Ballet Jooss. We saw *The Green Table*[37], topical and frightening. We were both in a state of anguish, he knew war too well, and I was beginning to fear it. As well, we were finding each other's company too desirable for our circumstances, though I didn't know very much about his life before that evening, when he told me that Adeline was an invalid, a vague term on which he didn't elaborate, and that their niece lived with them.

Next morning he came over from his Earls Court hotel and took me out to breakfast before going off to see about his passport and arrangements for going to Hamburg to be given the Hanseatic

---

[37] Kurt Jooss (1901-79): German choreographer, dancer, and teacher, and the first respected choreographer to synthesize classical and modern dance. *The Green Table* (1932) was a portrayal of the horrors of war and the fatuous discussions of diplomats

Shakespeare prize. He had had grave doubts about accepting the award, and had discussed the propriety of doing so the previous summer when the invitation had been sent. He had written,

> "... You have answered me that the honour is offered purely in the cause of Art by a learned body to a member of the English musical profession; that it implies no political propaganda and that I shall feel free as an honourable man, if I accept, to hold and express my views on the general state of Germany which are allowable to any British citizen. In these circumstances I have pleasure in cordially accepting the honour offered me in your letter."

A year later it was difficult to know if he should withdraw, but he thought the sensible thing was to go as he had promised. It was a disturbing visit, but a short one, and the prize of ten thousand marks could not be taken out of Germany, nor was he allowed to give it to any international fund for the relief or help of refugees. It stayed banked in Hamburg until long after the war, when its value had diminished to nothing much.

We met again on Midsummer's Eve, when he took me to a dance at Cecil Sharp House. It was a hot evening, so we left early and sat on Hampstead Heath. The elder flowers were out and made a bower for us in the scented blue evening, with London lying below and St Paul's a black silhouette against the not quite dark sky.

Next day I went back to the Island with Mary Norris and an Island friend, Dick Kenny. John met us at Portsmouth and he and Mary sailed across the Solent while Dick and I went by ferry. Next day was Michael's birthday and we had an impromptu fancy dress dinner party and the next morning Michael and I left for Portland Bill, where we spent the rest of the summer of 1938. John and Mary came with us and shared the last fortnight of his leave, a desperate romance for him, a generous kindness from her.

Michael was sent there with a small unit to work on rockets, Portland being considered a safely remote place for such secret experiments. We had never been to the Bill before and approaching it, it looked both sinister and barren. We had a room in a guest-house on the landward side. From the dining-room we had a long view over the curve of the Chesil Bank, while immediately below lay a patch of sea where the Navy was engaged in torpedo practice. This started at breakfast time and it was a frightening start to each day, watching the pale track of the missile as it tore underwater.

Portland is a strange place to live. It had, then, a Borstal in the old prison, a prison which still dominated the atmosphere of the place. I came to know the whole area very well as there was nothing to do but to go for walks. There is a tiny museum in the cottage that was said to be the house Hardy described as the home of the first Avice in *The Well-Beloved*. It was given to the Islanders - of Portland Bill - by Marie Stopes and her husband. When I asked the Curator about them she said, with restrained distaste, "We didn't like them. They used to bathe without clothes, *but with bathing caps on*." The most interesting building on the Bill is the church. Christopher Wren came to choose stone from the quarries for St Paul's, the quarry owners gave a banquet for him and after, when there'd been a prolonged drinking session, one of them asked him to design a church for them. There and then, the story goes, he drew plans and elevation on the tablecloth and so, following his drawings exactly, they built the church. Each quarry owner had a pew in which no one else was allowed to sit, but the owners never went to church. Presumably the convicts did, and many are buried there. I made friends with the grave-digger, a thin old man, who would sit with me on a table-tomb and tell me stories of escapes and failed escapes, and all sorts of Island lore. Pieces of Eight were still washed up after storms, he said, and could be found along the Chesil Bank; they rolled in and were always edgeways on, never lying flat among the stones. The quarry men had their own language, they'd never speak of rabbits, and if they met a rabbit on the way to work they'd go home for the day, for they were unlucky omens. The most dramatic story he had – one that he'd told to Mr Hardy, he added – was of an earlier grave-digger. This man found pick-axing a grave out of the stone below the shallow covering of earth in the churchyard was dreadfully hard work, and hardest of all when he had to made a small grave for a baby. So when he was old and the pick-axe too heavy, he took to scooping out little graves in the place dug long ago for the anonymous burials of convicts. One wet day there was an infant's funeral and the rain washed earth from the bones already there. The women who had come to mourn with the bereaved mother, and most of whom had children already buried in the same part of the churchyard, realised that all these children were tucked away among the dead malefactors. They were seized with rage. One of them picked up a thigh-bone, the others followed, and with bones and stones, screaming and weeping, they hunted the old man down the hill and clubbed him to death in the village square.

As for the quarrymen, they were all friendly, and glad enough to stop work to gossip. They had one joke, and it gave them unfailing amusement. After asking what the visitor thought of Portland, of the quarry, of the weather, and so forth one of the men would ask "if you'd like a little souvenir of the visit?" If one was unwary enough to say "How kind," they'd proceed to offer a fairly large boulder – "Something for your rockery, then," and seeing the expression of dismay on the visitor's face they'd double up with laughter. After a time the joke palled, and I'd say "Good morning" and not loiter for the presentation. All through the summer there were spectacular sunsets over the bay, towering black clouds and crimson skies slashed with purple reflected in the sea. War was obviously imminent and, as everyone in the Services knew, there were inadequate armaments. Rockets, which were then top secret, were known about locally. When one fell into the sea close to a fishing boat the angry crew came to see the angrier Colonel, whose cry when anything went wrong was for "buckets of blood". The fishermen wanted buckets of compensation, and had – somehow – to be calmed down and sworn to silence about what had caused the damage to their boat.

Along the West face of Portland there are high cliffs. I used to sit in a grassy hollow sheltered by rocks, and watch the gulls and terns flying and gliding, playing in the currents and streams of air. I used to sit there to read my daily stint of the *Faerie Queen*[38], which I had never read all through before, but as it was difficult to get enough books, a long slow poem was sustaining through the dragging weeks spent in that extraordinary place.

There was a little teashop cottage which stood alone near the ruins called Rufus Castle. It was kept by a woman whose husband was a lorry driver. When he came home at weekends in the summer he would bring her a bag full of glow-worms he'd collected the day before, so that she could put them in the garden. They were usual in some parts of the country. Obviously in Dorset, Hardy, in *The Return of the Native*, described how they were used to give enough light to gamblers on the common. Their small greenish fugitive lights had a magic quality. Like fireflies, they seemed strange to us: artificial light has been of man's making, lamp and candle, gas and electricity, so to find creatures which can become light themselves seems like conjuring. Phosphorescent seas, the Northern Lights, glow-worms and fireflies I have seen, but Will-o'-the-wisp and St Elmo's fire I have not. Probably they are lost to us for ever, for they belonged to wilder times, like the frost flowers and forests that used to pattern the windows after cold nights in houses warmed only by hearth fires, which did not burn through the hours of sleep.

I'd met one of the young naval wives whose husband was a submariner. His ship was missing for twenty-four hours and I spent some of that time with her. Our imaginations were stretched to a

---

[38] By Edmund Spenser

point of horror that was hard to bear; for her, with the additional burden of love and grief, it called for courage and for endurance; there was nothing to be done but to wait for news. It was a first lesson in a course many of us were destined to complete, but there was still a thread of hope to be clung to, a hope which was realised when the submarine surfaced and we heard that the communication system had gone wrong.

Soon afterwards I went to London for a couple of days and my journey was coloured by this episode. Radiant summer weather was perfect for harvest, and I sat in the train watching the fields being cut, the stooks of sheaves, conscious that this could well be the last time that I or the harvesters would see such things, so heavy was the brooding sense of doom through these months.

We were back in the Isle of Wight at the time of Munich. While many people felt humiliated or abased by that event, the Forces were thankful for a breathing-space to try to catch up on the armaments which they were lacking. Ever since the days when we had lived in Woolwich Arsenal when my father had been Secretary to the Ordnance Committee, through his time at Porton, and after, when he was President of the Ordnance Committee, I had been used to his fury when the Treasury turned down 'The Estimates'. He complained of unreasonableness, lack of imagination, idiocy and so on whenever these Estimates were presented and rejected. So now, when all he had foreseen of lack and of unpreparedness had come to pass, he sat champing in retirement in the Island.

In the winter Michael was sent to Jamaica where the weather was suitable for continued rocket experiments. He went off in mid-December, and as wives were not paid-for for such jaunts I stayed behind. I stayed with Mabel and my brothers-in-law at Brighton for Christmas, and on Christmas Day I had Michael's first letter, from La Rochelle. By the time his next letter arrived, describing the paradisal weather and telling me that the lorries all ran on rum as it was cheaper than petrol, I was back in London rather enjoying life in a furnished bed-sitting room. I had quite a few friends about, I was able to see Ralph more often, to go to concerts for which he gave me tickets, and to see as many plays as possible.

I find one note in my diary "sixteen people, fourteen cans of beer, two cans of tomato juice" – we were modest drinkers in those days.

I had been messing about in some sort of voluntary job called Youth City. I cannot remember how I got there or for what purpose. I was frightened at my first introduction to an office, about which I knew nothing, so I made a solemn statement about the filing system's badness and asked for it to be changed, for I found myself in some sort of command. This kept everyone busy for a day or two while I thought of other things for them to do, as nothing real seemed to be happening. It was all an emotional South Sea bubble so I was glad when Ralph sent me off to meet Maud Karpeles – Douglas Kennedy's sister-in-law – and to work with her at Bloomsbury House where refugees from Germany and Austria were looked after, accommodation and jobs were found and all possible help and advice were given. Maud worked in the children's department, and here I joined her in the lowliest capacity to do the department's filing – revenge for what I'd done to poor old Youth City's offices. On my first day Maud took me out to lunch at the local Lyons Corner House. "We'll go early," she said, "as it won't be so crowded." So we went at midday. By four o'clock we were still talking. "It's not worth going back to the office," she said. We took to each other, in spite of discovering that we'd been prepared to dislike or to be alarmed by each other. Maud couldn't imagine why Ralph had sent anyone as unlikely as an Army wife to help her, and anyway she'd been cross when he'd left her bedside rather too soon when he'd visited her in hospital after a recent operation because he was going to take me out. And for my part I'd no idea what I'd talk about with a rather elderly scholar. As it was, we found each other most congenial. Through

Maud I met Henry Nevinson, that clear-sighted, wise and splendid, aged war correspondent and, through him, Ernest Rhys, the inventor of the Everyman Library, which was a cheap and reliable edition of almost every classic one wanted to read. Having satisfied himself from our separate reports that we liked each other enormously, Ralph invited Maud and me to lunch with him. Of course I'd told Maud about my scenario and she was almost as excited as I was when he said that he had finished the music. I thought it had been abandoned, for he'd spent the summer working on a new symphony. So now he was ready to talk of production plans. Douglas Kennedy was to produce *Epithalamion* at Cecil Sharp House: he would arrange a play-through soon, and so on; delightful plans filled the foreground of the days. Meanwhile the English Folk Dance and Song Society were having their Winter Festival and we went off to an afternoon of singing which he conducted. Because I was completely ignorant of folk songs, he arranged a programme of his favourites, so I heard for the first time *Bushes and Briars*, *Searching for Lambs* and many other songs which were as lovely as he had told me they were. There were other EFDSS festivities that week, the Albert Hall performances, foreign and home teams of dancers, followed by a party at which Ralph was surrounded by old friends, sharing a sofa with the prettiest ones, and which ended with Maud singing an interminable ballad called *The Bloody Gardener*, which she had collected in Newfoundland and to which she was unduly devoted. By about verse twenty-six everyone went home. The next evening there was a Ball. All the foreign teams came in national costumes, the British in ordinary party gear, tails and best dresses. I was steered through intricacies of Playford dances which I had not yet learned, and it was all enjoyable. The winter passed in this lively and agreeable way, meeting new people, going to concerts mostly with tickets given to me by Ralph, and working at Bloomsbury House, a curious mixture of freedom to do as I liked, and seeing where the freedoms of others lay in ruin.

As the winter went on I found living in London so much to my liking that I decided to try to find an unfurnished flat cheap enough to keep as a base when Michael came back to England and our peripatetic life resumed its dictated course. Now that my parents were no longer in London there was no place to stay, and as we seemed fated to be stationed in the country I thought we could at least spend leave in London. Mary helped me house-hunt and it was she who discovered the attic flat at 7.5 Thayer Street[39] that I moved into in March. It was tiny, two small rooms with sloping ceilings, a bath in the kitchen and a lavatory, and later I made a garden on the flat roof outside the staircase window. At this time, though, I was occupied enough with getting myself moved in and settled enough to start entertaining there. In March, Maud took me to hear my first *St Matthew Passion* at the Queen's Hall. Bach was a name only for me, so I was launched into the deeps without any preparation. Then, very soon after, Maud and I went to the Leith Hill Musical Festival for the last concert, at which Ralph conducted part of the *B Minor Mass*. For me, I think it was fortunate that both were choral works so that there was the familiar element of words to cling to. Two such major experiences were as shattering and exciting as discovering Shakespeare had been. After this Dorking concert there was a party and Ralph introduced me to one of the young musicians, a viola player, Jean Stewart. She, with three other contemporaries from the Royal College of Music had formed a quartet and he had arranged for them, with a pianist, Joseph Cooper, and a flautist, Eve Kisch, to play through *Epithalamion*. Maud and Douglas Kennedy and I were the only audience that morning at Cecil Sharp House. I knew the poem so well that I realised how clearly Ralph had the words in his mind as the different dances, processions and mime were accounted for. He had made only one actual song.

---

[39] The entrance to what had once clearly been a mews was between nos 7 & 8. All the flats inside shared this number – my flat was the top one in Cottage South. Cottage North was a longer building and had more rooms than flats in it (UVW)

"When will this long weary day have end
And lend me leave to come unto my love…"

I did not know if he was asking this question of time, as I was, or whether it was simply in the context of the masque[40], where it was dramatically right, but as he had decided that I was to be the bride, Spenser's Elizabeth – for the poem was written for Spenser's own marriage – I had a secure feeling of sharing the honours with her. It's one of the few entirely happy love poems, a love on which no shadows have yet fallen, and on that day with the words that belonged to her and the music which was as much, it seemed, for me as for her, I was in a state of exaltation. Ralph took us all to lunch at Pagani's, Toscanini came in while we were there, we all chose zabaglione for pudding and after lunch Ralph took me on a frivolous shopping expedition in Bond Street. I had just put the cowslips I'd been wearing all day into a glass of water when the telephone rang. It was my parents, speaking from the Isle of Wight; they were both cross and tired and they told me they'd been helping to fit Islanders with gas masks all day. A few days later Jean came round to see me. The flat below mine was to let and she wanted to see it. Luckily she liked it, and proposed to move in the following week. Before she did I'd found some curious triangular insects, and taken them to the landlord.

"Mr Ray, are these bed-bugs?"

"Yes, but they're very *thin* ones."

The Town Hall sent their Pest Officer round. I went away for two days while both flats were fumigated. There were no more bugs ever, but I thought it better not to tell Jean about this until many years later.

She was a diligent girl and practised a lot. It was my first experience of quartet playing, and at one time I knew well the viola

---

[40] The masque was entitled *The Bridal Day*, and its first performance, delayed by the War, was in 1953

parts of a great deal of the repertoire and found pleasure in hearing their integration in the whole when the quartet came to rehearse. But I'd only started on this strand of my musical education when Michael came home from Jamaica. I had not told him about my lease of 7.5 – it wasn't, in any case, a proper lease but a cheerful arrangement with the landlord. So I met the train from Liverpool wearing a new dress for which I negotiated my first overdraft, five pounds which seemed to me dashing, to the Bank Manager modest, and brought him back to the flat, which was rather a successful surprise.

One of the amusements of our days together in London was to see *Hugh the Drover* at Sadler's Wells, when Michael met Ralph and Adeline.

With uncommon assurance, considering how new-to-me a subject it was, I had written a programme about folk song which was accepted by Schools Broadcasting. I met and liked the producer Evelyn Gibbs who came to lunch at the flat. Michael met all my new friends, Jean and the Nevinsons, Ernest Rhys, the Danish-Icelandic singer Engel Lund, and Evelyn, as well as people he'd known before, Mary and her fellow student at an art school where Rosemary was also studying, Richard Arnold-Baker, and the rest. I think, though, that he was quite glad when we went to Somerset to stay with his mother in the house, cottage she called it, that we had all tried to prevent her from buying, knowing that financial disaster would follow in spite of some eccentric economies. "So I got some very good dog-blankets for the servants" was one. But the house in Allerford was delightful. She had bought it chiefly because it had a large camellia bush in full flower when she went to look at it, but of course it was impracticable, too big, too cold, and all the rest, though at that time of year it was perfect.

Soon Michael was on tour again, with a small and experimental radar unit mostly in Suffolk. While he was away I stayed in

London off and on. By mid-July we were back in at Springvale. Ernest Rhys came to stay and took us over to tea with Alfred Noyes, who was an old friend of his. The chief thing I remember about that were two beautiful 'velvet' Breughels he owned, and peach trees heavy with, unfortunately, not-quite-ripe fruit. At the beginning of August, John's school friend Freddie Corfield and Douglas and Helen Kennedy's son, John, a young architectural student, came to stay. It was sailing and bathing weather, and there was a great deal of sitting about on the beach or on the sea wall. John and Freddie were both rather disillusioned professional soldiers and there were tremendous discussions about the future. Freddie wanted to go to his father's small estate in Shropshire to farm, John Kennedy would build new farm buildings for him as well as theatres and houses. Rosemary, now free for the holidays, would design theatrical costumes, our brother John had all sorts of plans for trying to become an archaeologist by way of getting into some expedition as an interpreter, for, like Michael, he had flair for Eastern languages. I had *Epithalamion* to look forward to, for production plans for the autumn were well advanced. We talked as if we had all time to play with and we all knew that we had not.

On August 8th John and Freddie left. Their leave was over. We managed to prevent my parents from going to London to see John off on the first stage of his journey to Burma so that he could have a little time with Mary. Then there were long days and news bulletins. About the third week of August my father, after various War Office consultations, was recalled and posted to Canada. He and my mother stayed at 7.5 to make their final arrangements. Rosemary stayed on with us while we moved from Springvale House into the Coastguard cottages. Our lease had come to an end, Michael's batman was recalled for regimental duty and Rosemary, much against her will, was to go to Canada with our parents. I saw them all off from Southampton on September 2nd and on September 3rd war was declared. Michael was at the fort at

Yaverland[41] more and more, sometimes staying the night, otherwise life on the Island was like everywhere else, sandbags and evacuees.

In spite of the alarms, despairs and waiting-about I managed occasional visits to London, 7.5 was still there, empty and desirable, also it was lovely to have a chance to go to theatres, to see friends, and to fill up the boring times when Michael was away on duty as he was rather often. Now that my parents and Rosemary were in Ottawa I was the only one available to go to see Grannie. She lived with friends, three sisters, in one of the older houses in Painswick. It was an admirable arrangement as they had known each other for years and were all fond of each other, sharing a circle of friends. Grannie, as a widow, as well as being older than the others, was deferred to, agreeably, and all was well. She remained a splendid correspondent and loved to get letters; even more of course, visits, so I would occasionally, and not nearly often enough, go down for a night to stay with them all.

John was in Burma. He managed at some time to go to Angkor Wat[42], and one leave he spent with a French beachcomber who had a little hotel on some coral strand by a pale green sea. He wrote of other escapades too. He managed to have various romances which involved moonlight expeditions and some risk of irate husbands. It was a good thing for he had spent too much of his youth shut up on the North-West Frontier, and this sort of life was far more suited to his temperament. My father was tremendously busy, using his long experience of armaments and of administration, and rejoicing at being once more in a world of action. Rosemary was miserable; Ottawa was no exchange for London. Before long she started to plan to get to Washington at least, if she couldn't get back to England. My mother hated Ottawa, and as usual made the worst of everything, though she did find diversion in having new arrivals to

---

[41] Isle of Wight

[42] Angkor Wat: a temple complex in Cambodia, regarded as one of the world's most important religious monuments

meals or to stay, and there was a prolonged misery in being made responsible for the child of an acquaintance who was sent to the safety of Canada. He was a dead loss, a terrible lad who cast as black a shadow on life as did the war news.

One night, when Michael was up at the fort, I was woken by an appalling noise. I looked out of the small window in our sea-facing bedroom and saw the coast opposite, Portsmouth and Southsea, lit by flame, gunfire, searchlights and the sound of something rolling down the roof made the further and nearer sounds into one alarming and unbelievable sensation of being in the middle of battle. I got up and called our maid who slept in the back of the cottage, and together we took shelter in the little cubby-hole that was between the cottages – a door on each side from the sitting-room to the dining-room where the two had once been separated. We could hear the guns and the aircraft all too well, but we started to tell each other stories to cheer ourselves.

Anne was an Islander, one of the many who in those days had never been to the mainland. Her story was about the first visit of the Overners as the Islanders called people from the mainland.

"When they first came here," she said, "we were going about on all fours." I asked her when this happened. "Oh, before my grannie's day, it was. Well, they didn't like it, the Overners didn't, so they said to us, the Islanders, that is, get up now, stand up. So we looked at them and saw what they meant, so we stood up. Look, they said, now isn't that better? So we said thank you, it's very nice, but – she held up her hands – what do we do with these?"

After the battle sounds died down we looked out of the window and once again the only sound of night was the familiar one of the sea. We found that we were both exhausted and we went back to our beds. The next thing I knew was that it was morning and Michael had come in, wanting a bath and breakfast. It seemed extraordinary to have our usual breakfast and to be sitting quietly talking of the terrors of the night in the calm sunlight.

Michael had to be at Yaverland most of the time, so we gave up the cottage at some time that Spring, not before I had seen too many dogfights, as they were called, over the water between us and Portsmouth, too many men falling from broken aircraft, remembering each time 'My enemy is dead, a man divine as myself is dead...'[43] I said it aloud, once, and two neighbours refused to speak to me ever again, but the pain of watching destruction is not easily converted to the assessment of "ours and theirs" even when a watcher is acutely aware of danger and of fear.

The island was full of Home Guards, a lively manufacture of home-made bottle-bombs was going on in garages and garden sheds and there were rumours that many Island feuds were being settled in merry abandon in the hedges and on the Downs. It became apparent that one should not go out after dark for these characters did not necessarily make certain that their targets were the people they intended, so, what with this and the restriction on Michael having to be within ten minutes of his guns, I moved to Brading to live with the mother-in-law of a friend, Helen Roach – Helen herself having taken her little girl to North Devon. All the children who had been evacuated to the Island were shipped back to the mainland, and there were troops everywhere. It was a brilliant summer as I remember it. Before we left Springvale I'd spent every day gardening for our friends the Vernon Harcourts. All except their elderly head gardener had been swept off to war, leaving them with a huge vegetable garden as well as lawns and flowers untended. Under the eagle eye of this head gardener I learned to weed beautifully, clearing endless rows of young vegetables. It nearly broke my back at first, but I soon toughened up and enjoyed

---

[43] Walt Whitman (1819-92): American poet and journalist; from *Drum Taps*. This line was included in Ralph Vaughan William's *Dona Nobis Pacem* (1936)

it, the results were visible, the beans and carrots and sugar peas prospered, and I lunched every day with the owners, sharing the delicious dishes that were, in part, the result of my toil. They'd had trouble enough, for Mrs Vernon Harcourt was German, though she'd long been naturalised, but her twin son and daughter by a previous marriage had a German name, and Gerd had been swept off to internment at the beginning of the war. The policeman who'd come to collect him had, with typical decency, waited till the end of the tennis party at the house before making the arrest. I found them both good company and sustaining to be with. One of their nice frivolities was spending the wakeful nights of raids gambling with their maids. "We always win their wages back," Bernard said, "a great economy. But we pay them double on Fridays." We had all had to get used to broken nights, and our Anne decided that tea was the great sustainer. Directly a raid started she put on the kettle and we sat in the bathroom – the cubby-hole wasn't big enough for three when occasionally Michael was at home – as it was on the ground floor at the back of the house. Before long we had become much less frightened, and strong tea and biscuits in the night weren't very enjoyable, so we changed back to staying in bed, watching the cold beauty of the searchlights.

At Brading we couldn't see much of the battles, but the huge thunder-clouds of the German bombers did darken the sky, and the practical Emily, Mrs Roach's cook, devised meals that were easy to eat on our laps, for the raids were usually at lunch or dinner-time, and we all three had them under the stairs, to the sound of gunfire. I still went over to Seaview twice a week to garden, and the other days I worked in a canteen in the village where the local soldiery came for their free hours. We were all absolutely baffled by the Northumbrians, who were incomprehensible, and we reverted to sign language for a few days, till we began to grasp a little of their dialect. Otherwise, people continued to picnic, go blackberrying and mushrooming, but tended to lurk in the corners of fields, for bombers limping back from raids on Portsmouth and Swansea would likely as not drop a few bombs in passing. Sometimes, if they saw anyone about they'd use their machine-guns, and this added an extra hazard to shopping: one learned to fall flat wherever one was, and usually wrecked a good pair of stockings in the process.

Just before we left Seaview I'd had a poisoned insect bite, and had to stay at home and keep my swollen leg up. So I was at home to see the rusty, battered French destroyers of the flotilla that escaped from Oran coming up the Channel. Swollen leg and all, with the rest of the inhabitants of the houses I went out to wave from the sea wall, tears pouring down our faces, for somehow the honour of France was apparent in these survivors, proudly carrying the tricolour.

The Island girls were not very attractive; in general, the right word for them was slumocky. After a week they'd blossomed into clean dresses and curled hair, and every matelot was seen with one on each arm, strolling happily in the streets of Ryde or Newport or even as far as Brading. They were great benefactors to the population.

Living in someone else's home is always difficult, more so when there was the tension of never knowing when Michael might have a free hour and be able to come for a bath, a meal or even for long enough to go for a walk. However, we managed all right, though I used to go up to London sometimes for a few days, and stay with Maud Karpeles in Hampstead. On one of these visits I was invited to go to Ralph's house, The White Gates at Dorking, for tea and there I met Max Beerbohm and his wife. I had no idea what Ralph's home would be like. I suppose I'd expected a small Georgian red brick house, or a long, low, early Victorian one, so I was surprised by the rather ugly bungalow and the large but not well-gardened garden. The marks of war were there already, a white scar of trench across the Downs, leaving the valley as a place for a battlefield. Inside, the big sitting-room with a gallery was quite the most untidy room I had ever seen. In fact I doubt if I'd ever seen a really untidy room before, but as the materials of disorder were books and papers it was congenial. The room, anyway, was big enough for it not to be an oppressive clutter.

Adeline was in her high-backed wheelchair. I'd met her, briefly, at a Wigmore Hall concert, and at *Hugh the Drover* to which I'd gone with Michael, but here in her own home she was alarming. I was, of course, curious about her, and a disabled old age is, at first, an impenetrable disguise. She seemed infinitely older than Ralph, who was at that time in his sixties, very upright and strong, whereas her fragility, her hands bent and crooked by arthritis, her straight grey hair and her face the greyish pallor of an invalid, seemed to remove her from life's ordinariness. It was a relief when the Beerbohms arrived. He was exactly as I'd expected, perfectly himself, neat and trim and enchanting. She was a faded beauty with hair the colour of winter bracken. Ralph and Max hadn't seen each other since Charterhouse, and there was a lot of creative "do you remember?" – Max speaking of one of the masters "and when his wife died he went into mourning in pea-green trousers" – then they went on to music halls, and the Follies, and songs and acts that had delighted them both, for which both had amazingly good memories. When I left, Ralph having hired a car to take me to the station, they came too, and said, "You must come and see us when you are here again." This was marvellous, though I didn't know if I'd ever be there again, and it cheered me as I changed trains at Waterloo and sped back to the Isle of Wight. Walking up from Brading station to Mrs Roach's cottage I could not believe that one day had enclosed such contrasts, and the Island seemed more like a prison than home.

The summer dragged on, with alarming raids and air battles. I slept on the ground floor, in the old nursery, and I used to listen to French cabaret music on my radio trying to drown the sound of the planes, wondering how they were getting on at the fort, wondering if the planes were over Dorking. Then we were suddenly moved, and with a small radar unit we spent the Autumn in Bude. It was all mysterious and we never knew from day to day when we'd have to move on. However, having been told we'd be there for a week or ten days we thought that it would be a treat to stay in a hotel, so we went to the Falcon. It was full of people who'd left London because of the raids and whose maids were supposed to be sending on their letters – dull company, but lovely to have unbroken nights. Cornwall in Autumn was warm and radiant. I spent a lot of time walking on the sands. Once I found that I'd got cut off by the rising tide so I had to scramble up an easy bit of cliff, only to find myself in a field full of black bullocks who were curious and surrounded me. I wondered which to choose of death by drowning or by horns. However, I lived on. I asked if we could have mussels – the rocks were covered with them – but the hotel manager said that the guests wouldn't like them as they were free. Michael was immensely occupied, but we did manage to go as far as Morwenstow to see Hawker's little church with a graveyard full of slate headstones. One day a girl arrived at the hotel, the only other young creature, so we fell into gossip. She was very dashingly dressed and turned out to be the Editor of a magazine called *Woman and Beauty*, visiting her husband who was in the army, and very good value she was. We all dined together and Michael taught her husband the approved gunner method of cleaning boots till they shone; he was finding this a difficult aspect of being a private.

After Bude it was back to Williton, still with the same little unit. I had one amusing excursion to Nottingham, with Mary and her mother. Mary was going to marry Richard Arnold-Baker, and the arrangements for the wedding were pretty sketchy. After a tedious bus journey from Newbury we arrived in a raid, found our way to the hotel where it was too late to have any supper but tea and something cold, mostly beetroot. In the morning the maid said, "Mr Arnold-Baker wants to know where the wedding is." I said, "Tell him, so do I". But it was Richard's brother, who'd arrived even later, and was to be best man. Luckily Mary and I met Richard, we in one taxi, he in another, and found it was the Town Hall at one. Having the two mothers each thinking their loved child was making a mistake and glaring at each other didn't help. The Registrar, because of the confusion (Richard, whose father was a German – later to be involved in one of the anti-Hitler plots – had taken his stepfather's name), asked him to step aside and in a loud whisper asked, "Excuse me, sir, but was you born in 'Oly Wedlock?" and Richard's mother bounced up angrily, saying, "Of course he was." Mary was asked her father's profession, and her mother said, "Well, he's in the Home Guard." And finally their certificate was written out with the wrong names, but apparently they were actually married. We all went off to lunch and then to the pantomime, and finally it was bedtime and Mary's mother came to my bedroom and talked all night about unhappy marriages. I had to be off at dawn on a bus to Oxford, where I stayed two nights with Jean and her parents.

I saw Ernest Rhys there and called on Basil Blackwell, who had published my first book of verse, before I started on the complicated journey back to Taunton. By this time I had a cold and no voice at all. The last lap of the journey was by train from Bristol and for some reason I had to go in the guard's van with a lot of soldiers who, as I could only whisper, whispered too. There was a bad raid going on, so I suppose they thought if we all kept quiet we wouldn't attract attention from the German planes.

Michael was posted to Leicester and I returned to London. His work was in the nature of eighteen or more hours a day, and he would obviously not be able to spend much time with me, even if I had found rooms near his headquarters. Thayer Street had been let and when I returned there I found the flat in a totally disgusting state. The tenant had painted my pale grey stained floors a thick plum colour, and everything was dirty. Much as I hate housework it was a labour of love to clean the place and a delight to settle there. Jean was back in the flat below. After driving ambulances in Oxford she was playing again, and we found a tiny little woman, Mrs. Morris, who came three mornings a week to do our cleaning.

For some odd reason, partly because I wanted to be free when Michael had leave, partly because I thought I should discover how others lived, partly too, because my mother's old friend, Betty Wilmott's husband could arrange it, I went to work for the Charity Organisation Society, the C.O.S., in Marylebone. It had been, in the past, a dragonish Society insisting on respectability in those it helped. By now this sort of censorship had more or less ended and we worked in a pleasant office staffed by young women of my own age, except for the Secretary who was middle-aged and seemed daunting. Now I can see what being forever on the giving end of the line may do in making the most generous sceptical, or disillusioned, if they are going to survive and not be a spendthrift of both pity and funds.

I learned to do casework, visiting people to discover their needs, and how we could best help them. Some had little pensions from other sources which we took to them each week, so I learned a good deal about London as well as meeting many lively characters during those days and living through nights of raids when none of us knew if we should survive, though most of us cheerfully supposed that we would.

One of my clients was an aged midwife who lived near Paddington Station. She was small and plump; she had a room full of dusty china ornaments. She gave me accounts of her most sinister cases, always ending, "And when's the Major coming on leave, dear? Don't you go falling..." When the nearby goods yard was bombed I went round the next day. She'd been taken to a Rest Centre in the middle of the night. "And it fair broke me 'eart. There was whisky there, and all the cheese rations, so everything smelt of Welsh Rarebit – terrible to think of the waste!" she said, over tea. As her sight was bad the cups were usually grubby, but I had taught myself to drink with my left hand, so I got the cleaner side. She was a tough little creature and much more angry than frightened during the raids, though eventually she was quite glad to be taken off to the country. I don't suppose she liked it when she got there as she was essentially a Londoner, but I never heard where she went or what happened to her.

Another of my clients had been a cook and was rejoicing in the first home of her own after a lifetime in service. She had very little of this joyful freedom for she developed paralysis agitans after two years, and it was thought dangerous, for she kept falling, once rather too close to the little range which kept her room warm. She was taken to the Workhouse, and a sadder place I have never seen. There were long dormitories with polished floors, tiny lockers on top of which nothing could be kept. Any relics of real life, a photograph or a workbox, had to be put away, and even the clothes the inmates wore were not their own. They were sheltered and fed and clothed. All that each life had been could survive only in memory as possessions were a nuisance to the authorities. The men were a little better off as they used to go out in fine weather, but the women seemed to have lost all desire to live, huddling silent on hard benches like little birds who know they cannot survive the weather. I was glad when Miss Hulls died, gladder far, many years later, when the Workhouse in Luxborough Street was pulled down.

Our most glamorous pensioner was called Jane Rouira. I sometimes took her money to her, in her lair – a darkened room with a four-poster bed, a ribbon-garlanded guitar, and various appurtenances of magic, Tarot cards and books on astrology and divination. She was used to a diet of new-laid eggs and china tea so rationing had made life, incomprehensibly to her, impossible. She was very entertaining, full of strange stories once the plaint against the unreasonableness of the grocer had been recited. One day when I called I found her in great pain and I insisted on getting a doctor.

She said that she was a Christian Scientist – but when the doctor arrived, she fluttered her five remaining eyelashes and thanked him. She had a strangulated hernia; her poor body was like old elastic, rumpled and crumpled and thin. I took her to St. George's and having seen her to the ward said goodbye, thinking she would never get through an operation. When I called two days later she was sitting up in bed brushing her pale, red-streaked hair and requiring the Matron to be sent for at once, in a tone of unappeasable command, for, she said to me, "The library service here is impossibly bad." After this episode she rather took to hospitals, and a couple of years, a broken arm and a fractured thigh later, she died peacefully in St. Charles's hospital where, she said, the library service was excellent and the nurses angels.

Some time after this I was sent to do a crash course in social work at the Society's Camden Office, where I spent two months. There had been a lot of bomb damage, whole rows of cottages, halves of streets demolished, and there were even poorer and sadder people than in Marylebone. Camden – the office was in Crowndale Road – was new territory to me, full of excitements. A chemist's shop near Mornington Crescent had a collection of oddments in the window including a dish labelled Mandrake. There was a notice on the door saying "Back in ten minutes" and the ten minutes lasted all the time I worked there. The big railway horses still lived under the arches and flocks of goats were kept in back yards. There were thick fogs, when every street became mysterious, all shapes were exaggerated and the horses pulling coal drays looked ten feet tall. One day, in such a fog, I lost my bearings and went into the nearest shop. I thought I was leaning on the counter as I asked my way, and then I looked down and saw it was a coffin. So I moved away. "Don't worry," the shopman said, "the stiff won't mind."

It was all very much Dickens's London, for I'd begun at last to read Dickens, and to understand the world of narrow alleys and little courts, of poverty and of the small unsinkable eccentrics who still lived there. An old woman who lived alone in an upper floor of one of the tall dark houses that used to be in Marylebone Road – one tap and some sort of lavatory for the whole house were across the back yard – had sent a message to the office, that she'd like "to be evacuated." She'd not had her boots off for ten days she told me, because she did go down to the basement in the raids, and a dark and lonely shelter it must have been. Everyone else in the house had gone and she couldn't stand it any more. There were various procedures for evacuation, and she was allocated to the Church Army's quota. "In spite of all these awful circumstances," I told them, "she's remarkably clean and even smells of Eau de Cologne." "How long have you been working here?" "Oh, about six months." "Well, you're pretty green, aren't you? Cologne, indeed! They drink it!" "It's probably nicer than meths," I said.

Not long after this the Citizens' Advice Bureaux were started, and some of us were transferred to work in it, still in the same house in Wyndham Place.[44] I liked the work much better, though it brought my journeys and explorations and the visits to junk shops near where clients lived, to an end.

The C.A.B. was started to cope with all the problems arising from wartime disasters, problems and mishaps of the citizenry. Most people lost clothing coupons and ration books, needed to trace relatives after nights of blitz, needed permits, needed Red Cross letters written to prisoners of war and a thousand and one other problems solved.

A brave girl had saved a child from drowning in one of the emergency water tanks that were here and there in the open cellars of bombed houses. She'd been dressed in her best clothes to go out with her young man, and the wartime materials had shrunk... could she? Yes, we got a new lot of coupons, as well as a glorious

---

[44] Until it was bombed and the CAB moved to more central premises in Baker Street (UVW)

mention in the local paper, for her. A woman came home from work to find the house she lived in cordoned off because of an unexploded bomb. Everyone else had gone and her cat was inside. We had the Heavy Rescue out and her cat Rodney saved, as well as her toothbrush and nightdress, and found somewhere for them both to stay. And so it went on, small dramas making the substance of each day.

One afternoon a grubby girl came in, with a dirty baby in a battered pram. "I want him evacuated now," she said, "he screams all night – he's got to be taken to the country." I couldn't do this myself, I explained, because the W.V.S. did all the arrangements for evacuations of children, and must it be today? Of course we'd do all we could, but not the actual arranging, so I telephoned to the W.V.S. and explained that it was urgent and they, used to such crises, promised to manage it somehow. So I told her this, drew a map for her of how to go – it wasn't more than quarter of a mile – and pointed out the direction. I went back to my desk, saw another two or three people, tidied up my papers and left for a week's leave with Michael.

We went to Kempsford, to stay in a country pub. The upper reaches of the Thames were full of water-lilies, there were meadow sweet, blue cranesbill and roses. It was very peaceful, we were both tired, so we idled and strolled in comfortable ease. We looked at the windows of Fairford Church and had tea with the Blackwells near Oxford. At the end of the holiday we went to tea with the Nevinsons who were living at Campden – in exile as he said, and in misery. Their house in Downside Crescent had been bombed, his pictures were in store, and he was away from the city he loved and his friends whom he needed. He knew war well; six campaigns as a War Correspondent had shown him things he had found worst and best in men. He seemed very old, very fragile and very beautiful, and we both guessed that we were meeting for the last time. Since we'd met first three and a half year ago, he'd written me the most enchanting love-letters; the times we spent together at Maud's or when he'd come to 7.5 were each remembered in his small, elegant writing, by now almost ghostly. It was desolate to see him so unhappy, knowing that he'd much prefer to be going back to the impossible discomforts of his ruined house than left to fade in the country. His wife, Evelyn, was bored too, but too optimistic and prosaic to understand the black realism, romantic imaginings, heroic memories and political despair which made up his mental life; and as to creature comforts and the cooking where they lived, she was not clever enough to make their rations even faintly appetising. So there he was, and there was I saying goodbye for ever over tea with dusty biscuits in the lounge of a dreary hotel.

Michael drove me to Leicester where I left him and went back to London by train. Next morning I heard that the woman who wanted her child evacuated at once had not gone to the W.V.S., but had taken him to the Embankment and thrown him into the river. It was a horrible business and it ended in a frightening day in the following February when I was a witness at her trial at the Old Bailey. I sat through two other cases, and when it came to the point I was asked very little. It seemed that she was known to be mentally disturbed and she was sent to a convent hospital for six months.

I met some strange people at the Old Bailey: the Pathologist who said that he had taken up his gruesome profession because he'd "always been interested in Botany"; the witness who worked in a wholesale meat factory and told me she always took a good piece of bacon home in her hat – "They don't make you take your hat off to search you"; the river policeman who won all his cigarettes by betting that he could tell which reach of the Thames bodies had been found in; and so on.

Long before that end to the story my father came to England for a fortnight. He had travelled over very uncomfortably in a bomber but no-one seemed to find it odd to convey elderly generals in bomb racks. He brought me a very pretty dress and other presents and, joy and delight, twelve lipsticks. I shared them with my friends, and we all enjoyed the luxury of good American war paint as a change from the poorish, hard-to-get, British kind. Father, whom I'd never seen as a man-on-his-own before, was in high spirits. He was much nicer, friendlier and more lively than I ever remembered him. I had of course offered him my camp bed, but he refused it, having other arrangements which I supposed had been made officially. Actually he was staying with a widowed friend, the sharer of an old romance, so it must have been a happy time. It had never occurred to me that he would break loose, and having seen him when he did I can only regret, for him, that it was such a brief interlude. I hope, but doubt, that there had been other times.

I was out and about a good deal, going to rehearsals and film sessions, sometimes concerts with Ralph, to films and plays and to National Gallery concerts at lunch times and to Proms in the evening – early evening in those days. Michael came and went from Leicester, and he was glad that I'd found 7.5. It was an easy base for wherever he was. He was promoted to Lieutenant-Colonel in September, so I found myself, improbably I felt, the Colonel's lady.

My friends were school friends now married, old friends like Kanty, new friends I'd met through Maud, Ralph or Jean; I was having an amusing life. My Aunt came up from Chichester sometimes to see her doctor, and Michael and I went to Brighton fairly often, singly or together, to see Mabel who was ill. She'd had a heart attack and had to rest, to stay in bed, to be idle and bored. Her old friend from Southport days, Leila, was often with her, staying in Rodney's house to which Mabel had returned after her Somerset venture proved too expensive and too lonely. Rodney was a busy surgeon, little at home, so Mabel invented her own occupation for these months. She had become interested in spiritualism. Always fascinated by the occult, she had, too, a great passion for romance and as, in this case, the two came together in generous absurdity, or so it seemed to her sons, they were content to let her fancy roam round possibilities they considered to be rather like her usual novel reading. Twice a week a friend who had some sort of mediumistic powers came to spend a long afternoon at Mabel's bedside. Her sons did not wish to meet this emissary, and never managed to, but Mabel told me about their sessions. A Red Indian spoke to them, lights shone and blinked round the walls of her darkened bedroom, a strange excitement among the beautiful eighteenth-century furniture she had collected. She lay propped up on big down pillows in embroidered cases, with her small hands folded on the hemstitched linen sheet, and by her side sat the tweedy, ancient lady, at whose command the voices told a story of a spirit-lover, much unlike the shooting, fishing, sensible doctor she'd been married to for so long, waiting impatiently to carry her across the threshold of the spirit-home he had prepared for this eager bride. As all the boys had been fond of their father they found this tale both ridiculous and painful, so Mabel told it to me. When she got better and was allowed to get up she would go off to real seances, and both these, and the earlier bedside sessions, had obviously mitigated the loneliness of her life. She had a lively sense of fun, a desire for pleasure, a love of entertainment, and these had had little scope. She was a good watercolour painter, a brilliant needlewoman, but these solitary occupations did not satisfy the frivolous young creature which a part of her remained. This was one reason that she and I got on so comfortably, for we both enjoyed parties and going to the cinema on the spur of the moment. Michael and she enjoyed sketching together, and she admired and respected and was slightly frightened of Rodney. Christopher, away in the Navy, had been a slow developer, less successful in his youth than the other two, and they had lived lovingly but impatiently together until she'd gone to Somerset. At Brighton she'd been hostess to Rodney's friends, with slightly alarming perfectionism. The house was filled with beautiful things, and nothing was ever untidy. Her silks and threads were kept in exquisite order, and her embroidery frame lived in her bedroom where she spent the lightest hours of the day when she was able to work at this craft, which she had taught herself.

She went off on Christmas Eve armed with bottles of claret and pheasants to dine with her spiritualist friends, and there she was taken ill and died. Michael was at Southampton now, in the 131st Heavy Anti-Aircraft Regiment, defending Portsmouth and Southampton, and we could not spend Christmas together but we met at Brighton on the day after Boxing Day for the funeral.

It was the second death close to me that year, for Grannie had died too. She had had a cold, the three sisters with whom she lived in Painswick had told me, but when I telephoned to suggest going to see her they'd advised me to wait till she was better. She died very suddenly and I'd found myself involved in all the funeral arrangements, telegrams to my parents in Ottawa and so forth. But before that I had to go to Painswick. Jean and I lunched together before I caught the train for Stroud. Then the bus took me to Painswick and the house and the friends. It was expected, of course, that I should go to Grannie's bedroom to see her. I was both reluctant and curious, though I had come too late to be any comfort to her. I'd never seen death before, except dead animals and dead birds which I can't bear. So I went nervously, where her friends went familiarly, into her room. There was this faint curve on her bed, covered all over with one of her fine linen sheets, so still that it did not seem real, a stillness greater I felt than that of an inanimate thing like furniture or cushions. Then one of the sisters folded back the sheet, and I realised with a pang of love that I had no need to feel fear of anything with her. She had comforted and cherished and protected me with her love and she showed me in her death the best meeting I could have with that stranger. She looked neither young nor old, the face of a girl, the white hair of an old woman, the calm of untroubled sleep, the face of someone whose serenity was that where everything was resolved. It was a sustaining meeting. I had been conscious on my journey that I had tended to neglect her in the last few years. She had stayed with us in the Island, but since travelling had become difficult we had seen rather little of each other, and I knew that I probably mattered more to her than anyone else. She was no fool, for all her gentleness, and once she had said to me, "I've been too unselfish, it's been very bad for other people as it has made them selfish." My grandfather, of course, my mother even more so. I realised that this was as far as she'd ever permit herself to criticise – sad, sad. She had loved fun and teasing, simple pleasures and talk, she'd not ever failed in generosity of heart or of time or of all she had. All this showed now, a charming goodness that made her dead face something to remember with gladness.

I knew she wanted to be buried with my grandfather, so the dreary pilgrimage to Charlton cemetery was organised, faintly lightened by overhearing her nephew ask the undertaker how much such a journey cost. His aged mother lived at Cheltenham and her soldier husband was, I suppose, another tenant at Charlton cemetery. I gave all the available friends and relations lunch at the Trocadero, which rather strained my resources, but I thought that some sort of feasting is a necessity for the living after funerals.

After Mabel's funeral, when we should have been together, Michael had to go back to Southampton, I to London. It was one of the times when we seemed furthest apart. Both Mabel and Grannie had lived in many ways far below their potential, been victims of the only-too-clear place of women in their circumstances. Widows, as I was soon to discover, are members of the dreariest club in the world.

Meanwhile, we all seemed to live inconsequently, taking sleepless nights and the longing for sleep in our stride; firewatching duties were a second nature. At an alert I tumbled out of bed, clothed in pyjamas, which I hated wearing. But I could pull on the siren suit which lay beside my bed over them more sensibly and easily than I could over the chiffon nightdresses I affected otherwise, then scramble into boots or sandals, according to the weather, snatch up axe, torch and gloves, and be out in seconds, in the familiar nightscope of searchlights and stars and the sound of guns and the rocket batteries.

It was a far cry from the long summer at Portland where I had lived with their early experimental days, from which they had grown to their protecting and devastating power. There was fear all round us, news bulletins, newspapers, but I was enjoying the pleasures of urban life and of meeting people. My diary is full of visits, of meetings with Ralph, with Bob Trevelyan, Leonard Strong and Evelyn Gibbs through whom I had met him, as I had Priaulx Rainier, the South African composer, with Nora Wydenbruck[45] and her husband Alfons Purscher, friends of my Isle of Wight friend Helen Roach – and concerts and theatres in quantity.

Michael had a week's leave in March which he spent in London, and after that I did not see him till Easter which I spent at Chichester with my aunt and uncle from where I went to Portsmouth for the day and so to Cosham where he was stationed; another day when we seemed far apart, barely acquaintances.

A week later I went to *Messiah* at Westminster Abbey. Jean was playing in the Jacques Orchestra and the Bach Choir was conducted by Reginald Jacques. The mezzo singing at that performance was Kathleen Ferrier. I remember her wearing a little cap of black sequins and looking beautiful while she sang with a warmth and involvement that was radiant. I kept meeting musicians, through Maud Karpeles. Old friends of hers, the Rosé Quartet, who were refugees in London, I had met at her flat before she was bombed out in 1941, and I went to some of their concerts. There I usually

---

[45] An explorer of the occult and translator of Rilke

met Paul and Nora Nathan. He had been a paediatrician in Berlin and like all other refugee doctors he had had to re-qualify before he could work in England, which he had to do in a language foreign to him, no easy thing to attempt and achieve in middle age. They, with Maud, Engel Lund, her accompanist, the pianist Ferdinand Rauter, Robert Müller-Hartmann, a refugee composer, were one of the interlocking groups of friends with whom I went to concerts. Jean and her contemporaries were another, and when Michael was on leave we tended to see people he knew already rather more than my newer acquaintances. He had a week's leave at the end of April, some of which we spent at Richmond, going to Kew and to Hampton Court for gentle, pottering days. By this time my sister Rosemary, having managed to extricate herself from the family and Canada to work in Washington as a decoder, had made a further break for freedom and had come back to England. Slim, elegant in gorgeous American clothes, she was longing to work in the Admiralty but they were well supplied with girls doing the work she had done in the United States, and she was firmly directed into the Land Army where she became acquainted with cows, early rising and a completely new kind of life to which she took with surprised pleasure and success.

Ralph came to London fairly frequently, and we were often able to meet for lunch or tea, sometimes at the M.M. Club, which the cellist May Mukle ran in a cellar next to Oxford Circus tube station. The food was moderate, the prices even more so, membership was five shillings a year, and there was always agreeable company to be found. Sometimes Ralph came to my flat, and this of course was much nicer, for I saved up rations and any special treats I found in the way of cakes or frivolities for him.

When Michael had a couple of days' leave at the beginning of June, we planned a holiday for the ten days due to him later in the month as we spent Friday and Saturday rather idly, dining out both nights.

I saw him off at Waterloo on Sunday morning after, luckily, happily, this interval of being together which we had both enjoyed.

So often during the past year we had felt like strangers. In London I was having a much more congenial life than I had ever had before, he a lonely and overworked time of responsibility. But we were luckier than many of our friends for we were in the same country and within reach of each other by telephone, and we had been able to meet fairly regularly, able too to spend his leaves together where we chose, not in the clutter of shared houses in the country to which friends burdened with young children were often exiled – a fate we had been diligent to avoid as we both hated family life. I had found it perfectly possible to be tolerably happy without his presence, though I had not imagined life without him.

The day after he'd gone back to Southampton my telephone rang very early and I heard that he had had a heart attack. I knew enough to say, "Don't move him. I will talk to his brother who is a surgeon, and please, please don't do anything till *he* gets in touch with you, and I will come down after I've arranged everything." Then the telephone went out of order and I had to go to my neighbour, Clare, and use her telephone to talk to Rodney, who was collected and efficient and promised to send a heart specialist over to Cosham as soon as possible, then to get Michael to a Brighton nursing home as soon as he was fit to travel. But all this took time, and when I telephoned to Cosham about eleven to tell them the arrangements, someone there said that Michael had been taken by ambulance to the hospital at Netley. By then I was frightened, and this move seemed to me irresponsible and dangerous, though I realised that facilities for nursing Michael in his small room in that busy Mess were pretty bleak. However, I could do nothing as I could not get through to Netley, but I asked Rodney to try when I had to ring back to tell him that all he'd arranged was now useless. I was glad that Ralph was coming to lunch, and I could only wait for news from Netley. I'd given Jean's number, as she had come in and as my telephone was still out of order. Ralph was, as usual, a comforting presence. It was not a telephone call that came, but a telegram, of the most unspeakable crudeness:

REGRET TO INFORM YOU THAT YOUR HUSBAND DIED AT NETLEY HOSPITAL AT TEN A.M. BODY WILL BE SENT TO LONDON OR ONE FIRST CLASS WARRANT ISSUED FOR YOUR ATTENDANCE AT FUNERAL SOUTHAMPTON.

I couldn't focus, couldn't believe that while I'd been telephoning, Michael was already dead, and how could he be dead when I'd seen him yesterday? Ralph said at once "You must come home with me." Before that he had to go to some meeting and how I spent the afternoon I do not know. I had to let people know – my brothers-in-law, my aunt and uncle, Rosemary, my parents in Canada, which I suppose I did, but those things are completely obliterated.

I went back to Dorking with Ralph, and found that a bed for me had been made in the big galleried living-room they called the hall. "We wanted you near us," Adeline said. She was very quiet and kind, so were her nephew Adam and his wife Pam who came and talked to me after Adeline had gone to bed. Then, finally alone, I realised that Michael was dead and that I'd never hear his voice again. It was this dematerialization that seemed most strange. A body is there, but the voice is not. Another realisation of that night was that there were two couples in the house, Ralph and Adeline, Adam and Pam and that henceforward I was going to be outside that normal state.

Next day I went to London for the day to collect some clothes, and heard that Jean's father had died, and the same week our little Mrs Morris's husband died too. Alone at 7.5 that afternoon I was aware of a presence in the room. I felt that Michael was making some insistent sign, some urgent hurried visit, but that we could not understand each other, or reach each other.

Adam took me to London on the day of the funeral, and Mary met me at Waterloo to go to Southampton. I'd taken great pains with my appearance: black I wore very often, but I wore a green straw boater Michael liked, with a veil, and I wore a rose. It seemed wrong not to make as good an effect as possible. When we went into the little hut of a church that was used by the Army I was entirely undone because on the long coffin they'd put his uniform cap. All hats do acquire a personality, a tilt, a look of the owner's wearing of them, and this was an old one I'd known for years.

I sat between Rodney, Michael's younger brother – the youngest, Christopher, was at sea – and Mary. Who else was there I cannot remember, but there were men who had served with Michael. One wrote: "He was the one person who held my whole-hearted regard and admiration... Michael had that rare gift of leadership so essential to the born officer. The welfare of his men was always his first consideration, and he was loved for it, no officer in the British Army was ever so sincerely loved and admired by his men as Michael was." I felt the grief and the affection of those who were able to be at the short service.

Mary and I waited about, then came home with a small oak box, all that was left of Michael's physical presence. Hands and eyes were no more, now, than memory. Next day I went up to Ranmore and scattered these ashes among the beech trees in the wood to the north of the ridge. I thought it was a place he would have liked, both secret and wild.

That afternoon Ralph took me to tea with his brother at Leith Hill Place. His brother lived there alone since his wife's death, and the house had not changed very much, Ralph said, since his mother's day. She had died only a few years earlier and had lived there ever since she had been a widow, some sixty years, until Hervey came home on his retirement. There was a white and gold Morris paper in the drawing-room, table piled with books, the family portraits were put away, and their places showed on the walls. Thin bread and butter, strawberries and cream for tea, all rarities in these days of rations. Hervey and Ralph were not like each other, yet their voices were alike. Ralph asked if he might take me to see the kitchen garden. Suddenly I could see Ralph as the youngest, asking permission from his elder brother to borrow the garden-door key, an echo from their long-ago childhood.

The kitchen garden was a delight, surrounded by high walls on which grew old-fashioned roses and espaliered fruit. It was four acres square, tilted southwards, and when there had been enough gardeners to look after it properly it would have made the household self-sufficient, with the cows and the pigs and the hens of Hervey and Ralph's childhood days. Cows there still were, though under the control of the Milk Marketing Board, and hens, but the garden was no longer under full cultivation. Pink cabbage-roses flowered on the walls, and the strawberries we'd had for tea were picked perhaps an hour before we'd eaten them. It gave me, as he'd intended, a glimpse of Ralph's early life for there is nothing like seeing the places where people have lived to make it possible to imagine them in early years. Also, another part of his wise imagination, it filled the rest of the day for me, for how can the rest of the day be spent when the first hours of it are used to scatter a husband's ashes?

The queer thing was that Mary, who was an extraordinary forseer, using cards as her medium, had been saying for about six months that my life was going to change. She'd foretold my meeting with Ralph. She'd been very mysterious about it and written it all down about a year before it happened; she wouldn't tell me then as it all seemed so improbable. This time we had both been so certain that John would be killed in Burma that it had not occurred to either of us that this wouldn't change my actual living conditions. We had not imagined Michael's death as a possibility though he was as much exposed to danger as anyone living in England. After this she gave up telling fortunes for years, as she had been far too accurate far too often. It was a gift that had become a nightmare. She had been one of our most frequent visitors wherever we lived, often staying for quite long visits, and she was very fond of Michael, as he was of her, treating her rather like a younger sister.

I went back to London after the weekend and, for some reason or another, to Cameo Corner. I'd first met Moshe Oved when Ernest Rhys had taken me to a PEN Club[46] luncheon at Pagani's. We'd sat next to each other and he'd shown me a hazel-nut-sized yellow diamond he'd brought with him. "Something to look at, in case I was bored," he'd said. His wife had been a pupil of Kanty's father and Michael had bought me presents at his shop, a pair of earrings, a turquoise, gold, and silver bracelet for my thirtieth birthday. Moshe was severe about choices, not allowing people to buy jewellery which he felt wrong for them. I suppose Kanty had told him and his wife about Michael's death, for he invited me into the back of the shop where he lit candles in a seven-branched candlestick and tipped a heap of unset jewels on to the table. "Look at those," he said, "because they are beautiful", and indeed they were, glinting and dazzling in the light of the candle flames.

For a few days I saw a lot of friends: it seemed that everyone was determined that I should not be alone too much, and I was, in any case, wondering what I should do and glad to ask for suggestions. It was clear that I'd have to earn my living. My parents sent me a hundred pounds so I was solvent for the time being and in no hurry to make any effort; the sad unpacking and disposing of Michael's things was enough to manage, as well as seeing the bank manager and such business. My plans, nebulous as they were, were brought to nothing because I woke one morning with an agonising pain in

---

[46] PEN Club; an elegant private Club in London

my toe. I hobbled to the Orthopaedic Hospital where I sat in Out Patients' for hot hours and later I was referred to an orthopaedic surgeon in Harley Street. He told me that I had broken my toe, which seemed curious to me, but I was in pain and anxious for something to be done. He strapped up my foot and off I went to meet Ralph to go to hear the first performance of *Valiant for Truth* at St. Michael's, Cornhill, and to be taken out to dinner after. The words were as apt for Michael, at that moment, as any words could have been. Without any religious belief, allegory does very well to crystallise feeling and there were a lot of us half comforting ourselves with the magical sound of trumpets blowing in welcome beyond the river of death.

I continued to hop my way through life with my left foot in a bedroom slipper, gyrating from film to theatre to dining out with friends in London interspersed with quiet days at Dorking for a week or two. I went to stay with my aunt and uncle at Chichester. It was my aunt's doctor who discovered the truth about my foot. He'd called to see her and I asked him to fix a new plaster for me, as the original one had become loose. I'd had a most difficult acrobatic time keeping my foot out of water when I had baths. He was curious, then furious, when he heard my story. "No x-ray?.. Get in the car at once and we'll go to the hospital and have one." No break at all, it transpired, but one of my tiny fine needles had got into my foot and was on a nerve that vibrated in my toe.

When I told this news both Ralph and his brother-in-law, R.O. Morris who lived at the White Gates, wanted to go and horse-whip the orthopaedic surgeon. Adeline said it would be better to get my five pounds back, but I rather favoured the horse-whipping. It was delightful to have such an eighteenth-century revenge proposed. But what actually happened was that I arranged to stay with Rodney at Brighton so that he could take out the needle for me, armed with the Chichester X-ray. Brighton was forbidden territory, as were all the South Coast towns, but I took a chance, and followed a likely-looking soldier through the barrier, calling out cheerfully to him as I passed the ticket collector, "I've got my own, darling," – hoping to suggest that I was a resident and his appendage. It worked, and my right to be there wasn't questioned. I spent a week after my little operation skulking in the garden or indoors hoping there'd be no spot checks on identity cards while I was there, and vowing never, never to go barefoot again when I had sewing things about, to count needles, and so on and so forth.

I had to have an even larger bedroom slipper to cover my bandage and I hopped and hobbled home, developed a taxi reflex which I couldn't really afford, because buses were impossible to manage, and finally, at Adeline's invitation, I went back to Dorking for a month, with the utmost thankfulness.

Life there was very quiet. Morris taught me to play backgammon which we did every evening after dinner. The best thing that happened was Ralph's invitation to bring whatever work I was doing into his study. This was surprising to me for I had thought seclusion and concentration, solitude and silence, were necessary for his work. He had cleared a space for me among the piles of paper and odd bits of gardening stuff, such as bean pods ripening, which might be used for seed, in the round bow of the small square room. There I sat on the window seat and had my exercise book and a long page of verse at which I was working. It was a curiously successful arrangement, for we were easily silent together, or when one of us had something to say, to ask, we did so without it disturbing each other. When Ralph got up from his table and spent a few minutes, or a quarter of an hour, working at the piano he didn't mind my being there to hear his experiments or confirmation of his thought. These mornings spent together were a consolidation of affection, a comfort and a pleasure to each of us. I think this shared retreat rather amused Adeline. It gave me the reassuring feeling of being wanted, missed when I wasn't there, which helped me enormously. I was discovering that being single again was difficult, seeing from the outside that the world is made for couples, which I hadn't particularly noticed when I was part of a couple myself. Of course, at that time, nearly everyone was separated by the war from their husband or wife. I did not know any other war widows. My married friends still had leave or letter to look forward to.   Being with so long-married a couple I could see the interdependence, the shared interests, problems, friends, memories and fabric of living that made up their marriage, with all its qualities and all its problems, time to wonder about a structure from which I was now excluded. Had Grannie felt like this when she stayed with my parents or indeed with Michael and me? Did my aunt, who had never married, feel sad when a bedroom door shut on us, on pillow talk, and all the companionable gossip of dressing or undressing? I slept in a single bed and thought of that little strew of ashes under the beech trees of Ranmore, wondering if I had reached an end or a beginning.

Chapter 5: John's Death

When I went to the Labour Exchange to look for a job I felt myself unqualified for anything much. No degree, no training, a small book of verse to my credit and that was about all. I stipulated that I'd do anything in London except work to do with machinery or figures, for both of which I have neither talent nor liking. The first job they offered was as an inspector of aircraft at Bristol, an idea so ludicrous that I said an immediate no. The Air Force should, I felt, not have to depend on my say-so for their safety. The next offer was a place in the Income Tax office. Our country, I pointed out, was in a bad enough mess already without having someone unable to add, subtract or divide mucking up the revenue, so they said weakly that it would be nice if I could find myself a job, and not come bothering them.

This I somehow managed to postpone for a long time, I suppose while my parents' hundred pounds lasted. My diary till the beginning of November was full of seeing friends, going out and about with Ralph and, of course, firewatching. Then the engagements became evenings only as I had started work.

Dr. Paul Nathan was looking for a secretary-receptionist, offering two pounds a week, white overalls, and work in Welbeck Street, absolutely round the corner from 7.5. Having stipulated that I should be free to go sometimes to the National Gallery lunch-time concerts, making no appointments on those days between12.30 and 3 p.m., we agreed on a usual 9.30 to 5 day, and I said that of course I'd stay late if needed. So I started on a new existence. Financially it was a bit limiting; by the time the War Office had settled that my pension would be £85 a year, a lot of Generals, who were father's friends, had gone into battle on my behalf. Defending the South Coast did not, the War Office maintained, constitute active service, and twenty-one years' service in the Army and so forth allowed this amount for a Lieutenant-Colonel's widow, so there it was. I managed: rent twenty-seven shillings and sixpence, gas and electricity were on shilling meters, no fares except for weekend trips to Dorking, which was about five shillings including buses to and from Victoria, Mrs Morris about ten shillings and all the rest for me. I had lunch at home every day, so that was easy and cheap, and I gave one dinner party of eight to twelve people once a week. My parents sent me stockings and sometimes food parcels. It didn't seem difficult, and there were plenty of free entertainments such as the concerts given by the Committee for the Promotion of New Music. I was often given tickets for concerts in which friends were playing, or by Ralph, to whom many complimentary tickets were sent. I dined out with others managing on comparable amounts, and even afforded cinema and theatre tickets. The work was interesting, too, chiefly because Paul tried to treat me as a student, telling me, or asking me, what I thought this and this might be, and why. Also I had access to the *Lancet* and the *British Medical Journal* to read all I could understand and to ask questions about. He had many refugee patients, friends from Germany who had settled in England and continued to go to him with their children as well as many English patients. There were three things I hated, the monthly accounts (typing bills and envelopes was horrid, boring and slow for a two-finger typist – writing up the case histories was fascinating so I didn't notice my slow typing there), sterilising the instruments, and holding the victims for circumcisions. This dismal ritual was a fairly frequent occurrence, so when it was over I used to make tea. Circumcision Tea was a feature of many mornings. Paul's patients were mostly under twelve or so, and the variety of major and minor troubles was extraordinary. Some were sad and serious, some rare, some funny. There were two Czech girls who arrived with very small and bright orange coloured babies, both girls were crying over these horrid little creatures and muttering about jaundice, but it turned out that they'd been beguiled by Ministry of Food propaganda and had been feeding the children on practically nothing but mashed carrots. Another time a Russian couple arrived with a tiny infant that had great black bruise marks on its back. They were almost at divorce point, accusing each other of hitting a defenceless baby.

"Has either of you Mongolian blood?" Paul asked.
"My grandmother was Mongolian," the girl said.

Then Paul explained that all Mongolian babies are born with these marks which fade after some weeks. A passionate reconciliation took place and the couple left starry-eyed.

Paul saw many sad cases, Mongol children, deformed children, and some very ill ones. But there was a lot that was cheerfully fascinating, diets and remedies, cures achieved and even some moral guidance. One little boy whose father was away at the war was completely out of hand: he was stabbing fellow passengers on buses with a hatpin. Ostensibly he'd come about his chilblains, but his mother was in a frenzy about his uncontrolled behaviour and Paul gave him a commander-in-chief's court-martialling about his non-contribution to the war effort which succeeded in making home life a lot easier, we gathered.

Paul and his wife, Nora, were very hospitable, and their parties were usually for musicians, though it was through them that I met Olga and Hugh Miller. Writing under the name Sagittarius, her sharp, satirical verses were a weekly pleasure in the *New Statesman*. Engel Lund and Ferdinand Rauter were there, often. I saw a good deal of them either at home or in Clarendon Road where they shared a house with an old friend of Engel's, Eileen MacLeod, who worked at the BBC.

Through Bob Trevelyan I met his cousin Rose Macaulay who lived round the corner in Manchester Square. She looked like a Roman boy, suddenly old, rather than an elderly woman. She bicycled rather wildly about Marylebone. She was very angry, for quite a long time, with the Fire Service. The people living in the flat below hers in Hinde Street had telephoned for help as they had a fire – something domestic and not at all to do with enemy action. The Fire Service, bored with inaction, were round there in a flash; they had a ladder up the wall and poor Rose was woken from her sleep, slung over a fireman's shoulder and carried to the ground. "In my nightdress," she said indignantly, "and I hit him with my fists and said, 'Put me down, put me *down*'." The final insult was that by the time she went back upstairs another fireman had hacked his way into her flat with an axe, and anyway, by then, her neighbours had extinguished their curtains or wastepaper basket or whatever had caused the alarm.

Kathleen Long was another neighbour, short, energetic, candid in her thoughts and opinions and cheerfully funny about her adventures as a Catholic convert. Once in the confessional, the priest, who had asked her her profession, misheard the word pianist. He made her a long speech about the wickedness of such work, misleading the citizenry, dabbling in such dark forms of power ... on and on he went, Kathleen getting more and more aghast, till the penny dropped. "Father," she cried, "PIANIST, not palmist!" She could, with a scarf over her head, have looked like a fortune teller, but never in her life would she have played around with black arts. Other arts, yes. She had an Epstein maquette, she bought pictures for her tiny flat, and at her parties I met Orovida, Pissarro's grand-daughter, a very large woman with memorable eyes.

Our little nightclub in the basement of 7.5 made lunches. The barman Ted and Janet, the beautiful Irish wife of the huge soldier, Dave who acted as chucker-out when he was on leave – rather often – our landlord, the shrill-voiced lady who sang in the club in the evenings, a scatty talented girl Kay, the huge near-Great-Dane, our cat Alex, Kanty, who was now living in Jacob's Well Mews behind 7.5, and of course Jean, and an older friend of hers, Clare Howden, who had taken the third of our 'Cottage South' flats, were the usual company to be found off and on in the basement. Ralph sometimes gave lunch parties there, Maudie and Myra Hess were occasional guests, both with such weak heads, he said, that half a glass of sherry each in Heneckey's bar across the road was enough to make them fall asleep over lunch. When he took Jean and me there, or we were taken by Bob Trevelyan, the barmaid was delighted. Not only did they buy us drinks neither of us could afford, but she found them charmingly friendly customers. There were lunch parties, too, after some National Gallery concerts. One, I suppose given by Myra Hess, was at the Garrick restaurant, just behind the National Gallery. I was invited because the Belgian quartet who had given the concert had used my flat for rehearsals, and the party was conducted in French, Ralph launching bravely and successfully into a long story about meringues and false teeth that did great credit to his long-ago French governess or to the months he had spent in Paris studying with Ravel.

On Ralph's seventieth birthday the National Gallery concert was devoted to celebrating him. I went to the concert and afterwards I met Joy and Gerald Finzi. Gerald's Shakespeare song-cycle, *Let Us Garlands Bring*, had been written as a birthday present and dedicated to Ralph. I had liked it, particularly the dirge from *Cymbeline*, which still seems the perfect and inevitable music for 'Fear no more the heat of the sun'. The Finzis had asked Ralph to lunch with them. When we were introduced they invited me to come too. I supposed that this was because I'd arrived at the concert with Ralph, but I discovered at lunch that it was because they had bought my book, as they bought all new books of verse as they were published, and had liked it, which was very pleasing. We took to each other, and before long I was spending occasional weekends at their house in Berkshire and they were frequent visitors to me, Gerald particularly, as he was working in London at the Ministry of War Transport and felt an exile in the city.

I spent a Christmas week at Dorking, gardening with Ralph, walking and playing backgammon with Morris[47], gossiping with Adeline, sharing the reading-aloud sessions, enjoying the luxury of hot-water bottles distributed to us all after lunch for the siesta that always followed the reading. Ralph's voice would trail off into a murmur, the rug over his feet, the purring cat on his lap would soothe him to sleep however exciting the book. Adeline, in her high chair, a footstool supporting her feet, red Indian shawl across her long black skirt, would nod and doze, and I, probably sharing a chair and a hot-water bottle with the other cat, would drift off too, or pick up my own book. It was unlike any other Christmas I'd spent, and all the better for being different. We were fire-watching regularly still, and Jean and I were taken through a tremendous exercise with fire bombs and smoke in a ruined building, crawling about getting filthy as we learned the use of stirrup pumps. When on duty we were sent to certain houses where buckets of water were supposed to be kept for our use; more than once we arrived to find the buckets full of vegetable peelings and rubbish – and the owners of the house surprised and angry when we reproached them. Jean and I did our fire-watching together; the third of the stirrup-pump team varied. We had the barmaid from Heneckey's for a bit but she had hysterics when there was any gunfire so she gave up and a noble Lord took her place. He very often failed to appear and said always that he'd had to go to a dinner. We pointed out that we too had dinner invitations which we did not accept on fire-watching nights. He resigned, and other third parties came and went till that job ended.

Ralph had been busy with film music, *49th Parallel* in 1940, *Coastal Command* in 1942 as well as incidental music for a broadcast of *The Pilgrim's Progress*, but the core and centre of his work had been his Fifth Symphony. Some of it had been written before the war, tried out as incidental music in a pageant in 1938. For a time, early in the war, he'd devoted himself to any minor war

---

[47] R. O. Morris, composer and teacher, was Adeline's brother-in-law

jobs in Dorking as well as to various committees – working for refugee committees – musicians, for C.E.M.A.[48] and anything that offered as well as being on the committee of the house where some refugees from Germany lived in Dorking. Like this he felt that, though he was too old for any active service, he was as involved in work relating to the war as he could be. But he had been working on the Symphony almost since I had known him; in one of his earliest letters to me, in July 1938, he'd written, "I am here on the Wiltshire Downs and the hermitage is succeeding, I think. But I must confess that the other thing has taken precedence of *Epithal.* You know I can't do things unless I think I ought to be doing something else..." I hadn't known that when he wrote those words and, anyway, he had finished *Epithalamion* long before he'd finished his Fifth Symphony. Spending so much time in the study with him, I knew a great deal about that Symphony, though I hadn't been able to go to rehearsals. It was as magical and serene, as fulfilling as any music I had ever heard, perhaps more so because I had already known it, because Ralph had both written and conducted it. I had heard him conduct many of his own works by then, and there is always something special about the hand that wrote the music controlling and directing it, the long journey from invention to performance comes full circle and, in this radiant performance, fears and despairs were cancelled, beauty and serenity were all. It was still light, the evening of midsummer day, when we came out of the Albert Hall. There was a party of us, who I can't remember; Adeline's sister Cordelia and one of her nieces, but who else? We all walked down to Chelsea, to the river. The day ended for me dining quietly with Ralph, the music still in the air.

Since the war began I had done a number of verse programmes for the BBC, short anthologies, which I much enjoyed collecting, though they seemed to take as long to type as they did to put together. Through them I met both Stephen Potter and Edward

---

[48] Council for the Encouragement of Music and the Arts (the fore-runner of the Arts Council)

Sackville-West by whom they were produced, and I had a fair number of my own poems printed in various weeklies. My second collection was accepted, again by Basil Blackwell, in 1943; though I had found I could earn my living by working for Paul it was not at all the sort of work I wanted to do for ever. Certainly there was variety, but I had to be there by nine-thirty and I had to stay there till five, all right for the war, but there were going to be years and years of life through which I'd have to pay rent and eat and buy clothes, so I grasped at what chances I could to earn money in more enjoyable ways. As to buying clothes – this was not much of a problem. We'd been rationed for ages, almost everything was on coupons so it was a matter of ingenuity and cunning to have any variety at all. Furnishing fabrics could be found, corduroy sometimes, for skirts or coats, pretty dust sheets turned up in small shops. Joy Finzi was particularly good at finding such things in Newbury and one cut up old curtains for housecoats or evening dresses. It was always marvellous to be given coupons; Adeline was generous in this and it was one form of gold-digging I pursued with abandon, Bob Trevelyan being my chief quarry as he so often said that he owned too many clothes. He did, too, for he kept appearing in lovely corduroy suits, mossy and silvery greens or smoky greyish brown, just the camouflage for sitting under the trees in Leith Hill Woods where he went to write his poems. He showed me some of his haunts there when I went over to spend the day during a September holiday at Dorking. The Trevelyans' house was the other side of the slope on which Leith Hill Place stood, looking over the same long view to the south. Chanctonbury Ring was visible on a clear day from a paved terrace at the Sniffolds. The nicest room in the house was Bob's library, books from floor to ceiling, comfortably arranged so that he knew where each one was. There I'd met his old friends Gordon Bottomley and Arthur Waley, whose translations from Chinese poems I'd known for years but whose six-volume translation of *The Tale of Genji* was new to me and had been a present from Bob, given in his off-hand way: "Well, as I've got two copies you can have this one." He gave me another present that year. I think he was both horrified and surprised to find that I had no classical education, so he made a translation of the Georgics for me, and wrote a long and stately dedicatory poem which gave me enormous pleasure, partly for itself, partly because it was immensely touching to think of all the hours of work that he had spent to share words and thoughts he had delighted in, making them available to one to whom they were lost in the silence of an unknown language.

The only change in this pattern for me was my parents' return to England. Father was still working, I think at the War Office, and they took over a flat belonging to Mary and Richard at Richmond. They were glad to have left Canada where they'd felt, at least my mother had, very much too safe. For my father it had been a very busy and a very interesting and responsible job dealing with armaments, travelling to see factories and meeting people. I don't think that they liked Ottawa much, the climate was too fierce in both its heat and cold, and my mother had avoided as much as she could the available social life. Once back in England she was able to see her old friends again, the only people with whom she felt comfortable. They spent Christmas Eve with me. The next day I lunched with the Nathans, had tea with my godmother, dinner with Engel Lund. Looking through the little diary in which I wrote my engagements I am not surprised to find that I had written on the last page, "The end of a year of being always in a hurry."

Of course, 1944 started in exactly the same way. New years do start with empty engagement books, but the pattern doesn't seem to change. The National Gallery concerts were a continued pleasure. It was wonderful to have a chance to hear so much chamber music and to hear so many performers, many of whom I knew. Those of us who lived within easy access of each other's flats spent a good deal of time together, going to plays and films, or sharing rations for supper parties cooked with extravagant invention. Invention was all we had to be extravagant with.

We had irregular letters from my brother. Burma was a dangerous place and he was somewhere in the thick of the fighting. It was on April 4th that my father telephoned to say that he had been killed. By some hideous mistake the War Office had failed to let him know before releasing the story to the press. It was quite a long time before we heard what had happened, and that it had happened ten days earlier than the news reached us. John had been with a brigade, his battery in support, holding a position to the north-east of Imphal on a road on which it was not expected that the main Japanese attack would be made. It was, and for five days this small force held the Japanese army. A fellow gunner wrote: 'During this time John acted as local C.R.A. and had the whole of the Brigade mortars under his command, as well as his Battery. His work was magnificent and time and time again enemy attacks were broken up completely by the devastating fire he arranged to cover the perimeter. For many of us the experience of being under such continual, intense fire was completely new and some may have cracked but for John's example. Where and when things were hottest, John could be seen, calmly walking from gun to gun, visiting O.P.s and posts talking to the men in them. His very presence alone encouraged men to remain firm and unafraid. On the evening of March 25th, John, laying a gun himself, fought a duel with a Jap 75m. which had been strafing the infantry. He knocked it out and the infantry cries of "Well done, Gunner" were indeed well deserved. Unfortunately, a little later, John was wounded in the face and went to the Field Hospital. At dawn on the 28th the enemy broke through the perimeter and reached the gun position, over-running the gun post, but were then held by gunners and the infantry fighting in the gun positions. John, hearing that his battery was being attacked, came out of hospital and joined us. No words can possibly describe what that meant to us and after that there was never a doubt of the safety of the guns. The position was extremely tense, and John with Major Smith of the mortars attempted to rally the infantry into re-taking the perimeter, themselves with rifle and bayonet led a desperately gallant attempt to do so, charging straight at the enemy. Major Smith was mortally wounded immediately. John reached the over-run gun pit and killed the three enemy who were holding it. He was killed clearing a slit trench just beyond the gun pit. The guns were never lost, and although badly shot up, not a man of John's battery attempted to leave his post, such was the spirit John had created in them. That same night, after being ordered to destroy the guns the men of the Battery, with the remainder of the garrison broke through the enemy lines, and after three days rejoined the main force. The Battery is again in action and ready to face the enemy – whatever success we have in the future will be a direct tribute to the Major, and his ceaseless work in preparing us for these times. John died gallantly, and not a single man of his Battery can ever forget his supreme bravery.'

Joe Kidd, the subaltern who wrote this, had shared the dreadful week, the lack of water, food and sleep and the days between the destruction of the guns and finding a way back to the main force. He had written as soon as he could for his letter was dated March 31st. There were more letters too, from other survivors, but this immediate description was the greatest kindness and help. The news of John's death shattered both my parents, though I suppose that they must have half expected it, as I had, for so long.

The next day I went to the National Gallery where the Griller Quartet played Haydn's *Seven Last Words*. I can never hear that music without the desolation of that day returning, the sorrow for a life spent so much in remote places, behind barbed wire on the North West Frontier, in the Waziristan operations, and then in the Burma battles of '42 and onwards. He had had a great capacity for life and he had had so little of the kind of it he liked most. He was twenty-nine when he died.

D-Day came, again everyone listened to as many news bulletins as they could. Torrents of words flowed over us, hopes and despairs flickered and were blunted, and the days were as busy as ever. I was glad to be working at something where cures and remedies were the object in a world where everything seemed to be breaking. One of the pleasures was my minute roof garden, full of summer flowers and a place where two or three people could sit and talk. One night I remember going out there, having been woken by an extraordinary sound. John Evans, the author of *The Escaping Club*, used to spend his leave at 7.5, staying with Clare in her flat on our staircase. He was on the roof already, and we peered about to see where the noise had come from. He obviously knew something that I didn't, saying, "I expected this would start". The rest of us soon discovered what it was all about, for doodle bugs[49] were the new menace. Most of Paul's patients left for the country so I spent the summer at Dorking, coming up to London for a short working day, staying up on fire-watching nights or for any particular engagement. At Dorking the small bedroom in which Ralph and Adeline slept was sandbagged, and that and the passage between it and the big room were the safest places in the house. Adeline's maid, Salter, would bring her mattress into the passage and Adeline insisted that I should put mine on the floor between her bed and Ralph's. Morris stayed firmly in his own room. The three of us in our dormitory often gossiped for half the night. One buzz bomb fell very close, we had heard it cut out and were all expecting to die. I remember that my skin felt like a tight dress, and I was glad to be able to reach a hand to Adeline and to hold Ralph's hand the other side. The long moment of silence was too long, the crash shook the house and the explosion was a quarter of a mile away, half masked by the clatter of glass as the study window blew inwards. We discovered next day that the bomb had fallen on a cottage far from any other house. People from London had come down for the night to get away from the raids; one man and a baby survived.

---

[49] German V1 flying bombs

I had, since the first meeting at Dorking, seen the Beerbohms fairly regularly. They used to ask me to tea, which meant a bus journey. Max would meet the bus, his suit, brown as partridge, looked elegantly urban. He'd engage me in conversation, leaning on the bonnet of the bus. Gesturing towards a strange figure dressed in black flapping away down a small path, he said, "My sister." He would then continue his discourse, and I, who'd caught the bus driver's eye for some minutes had to say, "You know, I think the bus has to go on." He'd remove his elbow, bow to the driver and we'd go to the house to tea and I'd hear all the latest news of the searchlight detachment at the bottom of the garden. Lady Beerbohm drew me aside one day and asked me to tell Ralph that she had a special bottle of Madeira that she'd hidden from Max for him. At tea-time, to my surprise, Max seemed to prefer something out of a bottle that said Wincarnis, or Emu Burgundy – whether it was what it said on the bottle or some specially disguised treat I never knew – but we did share tea once. On a spring day, I went out for a walk with both Bob Trevelyan and Max. We found an inn where they provided teas, we sat down under a pink may tree in full flower and had an astonishing war-time meal of an enormous plate of bread with real butter, and watercress. It was a hot day and we were all content with the moment. "What are you doing?" asked Max. I discounted my job. "Reviewing for the *Times Lit*.", I said. "Aha," said Max. "Slash 'em."

This extra had come into my life when Gerald Finzi had sent me to meet Edmund Blunden at Printing House Square. He was as nervous as I, it seemed, for as he talked he wreathed himself round a chair till I feared that he would never be able to uncoil. However, he did, and he sent me books regularly, all books of verse at first, later collections of essays and other odds and ends. I enjoyed this work, as it made me think what I really did think. I used to read the books all through, then brood over them for a week, then write, then labour to type my thoughts, the most difficult part of the proceeding to me, as I cannot control machinery with any comfort – my typewriter has always been more an enemy than a friend. Reviewing was, I thought, a hope for future work, as well as a pleasant though small addition to my present resources.

However, living for the moment was occupation enough, and it was lovely to be at Dorking so much. R.O. Morris, whose wife (Adeline's sister) had died about the same time as Michael, lived with his cats in the biggest bedroom at The White Gates. He taught at the Royal College of Music and once a week at Oxford. He also compiled some of *The Times* crossword puzzles. He had the household supply of drinks. One bottle a month each was the allowance to all Army and Navy Stores customers, and by common consent all three went to Morris. Adeline didn't drink at all, and Ralph never when he was working; when he was revelling it was quite another matter. Morris would invite me to join him for a glass of gin and lime before dinner when I stayed for weekends, then he'd pass on all the gossip of the week, domestic, mostly to do with 'the girls', two middle-aged ladies who lived in the annexe, though the cats' adventures or horrors to do with the hens came into the picture. The hens were supposed to lay eggs for the house, but they weren't very good at it; however Ralph became fond of them and would dig up worms for them. Neither he nor Morris, who were supposed to share this duty, cared for mucking-out the henhouse. This weekly chore was set for Sunday morning, so when I was staying I did it, with whichever one whose job it was supposed to be that week, in attendance, carrying a bucket of hot water for me. I crawled inside, shovelled and scraped and swilled, painted the legs of any hen with scaly-leg with some sinister compound, and felt a glow of virtue, shared unjustly by whichever overall-clad workmate was on duty. A regular treat, too, were the Saturday lunches at the local pub, to save rations and to give the cook a half day. I usually cooked the Sunday supper and often did some of the shopping. Adeline's frequent postcards to me were filled with instructions or about what she'd 'caught' in the Dorking shops, or about how I should arrange to meet Ralph for rehearsals or concerts in London. She was by then almost immobilised, moving from her indoor chair to one that could be wheeled into the garden, and dependent on her maid, but she wrote and spoke as if she shopped herself. She was a tremendous letter-writer, dealing with all of Ralph's correspondence, either on her own, or taking his dictation, with all the bills and cheques, and with her own family. She and her youngest sister Cordelia wrote to each other every day, and she cherished all her family to the most far flung limits of cousinship as well as many friends, most of whom I met over the years when I was so frequent a visitor that I was part of the establishment. I saw my parents fairly often, and there were, as there had been all through the war, emergencies at Chichester. My uncle was deafer and blinder than ever, my aunt fragile and the mainstay of the household was an elderly gardener. Various inadequate housekeepers perched there for a short time, and when each left for more comfortable jobs I used to be summoned to clear up and help to find another. One of them had been imported from Yorkshire, and indeed from my uncle's past. She was a tough lady whom my aunt disliked from the start. I thought that her taking over of my uncle's clothing and sweet coupons, which my aunt considered to be her own due, was enough reason for dislike and had eventually caused her dismissal.

We were walking down to Chichester.

"So she went?"

"Oh yes. You see…" My aunt hesitated and stopped.

"You see, I went into Fred's room to get his laundry – I thought he'd gone out…and …" – her face went bright red – "They were in *bed* together."

"Oh!" I didn't quite know what to say; it must have been a shock for my aunt.

"And she was wearing pink corsets."

Here my aunt broke into helpless laughter, and so did I. We stood on the pavement convulsed with mirth. But why, why shouldn't poor uncle Fred have his fun, I wondered. Then I remembered the clothing coupons. The harpy was sacked, my aunt reclaimed her dues, and my uncle had to meet his inamorata in town, and I had to find a substitute to cook and clean for them.

Michael's younger brother, Christopher, came back from foreign service, shipwreck, and other adventures: it was lovely to see him again. The return of anyone of one's friends from any campaign was a joy, any survivor a most welcome guest. He was tall and quiet, his voice was disconcertingly like Michael's, an echo which I was both sad and glad to hear.

That year Ralph's brother had died in the spring, leaving Leith Hill Place to Ralph, rather against his wishes, but Hervey had insisted that Ralph might give it away if he liked but his it must be. Ralph did give it almost immediately, to the National Trust, but for the weeks between inheritance and handing-over he found himself a milk purveyor, a landlord to tenants whose grandparents he had known working on the estate when he was a child, as well as becoming clearer-up. He arranged for some of the furniture, the pictures, Gainsborough's and Reynolds's portraits of Josiah and his wife, the Romney and the Stubbs to remain in the house, while the minor loot was given away to friends and young relations, and a few things came to The White Gates. Some Darwin cousins came to look at the house, and finally, to Ralph and Adeline's delight, his cousin Ralph Wedgwood became the National Trust tenant. He and his wife Iris did a great deal to the house – more bathrooms, more light, more comfort that they created, which astonished and delighted Ralph when he went to see them. He found that all this had happened without spoiling the house's atmosphere, but that it was far more beautiful than it had ever been since he could remember. He took me with him to the tenants' party they gave at Christmas, their son and daughter-in-law were there with five children, and the entertainer was a conjuror, Ralph's favourite party treat. It was pleasant to hear the Leith Hill people calling him 'Mr Ralph' – and in one case I heard 'Master Ralph'. And he, in turn, was delighted when he was told that the locals once again referred to the house, as they had in his grandfather's time, as 'Wedgwoods'.

Ursula at six months

Ursula aged 1

Ursula in May 1912,
with Grannie Lock

Ursula with her father,
Robert Lock, at Mountfield,
May 1912

Ursula at 18 months

Ursula in early 1914
- aged 3

Ursula's sister Rosemary and their
mother Beryl, Feb, 1916

Ursula with her brother John,
Leeds, 1919

Rosemary (far right), aged 10

Ursula in 1923
- aged 12

Ursula at Woolwich in 1927
- aged 16

Ursula in 1932
- aged 21

Captain Michael Wood

Colonel & Mrs R. F. Lock
request the pleasure of the Company of

at the marriage of their daughter
Ursula
with
Captain J. M. J. F. Wood
Royal Artillery
at the Church of St. Clement Danes
on Wednesday, May 24th 1933,
at 2.30 p.m.
and afterwards at the
Portsmouth Club, 12 Grosvenor Place.

R. S. V. P. to 25 Emperors Gate.

Marriage announcement
for 24 May 1933

Ursula's mother-in-law,
Mabel Wood, c. 1935

Ursula in 1936.
This was one of
Ralph Vaughan Williams's
favourite pictures

Ralph Vaughan Williams, 1938

Ursula, 1938

Rosemary, 1940

John, 1942

Dr Paul Nathan, Ursula's employer
during the war

Ursula, 1947, on the roof garden at 7.5 Thayer Street

Jean Stewart at her marriage to George Hadley

George Jean 7.6.47.

Ursula and Ralph at their wedding - 1953

Ursula and Ralph at their
wedding - 1953

Gilmour Jenkins,
best man at the
wedding

Ursula, her father, her
friend Mary and Mary's
son at the wedding

Ralph in 1952 outside Palais
Royale, Paris

Ralph Vaughan Williams
1954 in America

Ursula and Ralph at
Gloucester 1956

Ursula, Ralph and Sir John Barbirolli, 1956,
at rehearsal for the first performance of RVW's 8th Symphony

Ursula and Ralph leave for
a holiday in Austria, 1957

Ralph and Ursula 1957

Ursula with Eva Hornstein
(age 14) 1959

Ursula with
Sir Edward Heath 1972

Ursula with The Queen Mother, 1980

Joseph Ward, 1980

Ursula a classic pose

Ursula, with Stephen Connock
Charterhouse 1999

Ursula with Roger Buckley

Chapter 6: Peace

While I worked for Paul Nathan I was allowed to invite my friends to spend Thursday afternoons with me; this was his day off so I was alone with the telephone and appointment book without much to do, and this was a pleasant concession. Bob Trevelyan was one of my frequent visitors. He was a strangely divided personality, part of him was far too young for the age he had become, the part that had loved his Cambridge world of lively young men, of enormously long walks, of unbounded hope and promise, the prospect of a life devoted to poetry which would give him a place with the great poets of England. This was not an ambition for fame, but to be a 'true servant of the muse'.

Besides this young Bob, there was the old poet, with less hope, with many of his dearest friends dead and, as he told me once, a sad understanding of those most despairing lines:
> 'I see them all so excellently fair,
> I see, not feel, how beautiful they are!'[50]

For him this was true not only of the moon and stars, of which Coleridge was writing, but of all the natural world, which he found diminished, both the familiar Leith Hill woods, where he would still walk each day, or where he'd sit and write in his thick little black note books (pencil first, then inking in the lines he approved) and for the classical worlds of Theocritus or Virgil – all were lost in a long haze of memory and regret.

He wrote to me often about my work, letters full of technical advice and full of praise which was heartening. "You were very nice to me over my grumblings about your poem. I admire and love your gift for poetry so much that I suppose I want it to do all sorts of things I once wanted to do but could not and to do them in the way I now

---

[50] Samuel Taylor Coleridge (1772-1834): poet. His 139-line ode
Dejection was written in 1802

would have liked to have done them – but that of course is unreasonable, for in poetry no one way is the best. Yet though there is no general best way, there may be a private best way for each of us which we have to find out for ourselves, and can't always be sure of finding at once. But that's enough moralising. I hope you have found a title for your book. It will deserve a perfect one..."

This was only one of his generosities to me, though I think he was glad to find anyone with whom he could talk about poetry. He took a great deal of trouble about sending copies of my books to his friends, Desmond MacCarthy, Gordon Bottomley, Sturges Moore and others, whom I met at the Shiffolds when I stayed there. I had met Gordon Bottomley when I was at the Old Vic, the students had been press-ganged into doing plays at a matinée in aid of the Leper Colony Miss Baylis supported, and I'd been in one he'd written about a lot of milkmaids and a ghost. I don't think it was a very good play, and we had been a dismal lot of bare-foot cotton-frocked milkmaids on an unheated stage in a Parish Hall in mid winter, but I kept that dark when I appeared as a protégé of Bob's. Bob took me to visit Logan Pearsall Smith[51] who was in hospital; I was dismayed when, as we approached the little room in which he lay, Bob said, in a piercing whisper, "He's on his death bed, you know." However he was, even so, full of fierce criticism of Rose Macaulay. "She's trying to get into Papistry", he said, "but you can't be a convert now unless you can produce a miracle." "Oh?" said Bob, wondering about his cousin's talent in that line. "Silly Rose," he went on, "tried the wrong thing, women can't do water-into-wine – she hoped for a decent claret and got a bad rosé – silly thing to try..."

One of the many letters from Bob, between our Thursday tea times, often full of good advice about 'commas and things,' was one that

---

[51] Logan Pearsall Smith (1865-1946): American essayist and author who lived most of his life in England

answered my question about why the flow of review books had ceased:

"...having some time on my hands I looked in at Stanley Morison[52]. It was more or less as I had suspected. Your article on Francis Thompson had done the mischief. It seems that he and his colleagues had liked your reviews quite a lot; but when it came to F. Thompson – my dear, you can have little idea (as I have, who have seen and deplored it fifty years ago) of the English-Catholic infatuation for that unfortunate creature and his somewhat shoddy poetry. It's all very silly; but there it is. I don't think Morison minded much himself. After all he let the article through. I rather think that someone else higher up in *The Times* may have talked to him, and said 'Why did you pass that article?' Anyhow he seemed to be full of goodwill towards you, and said he wished to, and would, send you more work soon, preferably contemporary poets, whom he thought you were so good at reviewing – so I hope you will forgive him, though he is a sinner – but an amiable one. It would be well worth while keeping your foot in there; and you might do a lot of good. But oh, those Catholics, they are really far worse than the Anglicans."

I was reinstated, and just as well, for Paul Nathan died after a long illness during which I sat in his consulting rooms and gave patients addresses of other doctors. After helping his wife Nora to clear up his books and papers I was thankfully unemployed and I was able to continue to live in the modest way to which I was accustomed but without a regular job.

In many ways having very little money and living among others who were equally impecunious was comfortable. What we had not got was easy to do without, though I did have fairly frequent dreams of being in a warehouse filled with bales of silk and velvet, of the most desirable colours, any of which I could have. Waking to

---

[52] Stanley Morison (1889-1967): typographer and scholar; staunch Roman Catholic; editor of *The Times Literary Supplement* from 1945 to 1947

the frustrating realisation that there were, or were not, enough coupons left in my ration book for one necessary pair of stockings, was only faintly disorganising.

London in the blackout had been supremely beautiful. Moonlight and starlight were visible splendours. St Paul's in snow and moonlight was unforgettable and there were the wheeling searchlights tenting dark skies with their questing beams, which made a firewatcher's authorised presence in dark streets a consolation for lost sleep. Fear was there, too, but it was of a mixed kind, for all of us, and for buildings so quickly broken into a mess of dust and rubble with doorways leading from no rooms and opening into space. Soon bracken and fireweed, ragwort and brambles asserted their long-buried mastery, and a wild tangle of flowers and green covered the ruins. Was this what Roman cities were like, I wondered, after the colonisers had left their buildings to the barbarians? Now all this was ending, and different hopes, hopes for the future, were beginning to stir for us all.

When VE day came I had a supper party; Kathleen Long was there, and Jean, a young cousin of Adeline's, Bob de Ropp and Gilmour (Gil) Jenkins, who was head of the shipping part of the Ministry of Transport, where Gerald Finzi worked unwillingly and unhappily through the war. He had found to his delighted surprise that Gil was an amateur musician of distinction, now living most of the time in the office, exiled from his home in the country by the demands of his job. They had become friends and Gerald had brought him to 7.5 parties for the last few months of the war, and Gil was glad to find other company than his very busy and hair-raisingly responsible work had brought him. Nols (Arnold van Wyk[53]) was there – he had become one of our closest friends, living in Crawford Street where he divided his time between working at the BBC in the

---

[53] A South African composer (UVW)

Afrikaans section and writing music – dropping in to see Jeanie[54] or me at any time of the day or evening.

Anyway, at some time late during the evening some of us went out to walk through London; windows were open with lights shining as they had not done for nearly six years; people were strolling, some dancing, some sitting exhausted on the pavement outside pubs which had long run out of beer. We went into St James's Park where lamps were lit, the young leaves wildly green on trees beside them; Nols asked "What is this forest?" He had not remembered this, or any park, lamplit at night. Then the searchlights came on, no longer pursuing planes flying like moths in the upper sky. The beams wheeled and danced and made patterns. It was a strange light-headed evening on which it was necessary to be with friends.

Soon the prisoners came home. One morning Bill Hicks, one of my childhood friends from Cornwall, knocked on my door, fresh from a prisoner-of-war-camp in Italy, thin and hungry and longing for his home. Another dawn it was John's friend, Freddie Corfield, from a German camp, also thin and hungry, but much tidier than he used to be when he and John returned to Porton after the rigours of their O.T.C. camps. It was then that the realisation that there'd be no return for so many was most acute and beyond the delighted welcomes lay the awareness of the desolation of lost futures and lost friendships.

It was a few months before the nightmare episode of Hiroshima, a time of concerts, the first performance of *Peter Grimes* to which I went with Ralph, Proms with Ralph, and the usual amount of meals with friends, and visits to Dorking or to the Finzis at Ashmansworth. Everyone was trying to resume their lives after the long break, and to re-discover themselves, to think of choice and change.

---

[54] Jean Stewart

Hiroshima was an immense shock. Till then war had been horrible enough, but there had been a certain traditional element for most of us, feeling ourselves on the side of freedom, of dragon-slayers, however dreadful the means and the terrors. This black celebration of man's power, though the current argument was that it saved more lives than it destroyed by hurrying the conclusion of the war, changed everything. All the old horrors of poison gas which had dismayed me at Porton, came back, and the door had clearly opened on degradations of power that were intolerable. Napalm and defoliants lay far in the future, as did the smaller evils of pesticides and the loss of hedgerows; we still had many wild flowers in the enclosed fields, shelter for birds, and harvest sheaves gathered into stooks – but the lesser would go with the greater, and the words that had haunted many nights of raids, 'All pity staled with custom of fell deeds', would grow clearer and clearer through the oncoming years.

Meanwhile the great despairs balanced against minor and more present troubles. My parents were still living in Mary and Richard's flat at Richmond, uncertain about their future. It was very difficult for them to know what to do, for all their lives the army had decided where they had to live. Now, faced with an independence deferred since father's pre-war retirement, they had no roots and no ties. My father's brother and sister lived at Chichester, but being near them had no attraction. Rosemary was in the Land Army still, and at Arundel, but that would not be for much longer. I was, as I'd always known I should be, given the chance, a decided Londoner. They were in a state of unhappy dither. John's death had absolutely darkened their lives. Eventually they took a small house at Milford on Sea, where both coast and the New Forest were at hand, and where a cousin of my mother's lived with her husband who had retired from working in London, providing a link with the past for them. There they settled to a quiet life of gardening, a beach hut, drives in the forest and a circle of pleasant acquaintances who all adored my father and found my mother a problem. Rosemary, with the money John had left, started to farm in Shropshire as Freddie Corfield's tenant. She had a number of eccentric animals, including a head cow who liked to lie in front of the kitchen range whenever she could get into the house, and a cat who was the eldest kitten of my Alexandra.

Alexandra had picked me up one night, coming home from Bond Street tube during a raid. I had seen her, running along the street, and spoke to her. She followed me home, and when we reached the street door of 7.5 I carried her in – one of London's many strays, a displaced and hungry kitten, small, black, and clearly in need of care and protection. I fed her and left her to spend the night in my kitchen-bathroom. In the morning she was there looking fatigued, one dead mouse beside her, one pushed into the bath and drowned – we had in those days to leave water in our baths in case of fire. She settled down with Jean and me, explored the roofs and the club, and developed into a most beguiling and clever animal. She was very quick moving, light as a feather, and she enjoyed playing with the shadows made on a wall for her amusement. Jean and I shared her favours, her cooking, and eventually her kittens. There were two cats at Dorking then, a small brownish she, Pushkin, mother of many and frequent families of kittens, and Foxy, a grey cat with a sensitive face, long nosed and gentle, Ralph's particular companion in the study and during his after-lunch sleeps. Pushkin spent her time with Adeline, for she was tiny and light enough not to be an uncomfortable weight on her knee, or among the folds of the rug which covered her feet.

I continued to spend a lot of time at Dorking and Adeline seemed glad to know that I would always be available for any hours Ralph had to spend in London. Now that there was no longer any danger of raids he was able to go away more happily and not only for things he felt he ought to do. Morris had moved to London so there was more room in the house, and I could spend time there even if Adeline's sister Cordelia, the person she most loved, was staying in the house. Adeline's own life was restricted, by now she was practically immobile. Her chair had wheels and could be moved from the bedroom to the hall, and very occasionally she would choose to have her garden chair taken into the shade near the house. Otherwise she was indoors from week's end to week's end, reading, writing letters for Ralph or at his dictation, in a clear, rounded script, extraordinary when one looked at the crumpled and disfigured hands of the writer. She enjoyed seeing their friends, Bob Trevelyan or Cedric Glover came over sometimes from Holmbury, Max Beerbohm from Flint Cottage, Meredith's house at Burford Bridge where he'd lived since he was bombed out from his earlier wartime home.

There were visitors from Cambridge too: the philosopher G. E. Moore, staying with the Trevelyans, came to tea, and best of all, Ralph Wedgwood. He and his wife Iris were the parents of Veronica, with whom I'd been briefly at school. I met her again at the Canettis: he, Elias Canetti[55], had a tremendous knowledge of literature, philosophy and history, a reputation among writers and a wide circle of friends. Veronica had translated his novel *Auto da Fé*, for though his knowledge of English was masterly he would write only in German. His wife, Veza, was a passionately faithful supporter of all he did. A writer herself – her maiden name was Calderon – she had submerged her own career for his. She had beautiful dark eyes and feet so small that buying shoes to fit her was almost impossible, and there was something of the Arabian nights about her – she would have looked right dressed as a Turkish princess. She had a sharp wit and a critical mind, as well as enormous kindness. I spent a lot of time with them both, though it was difficult to persuade her to come out; the usual pattern was for me to visit her, and for Canetti to come to my parties.

---

[55] Elias Canetti (1905-94): Bulgarian-born writer. Doctorate in Chemistry, Vienna 1929. Left Vienna in 1937 and settled in England. Awarded Nobel Prize for Literature in 1981

Anyway, it was at their Crawford Street flat that I re-met Veronica, and we discovered that we had kept track of each other's lives in the intervening years. Hers had been one of scholarship and writing admirable enjoyable histories, and I found that she was as friendly as she had been as a twelve-year-old, and that she was still, so to speak, in a higher form than I was. Ralph was amused and pleased to discover this link between us and to know that it was from her that I had first heard his name.

In 1946 Jean, Clare and I, with another friend, Nigel Curtis-Raleigh, a young barrister, decided that the time had come for us to break out of English restrictions, rationing, and limitations, for a holiday. Nigel and I went by train and sea to Paris, Jean had a concert, so she and Clare left later, and flew. We all met in Paris for dinner and then went to find our night train to Berne. Although we were early at the station we found that the seats we had reserved were occupied, and that no amount of documentation of our claims was going to shift those already in possession. More carriages were added to the already long train, but they were boarded by a party of mountain climbers who used their ice-axes and so got in through the windows before the doors were unlocked. Eventually we travelled in the compartment in which our booked seats were, but sitting on suitcases. It was a very hot night and there were sixteen of us in the carriage. The usurpers relented a little when we handed round biscuits, and somehow we all managed some uneasy sleep. I woke up tangled in the arms of a very garlicky baker, and the others were equally uncomfortably enmeshed. However, when we passed the frontier there was a stop long enough for us all to buy ham rolls and bananas, a strange-to-us condition of plenty. We stayed at Spiez, and had one of the most glorious shopping sprees I have ever enjoyed a couple of days later in Berne. It was well worth the sale of silver entrée dishes which had been wedding presents with which my part of the trip was financed. There were pleasant strolls in flowery meadows, unlimited food and wine, bathing in a rather chilly lake, and the discovery that I absolutely detested mountains.

I had never been among them before, and I found them hideous, claustrophobic when one was below them, and vertiginous when persuaded into a funicular. The other three loved them, Jean and Nigel did some climbing. Of course, by the last days of our stay we found that holiday money was running out and the sums on backs of envelopes became more frantic and the euphoric habit of our first week of having apricot brandy for elevenses came to an abrupt end. I arrived at Victoria with two new dresses, stockings and lots of presents of such luxuries as soap, sponges, handkerchiefs and sweets and my twopenny bus fare home.

In 1947 Jean married George Hadley, a young doctor who had been a prisoner of war. Ralph and I drove over to Oxford, where Mrs. Morris had spent the night and had helped with the feast, and she and I, Clare and Ralph sat tightly squashed into one small pew. Jean, in a silvery dress, carrying roses from her mother's garden, looked as happy as if she had just played a major concerto – something that she was beginning to be asked to do.

I'd been encouraging her to buy clothes; as usual Bob Trevelyan had come to the rescue with clothing coupons, and I'd gone on about money being of little account when clothes for marriage were the pleasure to be considered. I'd infected myself with this unrealistic attitude and I went to Heals on my own behalf.

"I want a white, Indian carpet."
"Well – hush – I think – will you come this way?"

Such things were in very short supply. I was led upstairs, into a tiny room where it wouldn't have been surprising to find an old woman with a spinning wheel. There was my carpet – a rare treasure they said. I remembered to ask the price, after I'd said I would have it, and arranged for it to be sent next day.

"Thirty five pounds", they said. I agreed cheerfully, but after I'd left the shop I came to my senses and remembered that my account had three pounds odd in it.

Oh well, I thought, I can cancel it tomorrow.

On my doormat was a small brown envelope. When I opened it I found a note: 'As your great aunt Miss Mahoney's residuary legatee I have much pleasure in enclosing a cheque for thirty five pounds and ten shillings.' The carpet for me, ten bob for the man who brought it, gratitude to dear Aunt Hettie, Grannie's half sister whom I'd not seen for years, and had never known very well, and a renewed faith in fate. I needed that. Like Rosalind[56] I was fathoms deep in love, and though I did spend some time with Ralph at Dorking it was clearly a situation with none too much present and no future. It was difficult for him, too, for he was indissolubly and properly committed to the life he and Adeline had achieved, so the only way there was for me was to be, as it were, icing on whatever cake he had, and not a disruptive influence or cause for his or her disquiet.

However, there were diversions. The Three Choirs Festivals[57] were quite a new sort of jaunt. Ralph stayed with his friends Canon and Mrs Briggs at Worcester, I had a room in another Canon's house, with a view across the river to the Malvern Hills. This was the house in which Thomas Tompkins had lived when he was the Cathedral organist. Ralph had, on his brother's death, inherited not only the family house, but his brother's car, a large, old fashioned Rolls Royce – as well as a chauffeur, Beagley, who had worked for both his mother and his brother. This made such journeys as Worcester, Hereford and Gloucester comfortable and easy, but also late nights in London needed no longer to be related to the last train from Victoria. After my first Three Choirs Festival, this settled into

---

[56] In Shakespeare's *As You Like It*
[57] They had ceased in 1940 for the duration of the war (UVW)

the pattern of each year and was something to look forward to. There were always a lot of friends there and a lot of parties, also there were likely to be concerts we could miss and use these happy days for a sightseeing trip, into the Black Mountains from Hereford, to Llanthony, or up the Wye to Symonds Yat. From Worcester we went to the Wrekin, and as I was shocked to find that Ralph had never seen Wenlock Edge that was our goal. But he never did see it for it lay, that day, under a long bank of cloud and he had to be satisfied with a Housman echo on a signpost, 'to the Roman City of Uriconium'. We both knew Gloucestershire well, so there were favourite places to revisit. It turned out that Ralph and I might easily have met long before in the post office at Painswick, which he used when he and Adeline had stayed with her sister in a house, Horsepools, on the Edge, which had been lived in at some earlier time by Grannie's mother. Indeed we might have met when he was a private in the R.A.M.C. for we discovered that we had both been at Sutton Veny, on Salisbury Plain, in 1916. But, though I might have looked with favour on him had our paths crossed at that time, I don't suppose he would have considered me as a candidate for his affections as I had been then a five-year-old, walking beside my brother's pram.

During these years I heard a great deal of music, met a number of musicians, heard all Ralph's works in the making, as well as at plays-through and first performances. Sometimes I went with him to film recording sessions.

In 1947 Maud Karpeles started the International Folk Music Council. There was a conference in London, with Ralph as chairman, a post he relinquished to his deputy, Steuart Wilson[58]. I had been helping Maud with the plans and arrangements, and I much enjoyed myself meeting a number of foreign delegates. At

---

[58] Sir Steuart Wilson (1889-1966): tenor and later administrator at the BBC and the Arts Council. Head of Music, BBC (1948-9); Deputy Senior Administrator, Royal Opera House (1949-55)

another conference, or festival, I forget which, I was put in charge of the Vendée team, led by one of twin brothers called Martel, who were sculptors and lived in Paris. I took them sightseeing and had to call on my utmost resources of history as well as of the French language to take them round Westminster Abbey – Henry V, for instance had to be the king who married a Princess of France rather than the victor of Agincourt, and so on. But when a valiant and bemused baker in the team asked me what was the difference between Catholics and Protestants – "do you not believe in the Virgin Mary, then?" – I crumpled and took them out to tea. All our sightseeing was enlivened by a young dentist in their team who played his accordion whenever possible; we often danced at bus stops to his infectious music, and when I saw them off on a snowy morning we kept warm till the train left by dancing the Farandole all down the platform. The Martels became friends and I stayed with them in Paris the next year.

One summer John Schlesinger (whose mother played in a little orchestra, the Newbury String Players, started and conducted by Gerald Finzi) wanted to make a film. He'd made one already, in which the Finzi boys had taken part, and he was anxious to collect a cast for this new venture, I was to be the Finzi boys' and John's young sister's mother in the film, married to his uncle. His aunt was to be a sea witch, and John and some of his undergraduate friends had written the script. I was a day or two later than the others to arrive at Cadgwith, in South Cornwall. I was taken to the cottage where a film session was in progress. A tiny bedroom was crowded with people, lights, cameras and a double bed in which Joy Finzi, whose real job was to be continuity girl, was tucked up with a strange man. It was her only appearance in the film, and practically all that was seen of her was a modestly sleeved hand quelling an alarm clock. After this there were all sorts of outdoor problems; we had to have unwalked-on sands so some calls were for early dawn for the tides had not been taken into account in the script. Sometimes we had to spend a lot of the day in boats and the Finzi boys were the only people who could row. Once we were at Kynance Cove for a scene in which Kiffer[59], the elder boy, had to run through a cave as the tide was rising – the higher it rose the more exciting the picture and the more anguished Kiffer looked – though it was not with fear but with stomach ache. Finally, when he refused to do it yet again, we'd all been cut off by the tide and with the camera paraphernalia, picnic stuff and bathing things we had to scramble up the cliff. Another time Margaret Webber, the witch, nearly drowned. She was heavily draped in blackout curtains with crab-claw fangs stuck on her teeth with sticking plaster. As she sank slowly, weighed down by her clothing, the fangs equally slowly crossed, and looked superbly sinister. The cameras followed every breath and gasp till she sank and her horrified husband had to push the equipment aside to save her from a chilly death. Joy and I laughed a great deal through the fortnight at Cadgwith, though one day the tables were turned on us. We'd a free morning and planned to spend it lying on a rock watching the cormorants. Another of the party, a Frenchman who could row, came with us, and during the idle gossip of the hour it was discovered that both Joy and I believed that the tide was low in England when it was high in France, so the peaceful morning became a lecture session on tides.

Friends from Dorking, Genia and Yanya Hornstein, were in Cornwall at the same time and came over to see us with their three daughters. Genia insisted on bathing though the sea was as cold as I'd warned her it would be, and her Cyrillic screams and cries as she met the icy water sent her children disowningly over the headland.

The film was made in a fortnight – a holiday for the actors, a time of stress for the producer and a very cheerful memory though the

---

[59] Christopher Finzi (1934 -), son of the composer. His brother Nigel was born in 1936

result was not exactly a masterpiece. But it has been a subject for boasting: "When I was in one of John Schlesinger's films..."

Another year there'd been a little spring holiday in Paris, of which I'd spent the last two days with Kathleen Long at her favourite hotel in the Rue de Beaujolais – practically next door, I believe, to Colette's[60] flat. It was old-fashioned, full of pretty furniture, and my bedroom looked over the Palais Royal Gardens. It was in very easy walking distance from the Comédie Française, where I saw my first Racine play, *Andromaque*. It was excitingly moving to see the love scenes played without touch, passion blazing between people at opposite sides of the stage.

I had a small romantic encounter myself, that week. I was out sightseeing, trying to get into the Cluny Museum, which was officially shut, by waylaying a caretaker. I wanted to see again La Dame à la Licorne, which had delighted us at the tapestry exhibition in London, but though I was let in, the tapestries were not on show – rolled up, the caretaker said, and locked up. On my way back to the hotel a Frenchman stopped beside me as we waited to cross a road. He spoke, and for one happy instant I thought that he'd mistaken me for a native and was going to ask me the way to somewhere. Instead he asked me if I was married. I had not, at that time, become properly used to the idea that I was a widow, so I said that I was. "Oh dear," he said. "I've never seen anyone like you and I was going to ask you to marry me". I looked at him, utterly taken aback, and saw that he was like Jean Gabin, a film actor I much favoured. But it was too late to say "Well, I remember now that I'm not married, and I have two free days more in Paris." So, though he took my arm and steered me across the road, and this touch felt comfortable and almost familiarly right, we parted, with dignified expressions of esteem. It did me a great deal of good with myself, though it also left regret for where that adventure might have led if I'd had my wits a little more about me instead of lost

---

[60] Sidonie - Gabrielle Colette (1873-1954), French Novelist

with the strawberry coloured tapestries of which I had been thinking.

I had an idea that there might be some exciting poems to be found in mental hospitals – the lunatic, the lover and the poet. Accordingly I wrote to the Director of the Retreat[61], and I was invited to stay there. It was a touching place, and I liked their welcome for my idea. We unearthed a few poems, but after visiting a much larger mental hospital in Surrey, where I found a few more, I realised that this enterprise was beyond me and that I could not face the despairs that clung like sinister clouds about such places. Being unemployed I took on a day a week working for the Care Committee. This is a London organisation providing a liaison between schools and parents. If children fail to keep dental or hospital appointments, or are away from school for a time without explanation, the committee member attached to the school is sent round to find out what has happened. I was attached to a north London school for the mentally handicapped – no poems to be collected there, but the patience and imagination of the members of teaching staff were superb. While I worked there the headmistress was asked by a team of doctors at St George's Hospital to choose ten children from the school for a most elaborate enquiry into medical records, family background and history. I was given a list of names she had chosen, and the forms, and sent out on this difficult mission. It was enormously interesting, and the parents were helpful and hopeful. My years with Paul Nathan proved a great help and we were complimented on the forms the school returned. The sad thing was that no further steps were taken, none of the cases was followed up and the half-promised treatment was not given. One family I came to know well were remarkable. They lived in a frightful house behind Edgware Road. It had been badly damaged in raids and the landlord refused to do anything about repairs as it was scheduled for demolition sometime. The child I was concerned with, Eileen, was a twelve-year-old, a surviving

---

[61] In York (UVW)

twin whose sister had died at birth. Their mother had been suffering from blood poisoning when they were born. There were three boys in the family younger than Eileen, and their mother, an old-looking young woman, coped with wet rot, dry rot, flaking paint, crumbling plaster, little money, different meal times for everyone, including an individualistic cat, with unfailing good humour. There wasn't an unbroken chair in the kitchen, the lino was in shreds, and the untidiness was wild. But she was wise and cheerful, interested, hospitable and entirely admirable. The boys protected and cherished Eileen and all three had engagingly good manners, and all three did exceptionally well at school. I kept in touch with the family for years. Eileen died when she was in her late teens and the family were re-housed. Mrs Evans did not live long in the new flat, though long enough to see the boys on their way to good jobs and the eldest married. Through this work I saw a lot more of the London I did not come across in any other way, I met a mixture of people, some finding success for the first time, some doing well on the dingier side of private enterprise, some with the wit and energy of the frequenters of the tavern in Eastcheap. No Falstaff and no Prince Hal, but plenty of others with the spirit of Bardolph and Pistol. I went to a lot of houses, though nothing was quite as desolate as one of the old women I had visited in C.O.S. days, ill in a bare room in a blanketless bed. Some of the living conditions were comfortless, particularly in winter. Some were vastly better, with a gloss of plenty, and one or two had achieved cocktail cabinets, though not cocktails.

One summer Gil Jenkins and I stayed with Clare Howden in a cottage at Lambourn and walked along the downs past Wayland Smith's forge and on to the White Horse, and back from there through a huge storm. Another place I stayed at sometimes was Chinnor, where Evelyn Gibbs's parents lived. Her mother was a lay preacher just as charming as Dinah Shore[62] would have become in later life. Once, during the war, when I was dining with her and

---

[62] In *Adam Bede* by George Eliot (1819-80)

Evelyn in a Chinese restaurant in London she asked what I wanted most. Wishes are always fun, so I said "a fine lawn petticoat with masses of lace on it." Three days later one arrived from her. She had, like my Grannie Lock, delicious boxes of treasures; very high-level squirreling all her life had left her with resources to meet any emergency and many frivolous desires. Evelyn's father was a retired sailor, 'Tom Bowling' was his favourite song, and he had endless stories which usually started "Up the Yangtze River in, let me see, 08 ..." until late in life when he went to America and they changed to "When I was crossing Arizona ..." He loved theatricals, and the village had a playwright doctor, so, as everyone in the village was likely to be her patient, she had power to compel them to take whatever part she decided would suit them. In one of these plays Mr Gibbs was cast as Jeremiah and Mrs Gibbs had a very tiresome rehearsal period while he grew his hair to prophetical length and prophesied every kind of woe. He was a very kind-hearted man, but undertook kindnesses with a severe bark. I remember sitting by the fire with Evelyn one winter weekend, late at night, when he came in with a tray of mugs of hot chocolate. He handed them to us, saying firmly, "Of course the Navy should bring back the lash."

Another time when I was there, it was a weekend again, for Evelyn was working at the BBC, first in the schools department, then as the first editor of Woman's Hour, we were out mushrooming. We met an elderly man who told us that as a boy he'd lodged with an old couple in the village, "and the old lady's grandmother had hidden on the common to watch Prince Rupert's soldiers attack the village – the women and children had been sent to hide in the woods above, and he brought his troop in by the lower road ..." That was three voices back to the Civil War: the old man who told us, his old landlady, who in turn had been told by her grandmother about this raid. Evelyn said that, as a child, she used to have nightmares about men fighting on the stairs when she stayed at Chinnor, and when her mother inherited the house, and put in a bathroom, Roundhead breastplates were found in the garden by the workmen digging to lay pipes.

Chapter 7: Ralph, Marriage and Happiness

In 1948 Ralph's sixth symphony had its first performance. The general attitude had been that the radiant fifth was his farewell blessing. He became very angry when he found that the sixth was given as many political-prophetical interpretations as, by now, hindsight had added to his fourth, but it was a long time before he disclosed that the last movement, a sustained and frightening *pianissimo*, was his version of Prospero's great speech[63] to Ferdinand:

> '... the great globe itself,
> Yea, all which it inherit, shall dissolve;
> And, like this insubstantial pageant faded,
> Leave not a rack[64] behind.'

He was working, too, on his opera, *The Pilgrim's Progress*, a story that had been in his mind since writing incidental music for a series of tableaux acted by friends long before the first war.

I had another collection of verse published that year – my third. I was still reviewing for the *Times Literary Supplement*. But much of my life was involved with Ralph's, hearing all the performances of his works, including the music for the film *Scott of the Antarctic* to which I went with him, and being a go-between to arrange sittings with Epstein[65] for a bronze head (a friend of his, the pianist Shula Doniach, being an acquaintance of mine). I met Epstein and enjoyed enormously going to his studio and seeing both Lazarus, tall and shrouded, towering over the many completed bronzes, and the Cavendish Square Madonna and Child, before they were finished. He was lively company and sometimes sharp tongued. Kathleen was there too, as graceful as she is as the bronze lady with

---

[63] Shakespeare: *The Tempest*, Act 4, Scene 1
[64] Wisp of cloud
[65] Jacob Epstein (1880-1959): sculptor; born New York, took British nationality in 1905

gardenias. I guess that Ralph slept through most of them and when the head was nearly finished open eyes were added, so the finished bronze had a startled, bird of prey look which wasn't like him, though the shape and back of the neck and head are most touchingly and intimately exact.

R. O. Morris died, very suddenly, just before Christmas in 1948. He'd been to one of my parties a week earlier – a great concession, as he preferred dining at his club or having a friend to dinner, to party-going; but everyone there that evening was known to him and, rather to his surprise, he'd enjoyed himself. I'd seen him regularly since he came to London. I helped him to move house, from The White Gates, and I had stayed in the new house for the first week, to cook, mind the cats and generally 'settle him in' as Adeline said, and I often dined with him and enjoyed a serious tutorial on wine followed by an evening of backgammon. He still won every time. He had dreaded old age, and the years since his wife died had been ones of withdrawn and dignified loneliness in spite of his many friends. We had come to know each other well as Emmie's death had been a very little while before Michael's so we'd been considered to be at the same sort of stages of emotional convalescence by Adeline, and I think we had been very good for each other. Shared and regular gossip-and-gin sessions most weekends, shared walks and backgammon, shared mucking-out the hens had broken down mutual shyness and replaced it with much affection and esteem. I missed his amusedness and perception.

Each spring was filled for Ralph with local music-making. He had started a small choir to sing the *St John Passion*, usually in February. Rehearsals were at The White Gates, the performance in St Martin's Church, Dorking. Each Saturday after Christmas he rehearsed as many singers as cared to come in the *St Matthew Passion*, for which all the town and village chorus who took part in the Leith Hill Musical Festival joined forces for a performance, sometimes two performances, in March; and in April the Festival lasted for three days. He marked parts, prepared his scores, and generally devoted much of his time to all this, with frequent consultations, arguments and arrangements with the Festival Secretary, Margery Cullen. She lived at Westcott, gave summer parties in her garden, cherished a huge brood of nephews and nieces, played at all rehearsals and was utterly dependable in any musical emergency, kind, bubbling, and argumentative. I was much caught up in all this activity, and had dozens of odd jobs to do. One year I re-covered all the *Matthew* band parts, disgracing my beautiful work by spelling the saint with only one t – which was held against me for some time – and at one Festival, Ruth Dyson, the harpsichord player and pianist, who for the Festival became a back-desk fiddler and librarian, very inconsiderately went on tour to Scandinavia and Ralph promptly commanded me to be librarian. He helped me a lot, and I mislaid only one flute part, and that temporarily – but I have rarely been more nervous of anything than I was of putting out the music for each concert in the right order on the correct desks. Another year I was asked to give away the banners at one concert and to make the accompanying speech. I sweated over my few paragraphs for weeks, then, when I stood on the platform I saw that my dress was rippling as my knees knocked together. I remember thinking that were I ever to be publicly executed I'd see to it that I went to the scaffold in something made of very stiff brocade. Otherwise the Festivals were fun, the same collection of professional players and local amateurs joined forces and shared a very good meal – Margery Cullen's catering – between rehearsal and performance, and the soloists were all people I knew. It was a festivity as well as absorbing music making. Ralph both suffered and enjoyed – he achieved some remarkable performances, particularly of the Passions, making both so dramatic and alive that they were new each time as the best performances of operas or of Shakespearean tragedies are, however well the listener knows them.

Adeline was becoming more fragile, and these years were hard ones for her, for she was frequently ill, in pain, and having trouble with her eyes. I was able to help more and more with the domesticities as unobtrusively as I could.

Ralph, during the exciting though not always satisfactory discussions about the planned production of *The Pilgrim's Progress*, had a commission from his old friend Bernard Shore, the viola player, then an H.M.I.[66], to write a choral work for the 1951 National Festival of Schools Music and to my great delight they asked me to write the words. It was my first commission for this sort of thing and marvellous to collaborate with Ralph who taught me a great deal about what is singable and what is not. I'd been to so many rehearsals as well as performances of choral works by then that I'd more or less got the hang of the structure needed for musical texture, and I much enjoyed the work. When it came to the performance it was a nervous business, but when the music started there was, for us both, a feeling of relief and excitement in equal part, finally a sense of surprised unreality when Ralph and I took a call together on the stage of the Albert Hall, with Adrian Boult joining our hands, just in the place where, between a rehearsal and a performance of the *London Symphony* a few years earlier, Ralph had fully declared his affection.

It was a hectic spring, with *Pilgrim* rehearsals and performances, satisfaction and dissatisfaction about the production; with the two Passions to be performed; and then the Festival. It was a comfort to have Beagley and the car to take Ralph from Dorking to Covent Garden and back, and I spent much time making picnic meals to be shared on these journeys between one rehearsal and another.

All through these weeks Adeline was very ill. Ralph, torn between musical anxieties and home despairs, between total involvement in performance and total hopeless worry in between, was getting more

---

[66] His Majesty's Inspector (of Schools Music)

and more exhausted. When the first performances of *Pilgrim* and the Festival concerts were over, everything seemed better. I went with him one afternoon to a rehearsal in London of an early work of his that I did not know, *Toward the Unknown Region*, and we had tea together. Then I went home to have dinner later with Gil Jenkins and Engel Lund. As we were drinking our coffee, Ralph telephoned to tell me that Adeline had died that afternoon. Cordelia had come to stay, would I come? I went at once. Death, I knew, had been inhabiting the house for weeks, an almost visible presence, known to us all but not named. Now the house was all his for a day or two while Adeline's little and derelict body still lay on her narrow iron bed, an influence still to be felt as if she had not entirely relinquished her hold.

After her burial at Brockenhurst, in her parents' grave, Ralph started an immense clearing up. Desks and drawers were emptied of letters and photographs, which he tore up or burned, clothes and jewellery were given to Cordelia to distribute, while the long-familiar wheel-chairs and disused crutches were assembled for collection by the Red Cross. Ralph asked me to undertake the management of the house for him, but I felt that I should not move in completely, so I planned to spend long weekends in Dorking, short mid-weeks in London, for I believed that he must have time for solitude, grief and release, and to find his new pattern of living. He decided not to cancel any of his engagements, some of which were local and delightful, for he said "It's no good looking back, no good at all." But I think it was impossible not to do so.

For after fifty-four years of marriage it was strange for him to be alone. Adeline's long illness had disabled her body, but she had been the central figure in his life. Probably her immobility had made it easier for him to stay at home and work. He had used his limitations, and she had been a centre for him rather than a curb. I saw that it was hard for him to accustom himself to the new freedom, though I persuaded him to have a short holiday while some necessary redecorations were done.

We went to Hythe so that we could spend days on Romney Marsh, and to Dungeness where he'd once spent a few chilly weeks at the gunnery school at Lydd. Now it was a magical garden of wild flowers, bugloss and poppies, daisies, camomile, campion and horned poppies, while over the marsh lay the hazy bloom of flowering grasses. When we went back to Dorking the house looked different for the big room had been newly painted white, the old and ragged lino had gone, new chair covers were being made and it was summer weather. Soon he suggested that I should find a larger flat where he could have a room whenever he wanted to stay in London. This was a good idea, for Jean and George had moved, so had Clare, and 7.5 was no longer the entirely friendly place it had been, so I started househunting and eventually found a flat in Bloomsbury, big enough to give Gil a room, as well as having one for Ralph. Meanwhile, Covent Garden opera was on tour and we went to Leeds with Ralph's old friend Steuart Wilson and his wife Mary. Steuart was second in command to David Webster at Covent Garden and it was due to his passionate faith in *Pilgrim* that the opera had been put on there. I had become very fond of both him and Mary.

This trip to Leeds was fun, and besides the *Pilgrim* performance we went to *Fidelio*, and after that directly to Worcester for an early Festival rehearsal, and back to Dorking staying at Oxford en route with another old friend of Ralph's, and by now of mine, Pegs Spring-Rice, a doctor and amateur flautist who had played for him in many performances of the *Passion*. She, like the Wedgwoods (with whom we spent a long lunch time at Leith Hill Place a few days later) seemed to find it natural for Ralph and me to be gadding around together. We went to Cambridge too, which was my first visit to the town, and he was a superb guide.

When we went to Worcester for the Three Choirs Festival, by way of Dorchester and Tewkesbury, an ambling, sightseeing progress, he murmured something about marriage. I felt that we were better as we were, that there was no need for him to make an honest woman of me, but it did add a glow to the day, a delight to our times together, a secret undercurrent to the parties to which we both went. I stayed for that visit with my friends the Kittermasters in College Green[67]. Ronald was Headmaster of the King's School, and his wife, Meriel, sang in the choir at the Festivals. I'd stayed with them before when I'd given a talk about poetry to some of the school one spring, and we'd gone walking in woods beyond Malvern to find wild daffodils. It was a rambling house, one that felt as if it might be haunted in parts. The banister of the main staircase ended frighteningly in a huge claw-foot, an odd and sinister piece of carving, as if one bit of a very large dragon had been turned to domestic use.

On the way home we stayed at Stratford for two nights, partly to go to a performance of Ralph's opera *Sir John in Love* given by the Clarion Singers, a production we'd been to in Birmingham during the last winter. It was conducted by Anthony Lewis, a young David Galliver sang the part of Fenton, and the producer Tom Harrison was a friend, as was Katherine Tomson who trained the choir. All these people came into later chapters of my life. The other treat and pleasure was going to *Henry IV Part I*, with Anthony Quayle as Falstaff and Michael Redgrave as Hotspur. We went to a party at the Quayles' house after the performance and it was strange to meet him again, so many years away from my vividly remembered season at the Old Vic. Next day Ralph and I had a fairly brisk quarrel about the character of Hotspur, which led him to suggest re-reading the play, and as soon as we were back at Dorking he read it aloud to me. This was the beginning of re-reading all the plays. It took about a year, for there were many other books in between, but

---

[67] Gloucester

it was a major experience for us both and gave us even more to talk about than usual.

As I was so much at Dorking I saw more of Dorking friends, particularly the Hornsteins, Yanya and Genia. He had come from Odessa, she still spoke of her town of origin as St Petersburg. They had both been refugees from the Russian Revolution and had lived in Hamburg. As Jews, they had left Germany in 1934 and had come first to London, then Dorking. He made a business life, and she had become deeply involved in musical activities and both through the war had taken their share of civic duties, Yanya in the Home Guard, Genia on the refugee committee where she worked with Ralph, and in the local Citizens' Advice Bureau. Yanya translated Russian poetry with a tremendous mastery of the English language, which extended to an abandoned use of puns in ordinary life, which we deplored with equal abandon. I spent a good deal of time with them, both in Dorking and London, a friendship that gave us all pleasure and I think we were about equal in talkativeness.

In 1952 Ralph and I went to France for a short spring holiday. It had to be short for the travel allowance was only twenty-five pounds that year. We stayed in Paris in the Hotel du Beaujolais; he showed me where he had lived when he studied with Ravel, a world ago, we went to the theatre, looked at pictures and had modest meals, sometimes picnics. I showed him Chartres and he showed me Mont St Michel and Rouen and finally, after ten days, we left, absolutely franc-less and so lunchless, but we had London-bought first class train tickets. We were enormously glad to reach the boat at Le Havre where our English money was usable and to have a huge high tea on board.

There were other first performances to come home for. Ralph's *An Oxford Elegy*, at Oxford, with Steuart Wilson as narrator, and a harmonica concerto at the proms. A sadder engagement was Desmond MacCarthy's memorial service. He was an old friend of

Ralph's and we had all been concerned with buying Bob Trevelyan's library for University College after his death a few years earlier, after a slow and melancholy year of decline.

Another of Ralph's friends, Paddy Hadley[68], then Professor of Music and Precentor of Caius College, Cambridge, invited us to stay with him at Heacham for the first King's Lynn Festival at which he had commanded Ralph to give a lecture on East Anglian folk songs. It was a good lecture. I knew it well as I had typed his script which, like all my typing, was a labour of love, for in spite of having to type bills and case histories for Paul Nathan and my own verse, reviews and so forth, I have never liked or had mastery of the machine. But Ralph's writing was hieroglyphic and though he never adhered to the exact text of any lecture, he had to be able to read bits of it, headings and dates, which would have been a slowing up process if he'd only his own script to guide him. Staying with Paddy was delightful. We'd pottered down 'by Beagley' as car journeys were summarised, looking at places from Ralph's past, Saffron Walden where he'd played the organ for church parade when he'd been a private in the RAMC, and villages where he'd collected songs. Heacham is the centre of the lavender industry in Norfolk, and the fields were dusky blue with flowers, the air scented in sunlight, and Paddy gave us teas on his lawn and dinners in his garden. Between these feasts – Paddy and his cook took food seriously, drink even more so – we left Ralph with Angus Morrison, our fellow guest, and went to bathe from the shingle beach. Paddy had lost a leg in France, and I was touched to find he had no embarrassment at all about unstrapping the artificial part and taking my arm to hop into water deep enough for swimming. In fact he'd walked and even climbed with the leg left on the beach, accepting it as a good substitute with cheerful courage. I made him laugh when I told him about Clare Howden's son, Brian, who had come back from Burma, also without one leg. While he had stayed

---

[68] Patrick Hadley (1899-1973): composer, Prof. of Music, Cambridge University (1946-52)

with Clare at 7.5 he used to leave his spare leg, foot uppermost, in the driving seat when he parked his car to frighten would-be car thieves, a successful measure as his car was never stolen in spite of very uncertain locks on the door. I'd seen him a good deal in those days, and we had discovered to our mutual pleasure and surprise, I – that he had known my brother well, he – that John was my brother. These mutilations from two wars were reminders of both waste and gallantry.

The King's Lynn Festival was full of pleasures, marvellous places to hear music and to enjoy architecture, friends appearing from all over the place, usually meeting them in bars or dining-rooms in the town, Ruth Fermoy, the chief begetter of the whole enterprise bringing the Queen[69] to Ralph's lecture, her easy charm captivating Ralph afterwards. I enjoyed, too, the market in the square into which I disappeared whenever I could and from which I was extracted by a search party sent out by Ralph, headed by Scott Goddard, a music critic, while I was negotiating for some desirable mixing bowls.

It was moving to discover so many of Ralph's past journeys, not only in the folk-song places of Norfolk, but in going with him to a memorial celebration of Stanford's centenary in the Abbey, where he showed me the burial place of his great uncle, Charles Darwin. Although his life reached back to so many others that were by now names in history, I never felt our age difference to be of any consequence. It was more, as Genia Hornstein said, as if we had been brought up in different countries than in different centuries. Though the fact that he had been born eighty years ago came to the forefront that autumn with many birthday celebrations. One was a dinner given by the Royal Society of Musicians, and the most enjoyable of all, I thought, a concert in Dorking with William Cole, Ralph's co-conductor at many festivals, and Adrian Boult as conductors. Isobel Baillie and Arthur Cranmer, who had so often

---

[69] Later Queen Elizabeth the Queen Mother

worked with Ralph, were the soloists, and Cecil Day Lewis was narrator in the *Oxford Elegy*, as Steuart Wilson was in hospital. We had a dinner party between rehearsal and performance, Cecil and Jill Day Lewis, Iris and Randolph Wedgwood, Cordelia Curle and Gil Jenkins were there, Gil having become Ralph's regular Pilate, so to say, in his *St John Passion* performances. It was a cheerful party, a rejoicing concert and the evening ended with yet another party in the smaller hall, when most of the orchestra, some of the choir, and a number of other friends who had come to the concert shared the fun of Ralph's favourite treat, a very good conjuror. It was a really good birthday, and being eighty seemed a rejuvenating experience. We used up all the birthday-present champagne – the prevailing present that year – giving a Christmas party in my London flat.

There had been a strange moment in that flat when I was having coffee with Kanty[70], the telephone rang, and Gil told me that the King had died. As he spoke we saw flags, the existence of which hadn't before been particularly noticeable, being hauled down to half mast and by the next day all the shops had done the best they could about mourning. Boots was all mauve soap and purple hot-water bottles, the various little boutiques for underwear were dark with black bras and pants, and other such devices to signify distress. Gil took me to the lying-in-state in Westminster Hall, a deeply impressive sight. Ceremonial uniforms, princes guarding the dead King, the quiet procession of men and women all in black moving slowly and sadly past the coffin, each woman curtseying as she passed the catafalque and each man bowing. Above, the quiet lighting outlined the splendid wings of the great angels carved in wood older than many of the dynasties he had succeeded as monarch. But by the turn of the year the talk was of the coronation. There was to be a set of madrigals for the new Queen to match the *Triumphs of Oriana* of 1601. Ten composers were asked to choose their writing partners, and I was to be Ralph's. We'd been going to

---

[70] My friend from Westerham days (UVW)

Manchester for rehearsal of Ralph's *Sinfonia Antartica*, and naturally seeing a good deal of John and Evelyn Barbirolli in consequence. John was conducting *Tristan* that season at Covent Garden and we went to a January performance the night before we were going up to Manchester again. After sharing that music our half-and-half life seemed to reach its natural conclusion and marriage was obviously what we both wanted. We caught the breakfast train in a state of dazzled glory, though we didn't immediately tell John what he had brought about. It turned out to be amazingly difficult to find time to get married with *Antartica* rehearsals and performances in both Manchester and London, the ensuing parties, the Dorking rehearsals, and so on. But we did eventually manage it on the 7th of February. A tiny party came to see us done, my parents, Jean, Mary and Richard, and Gil, who was Ralph's best man. Ralph was much surprised when I'd said that I preferred a church wedding, for I was rather more pagan that he, but I explained, and he accepted my reason, that I wanted only the very best words to be used for us.

It snowed all next day, which we spent in answering letters about *Antartica* and fending off reporters who had discovered the news of our marriage. After *The Times* announcement on the following Monday a new spate of letters followed, all welcoming and delighted by our good sense. The ones that gave most pleasure of all were from the Wedgwoods who said they'd been hoping for this, and from Cedric Glover, a neighbour, friend and eccentric amateur musician, who wrote to Ralph 'so you have married your Anna Magdalena'.

We found the perfect house, 10 Hanover Terrace in Regent's Park, through the good offices of another musician, Mary Carter, who with her husband, Jerry Field Reid lived in a part of the house next door. Before we could move in the rebuilding following the bomb damage had to be completed, so once the Leith Hill Festival was over we went to Italy. Apart from my week in Rome as a twelve-year-old, this was my first visit; Ralph, in a proper old-fashioned way, considered that Venice was the right place for a honeymoon. We went by boat and train, with spring flowering abundantly, cherry blossom across Switzerland, acacias in Northern Italy, azaleas in huge terracotta jars on station platforms. We stopped at Bergamo, at Desenzano, and Verona, and then there was Venice. We had a little room overlooking the sea canal in a pensione next door to the house in which Ruskin had stayed, and a week or so of absolute pleasure. Sightseeing and idling, late walks ending with coffee and ices on a little floating restaurant opposite our lodging, and one magical day when the great banners were flaunting on the flagpoles outside St Mark's and there were no vaporetti, only gondolas, and most of them seemed to be brightly filled by wedding parties. It was marvellous to see in reality the places known well from so many pictures, so many pictures known from reproductions, and Torcello, about which Jill Day Lewis had told me, where we spent a day, coming home at sunset across the lagoon. Our holiday wasn't marred even by the money restrictions still imposed on travel. We had thirty-five pounds each this time, and we'd paid for our demi-pension in England, though not for the hotels on the way to Venice, so they'd been modest, but everywhere was wreathed in wisteria and roses and we were both feeling spaciously pleased with life.

We came back to London, to rehearsals of two of Ralph's operas[71] at Sadler's Wells, rehearsals for the Coronation for which Ralph had written a short anthem and arranged the *Old Hundredth* for both choir and congregation – an innovation for which he had to get the Archbishop's approval through the good offices of the Abbey organist William McKie. The rehearsals were exciting, and it was amusing to see how many rather grand soloists of all kinds had got themselves into the choir – Gerald Moore was one. "Well," he said in answer to Ralph's raised eyebrows, "I was a choirboy – once."

---

[71] *Riders to the Sea* and *Hugh the Drover*

I was engaged in getting a dress made for this excitement, pale grey organza with a thin gold line checking the airy stuff, with a wreath of gold leaves, and veils in greenish gold and darker yellow falling from it. Though it was an odd sort of garment to have to put on in the chilly early morning, it was scarcely less peculiar than seeing Ralph at breakfast at 6.45 wearing his tails and his O.M. The beautiful Cambridge Mus. D. gown, once owned by Walmisley[72] and later by Alan Gray[73], had darkened with age, the ivory silk to honey colour and the pink to a dark rose. We were rather sleepy, for the night before had been the first performance of *A Garland for the Queen*, a long concert with the old *Oriana* madrigals followed by the ten new ones, and we'd had an agitating time before setting out, with Gerald Finzi (and all the Finzis) as well as Edmund Rubbra changing into tails in our flat, a hurly-burly of lost cuff-links, studs mislaid and cries for Joy and me to help with starched white ties. By the time we arrived in the Abbey at eight o'clock all tiredness evaporated as we watched everyone arrive, the velvets, jewels, uniforms, tabards, coronets, and fealties of history made the morning absolutely absorbing. When, at the end of the service, the familiar tune of the *Old Hundredth* filled the Abbey with voices and with heraldic splendour of the great trumpet descant, it seemed with the ancient architecture, the glowing rose windows and the noble language of the service that our moment touched Shakespeare's histories.

The summer was busy. Ralph was at work on a new Christmas Cantata[74] for which I'd helped him choose words, and for which I had to write bits when we could not find what he wanted. He was conducting at Bournemouth, where Charles Groves was in command of the orchestra, and the Three Choirs at Gloucester, and between all these journeys there were a number of things to arrange

---

[72] Thomas Walmisley (1814 – 1856): organist and composer
[73] Alan Gray: organist at Cambridge University and RVW's organ teacher in the 1890s
[74] *Hodie*

about the move, disposing of my flat and selling The White Gates
which we did eventually to Bill and Winifred Cole.

The move was not too bad, for all my things and the extra furniture
we needed, for which I'd hunted in sales, a pleasure of intoxicating
pursuit and capture, were moved first, so the lot from Dorking
could be last, leaving Ralph undisturbed until he and the one cat we
had, Zebedee, could walk into a tolerably ordered home. Gil had a
room on the top floor, Ralph undertook the arrangement of his
scores and so forth in the huge box-room in the pediment and I
tackled the garden which workmen had left as a desert of rubble,
though a superb magnolia and two laburnums had survived. I
wanted immediate results, so turf was laid and I rushed to and fro
from the Clifton Nurseries with quantities of plants. Our friend
Frank Hollins, another civil servant with a passion for music,
moved into the mews house at the end of the garden, and so began
the happiest years of our life.

Soon after we were married we had to make new wills. Ralph had
said that everyone must have supposed that he had married a rich
widow as we'd swept off from a bungalow in Dorking to one of the
most delectable houses in London. "They'll think *you* married *me*",
he added, "to go to the Coronation." Maybe, but apart from my
commission fee for my part in the *Garland*, which anyway I'd spent
on a necklace at Cameo Corner, with Moshe Oved's warm
approval, and at Joy Finzi's advice ("It will all go on kippers and
stockings otherwise", she said), I had precisely twenty-five pounds
in my bank and my widow's pension had ceased. So Ralph really
had endowed me with worldly goods, as well as a very beautiful
seventeenth-century cameo ring.

Discussing our will the lawyer said to Ralph, "And who do you
want to write your biography?" We looked at each other in dismay.
There had already been books about Ralph's music, but biography
meant after death. "You can do it", Ralph said cheerfully. I had

thought of his death every day of the war, and all through the last months of Adeline's life when fatigue was a lasting shadow on him. Since then I'd supposed that we'd perish together, or be whirled to the clouds in a chariot of fire, so these words fell like cold stones. "I can't write about music," I said, fending off the problem. "Michael, then, can do that part," Ralph said. Michael Kennedy was a young music critic, a friend of John Barbirolli's and ours, and so it was put down in that will and forgotten.

It was a delight to live in Hanover Terrace. It is a large and beautiful house, the front looking over Regent's Park, red may trees, an early flowering chestnut and the lake beyond. At the back, a garden the width of the house, and the mews house at the end of it. A big study on the first floor at the back gave Ralph a pleasant place for work, and a Steinway piano, chosen for him by Kathleen Long, allowed us to have plays-through of new works, parties with music and such luxuries.

While at 7.5 I'd had some madrigal parties for a few friends; now these expanded, and from autumn to spring we had them every month. Ralph loved this music and we gathered about twenty-five or thirty regulars who came, anything from fifteen to twenty of them at a time, to sing, mostly string players, but other musicians as well, some amateurs, and no professional singers, all to enjoy and explore these ravishing mixtures of verse and music. It is a literature I love, but as it was in the old *Linden Lea* days, I could not sing, so I was only audience. Madrigals are for performers rather than for listeners, but knowing most of them as verse, I was enchanted to learn them as music. When it was Christmas, and besides our regulars, now more-or-less-singing husbands or wives came, and other friends. We had a very potent cup and party food, and were allowed by Ralph, who was strictly for music-making ordinarily, more time for gossip and frivolity.

I realise that I talk and think a lot at parties. Perhaps this was something learned during war years when congenial people found each other mutually supporting, and when sharing what each of us had was comfort and pleasure. I like my friends, as Ralph liked his, to meet each other and to enjoy each other's company. But we had a lot of quiet days of work and concentration, a lot of sudden inspirational outings to operas and films, and the mixture worked beautifully as far as writing music was concerned. He was full of invention and new works were achieved in spite of the beguilements of London which he enjoyed as much as I did now that he had returned to live in town once more, from what he had recognised, in the early years at Dorking, as exile.

Our masque, *Epithalamion*[75], which had been a performance casualty at the beginning of the war, had been brought out of a drawer at Hubert Foss's[76] instigation. The first idea was for a Hampton Court production, which would have been the right setting for it, but eventually it was changed to a television performance. The small screen and black and white photography did not work well, though we were lucky in having Cecil Day Lewis and Denis Dowling as narrator and singer. Originally there had been one song only:

> Ah, when will this long, weary day have end
>
> And lend me leave to come unto my love.

Ralph added two new ones, an aubade:

> … hearken to the bird's love-learned songs
>
> The dewy leaves among,
>
> For they of joy and pleasuance to you sing …

and a night piece, where Spenser, who wrote the poem for his own marriage, spoke for himself, or for us:

---

[75] Originally *The Bridal Day*; later arranged by RVW for choir and orchestra as *Epithalamion*

[76] Hubert Foss (1899-1953): Head of Music Department of Oxford University Press (1924-53); wrote book on RVW (1950)

Now welcome night, thou night so long expected
that long day's labour dost at last defray
And all my cares which cruel love collected
Hast summed in one and cancelled for aye.

As we settled into Hanover Terrace this was our shared frame of mind. The extraordinary peace of being able to live happily ever after infused everything we did, even when we were sharing hours and days of recording sessions at Kingsway Hall, as we did during the winter.

Then my utmost concentration had to be called upon to follow scores with Ralph while Adrian Boult, with the London Philharmonic Orchestra, recorded all his (then) seven symphonies. Living, as it seemed to be for ever, in the Kingsway Hall is a curious experience. One is not sensible of any time of day or season among those dusty blue-green seats, even less aware of anything but the immediate present in the dustier vestry, among even dustier memorials, listening to the playbacks. It was then, and at many later such sessions, a discipline of listening, learning about balance and becoming conscious of the complicated structure of every movement – very educational for a non-musician, as I am.

Ralph's pattern of work did not change, but there seemed much more time for diversion. His, and often my, daily strolls were in the park. He took to occasional bouts with the mowing-machine until Frank Hollins decided that both Ralph and I were hopelessly bad grass-cutters and took over for us. Best of all Ralph came to feel that holidays abroad were a natural part of each year.

In 1954 we went to Florence, from there to Siena, and San Giminiano, all places Ralph had been to in the years before the first war, so he showed me their sights. At Siena I was excited to find both the Black Sybil and the three faces of the White Goddess, girl, young woman and crone, among the rondels on the Duomo floor.

But in all the places we saw, from Pisa to Florence to Siena, it was all new to me, yet each place was full of the recognition of buildings, sculptures and pictures I had longed to see. We had gone by train for the first part of the journey; from Florence we went by bus. All of the countryside was flowering: broom and sainfoin, white iris and little gladioli, wild roses and many brilliant wild flowers filled the roadside verges and the fields behind. We went on by bus from Siena to Rome. Rome had changed from the city I half remembered from 1924, but the sightseeing places were the same, and we explored a great deal. It being Ascension Day while we were there, we had hoped for a lot of music, but all the choirs were busy preparing for a canonisation so we didn't hear anything special. We had lovely weather for idling among broken columns in the Forum, exploring the water and shadow garden at Tivoli and at night all the church domes were lit by little candles. We went to the opera and to the cinema and sat about in cafés. It was a very good holiday.

We had another expedition to look forward to, because Keith Falkner, an old friend of Ralph's, a new one of mine, was a professor of music at Cornell University and, to gratify Ralph's desire to see the Grand Canyon, had arranged for us to spend the autumn term at Cornell and for Ralph to go on a lecture tour that would take us to the West Coast. Ralph had been to America twice, but only in the East, so this was exciting for us both. There were two new works of his to be heard before we left: one, a violin sonata, which was to be broadcast on Ralph's birthday, while we would be away, so Frederick Grinke and Michael Mullinar came to play it to us and to some friends; and at the Three Choirs Festival at Worcester Ralph conducted the first performance of his Christmas Cantata *Hodie*. He was very nervous, but soloists and orchestra were all friends, and there were many people we knew there to support him, and of course all was well.

I think that many people suppose that first performances are all rejoicing excitement for composers, but it's not at all the case. There is a lot of terror, an exposed feeling as something that has for so long been a private expression is made public and must be seen in the context of its time and place and as the inheritor of a musical tradition. But this is not so much a matter of immediate concern as is the actual performance – will that difficult opening come off? (Ralph's criterion was always: does it come off?) – will the harp be heard enough? – and so on and so on. One waits for all the places about which there have been questions at rehearsal. All this tends to lessen the impact of a new work for those closest to it. Indeed the greatest impact may well be at a first rehearsal when the tunes long heard on the piano sweep into their proper volume on the instruments the composer heard in his mind as he wrote.

Hodie was safely achieved, and with glowing notices to cheer us we set out for Liverpool and America. I found the voyage awful. My only experience of a sea voyage had been the one to Malta, and this was just as frightful, anyway for the first days. Ralph was a good sailor and had a merry time with Gerald and Enid Moore who were on the same voyage. Eventually I emerged for the last few days of the trip, but I found the endless sea and sky pretty boring. Of course it must have been much more worrying for the explorers who were not certain of land, but I did find myself thinking that we might slop over the edge and see a monster standing on a tortoise, standing on a snake as we poured down to some abyss with the ship folded into the waters. So the first seagull was a welcome sight, and the lights of the shores of the Hudson River a matter for gratitude. Then the towers of Manhattan were startlingly beautiful in the dawn, and Keith Falkner and Professor Donald Grout were on the quay to meet us and to take us sightseeing. Noone had told me that all the streets of New York ended in sky; this gives the tall city an unexpected lightness that I found delightful and unexpected. The shops looked gorgeous after our still meagre supplies of luxury, but there wasn't much time for shop gazing. Keith and Donald whirled us round the more obvious sights and next morning drove us through the blazing colours of the fall, a landscape of white towns and little lakes, to Ithaca and Cornell. We were to live in the Country Club where we had two rooms, each with a bath. One was provided with a piano and a table for Ralph's work room. In the other we slept, cooked, and had our meals. This was perfect, because it gave us an experience we might have had if we had lived together as young people sharing a bed-sit, though we had the luxury of a bathroom each and more comforts than would have come our way as impecunious students. The members of Cornell Music Department were our hosts, and as welcoming and friendly as could be. The wives took me shopping, introducing me to the then-to-England-unknown supermarkets. We were very much entertained. Ralph's first lecture went well, and his second even better. It seemed no time at all before we were off on our travels. The first journey was to Toronto, and Donald Grout drove us by way of Niagara where we spent a dizzy weekend, not only seeing everything there was to be seen, in the way of Fall, Whirlpool and Museum, but being put through a course of American short drinks, a matter Donald thought we should know about before we started to cross the continent on our own, and into which he went with us with all the thoroughness a devoted musicologist devotes to an exhaustive study of a subject he has long enjoyed.

We went by train from Buffalo to Detroit, for Ann Arbor, then to Chicago, Bloomington, and from Saint Louis we travelled non-stop to Los Angeles, a journey that taught us about distance as the days and nights passed and the desert lasted. We spent a few days in the comfort of a Santa Monica hotel with a swimming pool, surrounded by palm trees and hibiscus bushes. Not so large, though, as the Olympic pool at the hotel in Santa Barbara where we spent a week having a holiday in blissful summer weather. During the time we were there winter set in officially. I was surprised when we, with my Canadian cousins who had come to meet us for a few days, lunched in town and found that all the ladies were dressed in smart tweeds and carried furs although the temperature was still in the high eighties and we were still in the lightest of summer clothes. In one of the big shops – the shops in America were mostly delectable – a Christmas tree made of mink tails and diamante was a curious and shocking object, as well as reminder that it was already November, though the humming birds and the flowers suggested an everlasting summer. We saw pelicans flying out to sea each morning, and my cousin Molly and I braved the icy sea because I wanted to have bathed in the Pacific.

We went back via the Grand Canyon – its theatrical magnificence, particularly at dawn and sunset when the shadows heightened the illusion of architectural remains lying in broken splendour beyond the great depth of the gorge, was impressively terrible. Cornell, after these travels, seemed small and familiar, though we had not much longer to stay, as there were visits to Buffalo to be made for rehearsals and a concert. That was the only time in my life when I was given so many orchids that I did not know what to do with them all. We flew back to Cornell in a tiny plane, bumping through autumn winds over golden and scarlet woods, for more concerts, farewell parties and an astonishingly long and delicious Thanksgiving dinner to which the Grouts invited us, and a great packing up for our flight to New York.

There we spent a dizzy week with one day at Yale for Ralph to lecture and to be given a medal and a thousand dollar prize, most of which he spent on buying clothes for me, an activity we both enjoyed. We had a dreadful crossing in the *Queen Mary* over the rough winter sea. Julian Huxley was a fellow passenger and he advised pink gin on the hour every hour as a cure for sea sickness. I don't think we managed it every hour, but I survived on it, and Ralph, in any case, enjoyed being a good sailor. We were home for Christmas for our usual carol party, and for Ralph to have more time than he had had in America to work on his new symphony[77].

---

[77] The Eighth

He took it with him when we went to Cornwall in May. He knew the south coast from the days of undergraduate reading parties, but the north was new to him. We stayed at Mawgan Porth, near Newquay, a place I'd known since childhood; every rock on the beach was familiar, and the flowery cliff tops and lanes were at their best. My old friends Mrs Hicks and Bill came over to lunch, and Mrs Hicks took to Ralph and flirted with him extensively. Later in the afternoon when they were leaving she said: "He's much too good for a chit like you." I suppose it must have seemed odd that someone she'd known as a difficult child and a shy sixteen-year-old was now having a fascinating life of quite extraordinary bliss. Ralph had enjoyed her company, and they'd both amused and pleased each other.

That summer we missed the Three Choirs because we joined a Swan's tour to Greece. Ralph had been stationed in Salonika as a private in the first war, and had seen little more than the snowy slopes of Mount Olympus. It was a beautifully arranged three weeks with lots of time for swimming. Ralph had a new bathing dress, his first since the twenties, and there was time at each site for lingering and idling. The weather was perfect, and when we sailed back for Venice the banks of the Corinth canal were covered with wild cyclamen. We had a few days in Venice where Frank Hollins met us and drove us home through France. We stayed in Vienne and drove up the west bank of the Rhône, and through many little roads till we reached the willowy Loire, where we loitered and went sightseeing. I had long wanted to see the Plantagenet effigies at Fontrevrault, particularly of Eleanor of Aquitaine. She was as splendid as I expected, lying holding an open book, more likely love songs than psalms, while swifts flew through the arches of the great deconsecrated church above the restless, tiresome and heroic kings and queens now anchored in time and buried in history. We saw the Renaissance garden at Villandry, where only one bell remains of a peal of four that were given as a memorial to a son of the house who was killed at Agincourt. We stayed for a night or two in Tours, and saw the house where Ronsard lived in his old age and his grave. The woods were turning to autumn browns and yellows, and the willow leaves falling on to the sandy river banks as we left Chinon, Azay, Chambord, Saumur and Blois, and then to the Abbey of Solèsmes, and so home by sea, to be met by a foul customs man who turned out all our suitcases of crumpled summer clothes on the quay at dawn. We had a bottle of Calvados each, and some cheese, nothing smuggled to cheer him, but a tremendous store of visual memories of places of legend and of history.

There was more travelling, for in October Ralph was engaged to give the first Arnold Bax memorial lecture at Cork. We flew to Dublin and were met there and driven to the station. Gil Jenkins, in his capacity as Permanent Secretary to the Ministry of Transport, had made all the travel arrangements, and everything was done in splendour; our plane had been delayed by fog so the train was held for us, and because there was a restaurant car strike an aeroplane lunch was given to us, and finally the train started, then almost stopped to allow a running benefactor from the airport to hand a bottle of wine through the window, a welcoming introduction to a country I'd never visited before. Cork was fun, a good lecture, sightseeing including Blarney, though we both decided against the gymnastic dangers of kissing the Stone.

1956, and Ralph's Eighth Symphony meant more visits to Manchester, more evenings with the Barbirollis and Michael and Eslyn Kennedy, all lively and conversational. In fact there were plenty of little journeys, usually for concerts, but we managed to use them for sightseeing as well; after a concert at Hastings we were able to spend the next morning at Battle Abbey, going to Oxford and to lunch with Bruce and Elena Richmond at Islip on our way.

Sometimes I had to visit my parents at Milford, and whether for the day or for a night as well, I found that coming home to Ralph was an absolute joy. My parents never seemed able to enjoy life easily, unless it was in retrospect. I think my mother came to believe that the past had been wonderful and that the present was a diminished state of being. It seemed strange to hear her speak of times I remembered as doom-laden, of holidays when we were all at home, and John and I at least were wondering how we should ever escape into real life, as idyllic. Memory had not changed them for me, but a rosy cloud lay over them for her. Father said nothing much, but he was clearly finding it hard to make up for the livelier times when he was able to work with colleagues. However, they gardened and we discussed all our mutual friends and relations. Also, Rosemary had married and at last they had grandchildren, which seemed to me, in principle, a curious desire for people who never showed any particular liking for children anyway. As she lived then in the Isle of Wight, they were happily in visiting distance. But the joy of getting home to the easy freedom of our lives and talk, to the excitements and problems of the works in progress, and to the comfortable pleasure of shared friends was like coming from winter into spring.

We had had, ever since we came to London, a delightful arrangement with the Finzis. We were their town house, they our country estate. Ralph had, when we married, asked me marvellously endowing questions – did I want a lady's maid? – did I want a country cottage? I can't think what novels he could have been reading to make the first offer. Though a charming idea, my surprise at the thought made him laugh. To the second my reaction was absolutely no. I like freedom for variety; living in two places at once is my idea of no advantage at all. One house, one garden, are enough, and anyway I don't like the country in the winter unless seen from total and centrally-heated comfort. This arrangement suited us all, as staying at Ashmansworth was easy, happy, conversational, comfortable, with a lot of shared pleasures in little excursions, lots of places to sit, hundreds of books and enough tables for everyone to have somewhere to work. It was much the same when they came to stay with us.

Another visitor to Hanover Terrace was Ralph's cousin Frances Cornford[78]. I loved her visits. I knew her work well, I had reviewed some of her poems years earlier, and she was a familiar character from her cousin Gwen Raverat's *Period Piece*. She was small, vivid, wildly untidy – we once spent half the night looking for "the only copies of my poems" which she swore were in the house. But it was outside, by the steps, that they were found next morning by the milkman. "I must have put them down when I paid the taxi", she said. Parcels followed her to us, and from us when she left, anything from dresses to brush and comb, and once, after she'd gone from us to America, her address book. She and I were amusing ourselves with translations of Louise Labé and other things, and it was fine to have time to discuss such work together. She talked of Ralph as she remembered him as a young man, of Leith Hill Place and of his mother and sister, of Adeline too, for her stepmother had been Florence Maitland, Adeline's eldest sister, widow of the legal historian Frederic Maitland whom Ralph had known and deeply admired when he was an undergraduate reading history and Maitland was Professor of Laws of England. I caught a distant view through her eyes of many aspects of Ralph's past.

For several years we had gone to operas at Cambridge. A lively group of undergraduates, not all of them reading music, had been involved in productions, among them Ralph's *Sir John in Love*, and most memorable of all *The Pilgrim's Progress*, which was produced in the Guildhall by Dennis Arundell, with Boris Ord conducting the Cambridge University Music Society. It had been all Ralph had hoped for originally and of which he had been disappointed at Covent Garden. It had the extra qualities of Dennis's splendid and imaginative use of the quite dreadful Guildhall stage, all steps and no backstage, which he somehow

---

[78] Frances Cornford (1886-1960): poet

turned to advantage, and a particularly talented group of young performers. When their Cambridge days were over they felt bereft of this pleasure and some of them asked if they could come to see Ralph about it. So, on 19th June 1956, over quite a lot of sherry, the New Opera Company was invented. Among the founder members were Peter Hemmings and Brian Trowell, and it was largely Peter's enthusiasm and organising ability which created the possibility of such a venture. Among others who'd been in the operas at Cambridge were Christopher Bishop, Kenneth Bowen, Leon Lovett, and John Noble, all later to have distinguished musical careers.

There were more pleasures that summer, a few days with Paddy Hadley at Heacham for the King's Lynn Festival following a week at Cheltenham where we stayed at a small hotel at which the Kennedys were too; our room was in the annexe. When we arrived I found to my surprise that the annexe was a house that had belonged to my great aunt Alice and that our bedroom had been her dining-room. I half expected to see her there, reading the paper, dressed in black, her head covered with little streaked half-white, half-auburn curls, tiny feet in satin slippers on a footstool, and to hear Grannie's shocked voice: "Alice – how *can* you? at *your* age – *The Daily Mirror* ... !" Grannie always read *The Times*.

In those days the Three Choirs Festival was at the beginning of September. At Gloucester we had a room in the school house, usually lived in by unmarried schoolmasters. It was run by a delightful housekeeper, Mrs Cunningham, and for the Festival week she had a houseparty that felt as if it was an end of term spree at a very lively co-ed school. Our fellow boarders were the Finzi family, the conductors from Worcester (David Willcocks), and Hereford (Meredith Davies), Howard Ferguson, Eric Greene, and the treasurer of the South Western Arts Association, Harold Browne.

As our room was on the ground floor it was much used as a meeting place, a place to dump coats before meals, and so on, and for much sociability and gossip. It didn't improve the beds when three or four people sat on them at a time, but it didn't matter much for after all the music and all the gadding nothing would have kept either of us awake. Gerald and Joy Finzi, Ralph and I visited Rutland and Kathleen Boughton[79]; we spent the morning drinking coffee in their kitchen, a memorable encounter, for Rutland said something I've never heard before or since – "I've done everything I wanted to do in my life." The rest of the week was as usual, with works by Ralph and Gerald, Herbert Howells and Howard Ferguson among others. There was the usual *Gerontius*, to which Ralph went; by now my Elgar allergy was common knowledge to my friends, so I was exempt and I spent an amusing evening of gossip with Eric Greene who wasn't singing in it that year. It was a delectable week for us all; the weather had been golden, friendship abounded, the performances were good, and no shadow of the future fell on any of us.

We were going to Majorca a few days later; in the interval between Gloucester and the South, Ralph Wedgwood, Ralph's cousin and oldest friend, died. They had been able to see each other often in the last years at Dorking. Happily we had spent a day with him and Iris at Leith Hill Place a few weeks earlier, and the two Ralphs had been content in each other's company, sitting together on a sofa in the house which, at different ends of life, had been home to each of them.

Majorca was delightful. We stayed at Bendinet, at a hotel on the rocky shore a few miles out of Palma. We had the only top story rooms, a bathroom of our own, and a tiny extra room with a table for Ralph who was working on his ninth symphony. I swam a great deal, sometimes across the little bay to a tiny restaurant with enough money tied in a handkerchief to have grilled prawns and a

---

[79] Rutland Boughton (1878-1960): English composer

champagne cocktail for elevenses. As lunch was late, and Ralph liked a very early breakfast, there was time to swim back and collect him for a bathe before lunch, then siestas, more writing, a swim, a walk, dinner, and chairs in the garden looking at the clear stars, the Pleiades and the Milky Way. Gil was still Permanent Secretary of the Ministry of Transport and he was able to send us letters immediately by one of the regular planes with news of Gerald Finzi's death. He'd had Hodgkin's disease for some time, and he, as well as his family, knew that he had not long to live. It seemed strange to think how short a time it was since we had all been so happily together, and we both knew how much we should miss him from our lives.

We spent nearly a month in Majorca, which was a good place to work, with a little sightseeing and some highly entertaining times with Robert and Beryl Graves. An ex-pupil of Ralph's, Peggy Glanville Hicks[80], was staying with them, intending to make his novel, *Homer's Daughter*, into an opera. We thought that she was in New York, so it was a surprise to find her in Palma, though really it's silly to be surprised by anything like that, for in some mysterious way all the people one knows know people one never realised they knew, and so on, in a widening circle.

Ralph had been making too much money for us. Our dear accountant, Bert Sturgess, with a lot of discussion about aims and objects, helped him to set up a Trust by which his Performing Rights could be ploughed back into music. It took two years to get all the legal clearances needed, then the Committee was formed and Ralph asked Gil to be Chairman. The Committee was half musicians, half non-musicians, and we had our first meeting at the Musicians' Benevolent Fund offices, for the Fund's Secretary, Frank Thistleton, took on our Secretaryship. The first thing that Ralph did was to organise a concert of Holst's music at the Festival Hall, and to choose the programme for it. This was not very well

---

[80] Peggy Glanville Hicks (1912-90): Australian-born composer

attended, but it made a great impact as some of the then lesser-known works had not been heard at all recently, and were new to a number of younger people. It was a fine launching for the Trust and it gave Ralph a great deal of pleasure to be able to do this, particularly as Adrian Boult, his friend and Holst's, conducted.

Other plans were, at first, for support for various societies and for concerts of music by composers who were, Ralph felt, neglected. Later, the personal applications came, and there was more work for the Committee to do. As the Trust's revenue is from this private source, the Committee have been able to be entirely flexible in their work, to back their own judgement and to help, in very many ways, both professional and amateur music making. It gave Ralph enormous pleasure, and he was deeply grateful to Bert Sturgess whose knowledge, practicality and patience had made such a wide-ranging Trust possible. I have not missed any of the meetings and, like all the Committee members, I found that spending money in this way is a great pleasure. Also, we were spending it on what we wanted and not having it taken away in tax, a matter which gave Ralph great satisfaction.

Ralph's symphony was his major concern, and through the winter and spring that, and a few other works, kept him busy, but we went to Brighton for a few days in the spring after I'd had Asian flu, luckily not until after Ralph had conducted the *St Matthew Passion* at Dorking. The two Passions were all he did there now, having given up conductorship of the Festival to William Cole. Our only other spring journey was to stay at Haddo, near Aberdeen, for a few days and a concert – a most lively adventure, and one we both enjoyed. June Gordon[81] had prepared a very satisfying performance of the *Sea Symphony* and Ralph conducted Parry's *Blest Pair of Sirens*. There was a large party of musicians staying there, mostly old friends, and the mixture of the grand house and the warm

---

[81] June Gordon: Marchioness of Aberdeen studied at RCM and founded Haddo House Choral Society, Aberdeen

informality of the way it is lived in and used for music was, and is, enchanting.

I had a new job to do, for Ralph wanted fresh words for his light opera, *The Poisoned Kiss*. The original script had been written for him by Cecil Sharp's sister Evelyn, who married Henry Nevinson, and after her death he bought the rights from her niece, Joan. The songs were all right, but the dialogue was very longwinded and heavily laced with old-fashioned jokes. We scrapped this and I made a much shorter version in pantomime rhymes, quite difficult but amusing to do. I had, about this time, another commission: Elizabeth Maconchy, once a pupil and always a friend of Ralph's, wanted a libretto for a one-act opera. Her husband, William LeFanu, suggested an idea he'd found in a story by Crebillon *fils* about a young rake who was turned into a sofa (I think it is, uncomfortably, a chair in the original) until, as we delicately put it in the programme note, he was released when the act of love was consummated on his changed form. It was a lighthearted script, and we all had a great deal of fun with it. Betty came to play it to us as her part of the work grew. I have always found that, if I'm going to work with any composer, it must be 'prima le parole – e poi la musicà'. One of the things I did in this, which was set in the ante-room to a Paris ballroom in the 1860s, was to write a big drinking song, burgundies for basses, clarets for tenors, rosés for altos, and the sopranos had white wines. I put a lot of research into this, working with every single wine catalogue I could lay hands on; some wines have singable names, others are impossible. Unfortunately the song proved too long for the structure of the scene and all that is left is the champagnes-for-all chorus.

Ralph hadn't been feeling well; we went to Austria for a holiday, hoping it would revive him. I felt that it was our least successful abroading. I do not like mountains or pine trees or the German language, so even Innsbruck, Salzburg and Zell-am-See didn't take well. We went to see a 'glacier' which was horrid, and I kept looking with longing at signposts to the Brenner pass and the distant joys of Italy. There were pictures to see in Munich, but even so we felt dispirited, and Ralph was clearly not well, so we went home early. It turned out that he had anaemia, which was soon put right. But he still was not well, so after a few weeks he went to the Middlesex Hospital for X-rays. While he was there, Genia Hornstein came to stay at Hanover Terrace; with her there, and Gil, I felt I could leave as my father was suddenly ill. Rosemary and I were both able to go to Bournemouth with my mother when he was rushed to hospital for an operation. Their doctor, John Salkield, like ours, Ray Rowntree, was a friend, and unfailingly kind. He had to tell us that Father was found to have an inoperable cancer. Luckily Father never came round from the anaesthetic. We sat with him for a day and a night. Rosemary had the added complication of her youngest child, a small baby, but she managed to be there most of the time. It was very strange, a tremendous shock, and my mother could not face the unexpected horror of his death. I could feel her powerful hold over him, willing him to live. The doctor and surgeon said that he might regain consciousness and survive in pain for a day or two, but even this did not persuade her to let him die.

Eventually, and I do not know how, I knew that I had to do something, and I put my hands on his shoulders and said very quietly, "It's all right, you can go now, you don't have to stay, you are quite free." I felt my will fighting hers, then suddenly the hoarse breathing stopped and he breathed quite quietly. I went on talking to him, and suddenly the room felt as if a number of invisible people were with us. He sighed, and stopped breathing, just as it became light. I opened the windows, and there were no more unseen people in the room. Father was lying quite peacefully. The nurses came into the room, and we took my mother back to the hotel, to sleeping pills and rest and despair. I felt very tired, and going up to my room I saw brilliant light over the sea, and a single seagull, white and golden and distant flying over the water.

I had to get home to Ralph. My mother's old friend Betty Wilmott came to her, and she and Rosemary took her back to Milford. Ralph was temporarily better and insisted on going with me to the funeral. It was marvellous to have his support and help.

By the end of August we knew that he had to have a major operation. He thought that it was a bad idea to be in the Middlesex instead of at the Three Choirs, but we managed to go to several things he wanted to hear first, the New Opera Company's performance of Arthur Benjamin's *A Tale of Two Cities*, *Antartica* at the Proms – and then the day for the Middlesex came. He insisted on taking the score of the symphony with him, though I said that I doubted if he'd be allowed ink in the hospital, but I don't think that the authorities had ever envisaged ink and a full score as a threat to their sheets, so there was no forbidding rule to be infringed. I was far more nervous than he, and stayed late with him. The next morning Jean drove me to the hospital as she had driven me home the night before and I saw him again, doped and rather cross, and mentally made as many farewells as I had all through the night at home. It was a long day, and I didn't know how he had fared for eternities of time. But when I was allowed to see him again he was recovering consciousness in such a filthy temper that I began to feel reassured. Next morning, before eight, I was woken by the telephone. It was Ralph, asking how I was, had I slept? "I've just kissed the night nurse goodbye," he said. "Where did you put my work? I may want it after breakfast." I knew, then, that he'd make a brisk recovery. He had one failure only. Jean, visiting him, dared him to kiss Matron before he left the Hospital. George, who knew the Matron, gave him honourable discharge from the dare, but it was his only known failure. We went to stay with Joy Finzi for convalescence. A gentle and easy autumn holiday, most of which Ralph spent working.

It was Ralph's eighty-fifth birthday in October, and the Festival Hall was packed to the roof for his birthday concert. It was exciting and moving to see everyone stand as he came into the ceremonial box. There was a party after, and more concerts and parties at Dorking, but the actual day we spent at home. I borrowed Jean and George's two elder girls, Maggie and Nicola, to answer the door to telegraph boys and postmen, which they enjoyed, rushing up and down stairs with bigger and bigger batches of letters or congratulatory messages. We gave them as many cocktail sausages as they could eat to sustain their efforts. Ralph and I dined out alone that night, and drank the health of the new symphony.

He was as busy as ever, in spite of some phlebitis. Our winter was full of treats and pleasures, and an extraordinary amount of concert-going, some for performances of Ralph's work, some for other music we both wanted to hear, operas, films, and somehow, through it all, a steady pattern of work continued. Perhaps the most concentrated work of all was at the turn of the year, when Ralph wrote nine songs in four days, settings of Blake poems, commissioned for a film of Blake's pictures and drawings.

In February the usual Dorking performance of the *St John Passion* was quite the best he'd given, and in March there were two *St Matthew Passion* performances, the first conducted by Thomas Armstrong[82], the second by Ralph. The different approach and slightly different tempi of the two conductors kept the choir on their toes; Kiffer Finzi and Noel Taylor managed to make a recording of Ralph's performance. For me, this was the best interpretation of the *Passion* I have ever heard. It varied a little from year to year as he thought of different aspects of the music, but it was always as exciting, as vivid and as dramatic as any opera. From both professionals and amateurs he conjured a great sensitivity to both the music and his understanding of the music.

These events over, the weeks before the symphony were pretty busy. We had a piano run-through at Malcolm Sargent's flat. Roy

---

[82] Sir Thomas Armstrong (1898-1994): Organist and teacher; Principal of the Royal Academy of Music 1955-68

Douglas[83], who'd played, copied, and generally devoted his time to this work (as he had to all the major works since 1947, as well as some earlier ones), Ralph and I got into a taxi for this excursion with the manuscript score in Ralph's case. I had a sudden idea. "Who are you going to dedicate it to?" I asked, "because it seems to me a good idea to settle that at once." Roy caught my eye, then we both caught Ralph's. 'The Royal Philharmonic Society', who had commissioned it, had their dedication written boldly across the front page as the taxi waited at a traffic light.

Gerald Kelly came with other invited friends to the preliminary rehearsal, and said that he must paint Ralph again: "He is much more beautiful now." Ralph grumbled about this, but promised two sittings before we went abroad. The symphony was played at the Festival Hall, and followed by a party, but it wasn't the moment for a party, there was too much strain, emotion and agitation, and next morning, as Ralph had half expected, the notices were cool. Ralph said: "They can't bear me still being able to do it." However, the people whose opinions he most valued were full of the right sort of praise and understanding, and dear Roy came for a long conference on the alterations that Ralph made after a proper hearing.

As before, in 1951, the sittings with Gerald Kelly were great fun; he was tough with Ralph, and Ralph almost tougher with him, and they both enjoyed that. And then, Gerald was full of gossip, Jane[84] came in to see how things were going, and I watched him at work with the pleasure one takes seeing a brilliant craftsman.

We had taken one of the houses at Forio, in Ischia, owned by the Waltons. We flew to Naples where we spent three wet days, mostly in the museums, though there was one morning when we dashed to Herculaneum between storms. One evening we saw a baddish

---

[83] Roy Douglas (1907-): Composer, arranger and editor, who worked closely with Ralph Vaughan Williams
[84] Lady Kelly

opera at the ravishingly pretty opera house. The season was nearly over so we'd missed the more interesting works. Then we crossed to Ischia, the Waltons met us, gave us lunch in their house, and then took us to ours. It was a chilly, rainy spring, but even so it was a lovely place to be, with a big sitting room and a fireplace, so fires every evening, views of the sea, wild flowers, and lots of time. We were working on an opera[85] together. Roy had played the first act to us from a first piano draft and Ralph was working on the second act as I altered and improved, took in or let out, the libretto. Su Walton took us for drives and showed us the island; as William had had to leave for England he'd lent Ralph his piano. We went for a few mild walks or we sat in some sheltered corner of the garden whenever the sun shone. It was a surprise when, in our last week, the weather changed to summer. The white flowery cistus that covered the ridge behind the house burst into flower, and the fireflies arrived. It was warm enough to bathe, warm enough to have our meals outside, and really hot when, sadly, we left for Naples and home.

Ralph was always good at impulsive plans. One June morning he said that it was time to have a look at England. We had been opera going since we'd come home; the splendid Visconti production of *Don Carlos*, as well as *Tristan*, and other urban treats, so we went off for a couple of radiant June days, spent a night at Lincoln, a place I'd never seen, and then the next day drove in a locally hired car across the Fens – all new country to me, but long familiar to Ralph. We stopped to have tea with his cousin Diana Montgomery-Massingberd, now a widow living at her family house, Gunby Hall. She had been my hostess at my first dinner party when her husband was G.O.C. at Salisbury. She had been to see us at Hanover Terrace, where it seemed odd to be her hostess. I loved seeing Gunby, a house Ralph had talked about as one of the places he'd often stayed at, both as a child and as a young man, and had always enjoyed, for there had always been much music making with Diana

---

[85] *Thomas the Rhymer*

and his other cousins. We caught a breath of that happy past with all the other pasts that day, Tattershall and Boston, Spalding and Crowland, golden in June light, and finally Peterborough and a train back to London.

We were caught up in two battles in July, one, to save the Nash Terraces from demolition, a mad and terrible plan that had to be fought. The other was to save the Third Programme. Neither should have been necessary but they absorbed a great deal of energy. The Sound Broadcasting Society's secretary was Erica Propper; she had organised a press reception, collecting every chair in the house for journalists from about every magazine, weekly and daily newspaper. We gave them drinks while we waited for Ralph, Sir Laurence Olivier and Michael Tippett to come back from their interview with the BBC to report on their mission – and the press gave full coverage and full support – and we still have a Third Programme and the Nash Terraces, but that was a long campaign.

Simona Pakenham had collated some of the Christmas episodes of miracle plays for a performance at St Martin-in-the-Fields the following winter, and she asked Ralph to arrange the music for it. This was a pleasant, not too exacting, task; he was devoted to Simona and he had liked her book on his music. He thought this could be an agreeable summer occupation. He had finished the first draft of our opera, and there was a 'cello concerto hovering in his mind. Meanwhile the Cheltenham and King's Lynn Festivals were looming. Cheltenham was, as usual, a great meeting place for friends. Once more we were in Aunt Alice's old house, drawing-room, not dining-room this time, and the ghosts were of her black Indian furniture and brass trays, conjured up from recesses of memory where I had not known they were buried. The Kennedys were there and the Barbirollis, with all of whom we dined one night after a concert, driving to their hilltop hotel through the spectacular glories of a great sunset blazing above the Severn.

As Ralph was not well (he'd had phlebitis earlier in the year, and it returned), we had to miss King's Lynn, but later, when he was better, we went to stay with Joy Finzi at Ashmansworth. She drove us all over the country, over Salisbury Plain, to Avebury and Yarnbury, places that we had both known in our separate pasts, and down into Dorset where we stayed in a village pub, and so to the coast where we planned to spend a few days in the autumn. We called on Sylvia Townsend Warner and Valentine Ackland, and picnicked by the White Horse with Ruth and Tony Scott[86]. It was a lovely week, but we had to go home, for Adrian Boult was going to record the new symphony[87] and Ralph wanted to be at all the sessions. He was looking forward to hearing Adrian's performance, and the spaciousness that he knew it would have.

After a working day, he started to feel restless and not well, nor could he sleep. In the early dark morning Gil telephoned to our doctor Ray Rowntree, who came at once, and he and I were with Ralph when he died. It started to get light, and I opened the windows to the early day, not yet realising fully that nothing mattered any more.

I would have been grateful for suttee[88], and it struck me that perhaps this was how martyrs must have felt, their place on earth having become of no interest or value. The imminence of death would have held no terror, nor would its means have had any power to frighten or pain me then.

On some practical and other level I was able to see to it that Adrian Boult was told before he went to the recording studios and that as many as possible of our friends were told, by me, by Gil, by Frank Hollins and by Genia Hornstein to whom Gil had telephoned and

---

[86] Anthony Scott, a composer, whose work Ralph admired – as well as a friend of us both (UVW)
[87] The Ninth
[88] suttee, an Indian custom whereby widows commit suicide

who came at once. I knew that the news must be given publicly some time, but I hoped not before evening, but someone told the BBC and the one o'clock news told everyone. Poor Adrian, John Barbirolli and others were rushed to make broadcasts that evening and Gil was talking to the Dean of Westminster about an Abbey funeral. This I could bear, for Ralph and I had dined with the McKies that summer, and sat in the Abbey late at night, with a few lights catching arch or pillar in the shadows while William played for us. It seemed right for Ralph to be among the people of history, and I knew that at night, at least, the Abbey is a place of great calm. The next weeks were filled with letters, about two thousand came, and eventually I answered them all. It was a helpful discipline to have to do so. I had to help, too, with the choice of music for the Abbey, with the form of service, and eventually even going to the RCM each day as they had generously offered to deal with tickets for the service, but nearly everyone was on holiday and I was probably the only person who knew who many of the applicants were. All this was a curious half reality, a cool efficiency which surprised me. The whole reality was finding solitude at home, and deciding that whatever happened I must behave in a way that expressed a gladness for what had been, rather than a misery that joy had ended, which would have been unfair to Ralph – for he had not, as it were, died on purpose. I do not, and did not, believe that survival or non-survival has anything to do with religion, nor that it matters much. If there's more, it will probably be surprising, if nothing, one will not know. Only, I hoped, that if there was more, that time may not matter, and that Ralph would not feel as bereft as I.

On all important occasions, there must be some human ceremony to sustain the survivors. The Abbey gave us this, and among so many friends, with so much music, the point I had on which to fix my thoughts was that the clergy were wearing the dark velvet robes made for the funeral of Charles II. Ralph's mortality was now a part of history and his ashes lay next to the burial place of Purcell..

Chapter 8: Aftermath

What happens afterwards? Afterwards, except for that hour or so in the solicitor's office when the word biography was first spoken, and the night before Ralph's operation which had been a counting of blessings, had not been a subject to which I'd given any thought at all. But now everything that had been comfortably part of life, boxes and drawers of manuscripts, letters that had escaped the waste-paper basket, even contracts and copyrights were of a new importance. Everything had to be sorted out and nothing could be thrown away. I started on the work very slowly. Among other things I found tucked into drawers and lying among manuscripts almost every letter I'd ever written to Ralph as well as the certificate I'd carried in fire-watching days to say that I might break and enter in pursuance of my duty – though I could not imagine how he had come by that, unless I'd left it at Dorking sometime. Each one, when I had the courage to re-read it, recalled the time in which it had been written with vivid clarity. A time when there had been a present and at least a tomorrow. I collected some of the manuscripts, others I left till Roy Douglas and Michael Kennedy could come to help, for unless it had an indication in words I could not recognise what works they were.

Michael and I, at first, supposed that we would share a book, but we soon discovered that there would be far too much material for that, and that two would be necessary, one a personal life, the other musical. We went to see John Brown of the Oxford University Press at Amen House to discuss our plans and our problems. He promised help and gave it richly by advertising for us in a tremendous number of papers. The response, letters from Ralph and memories of him, poured in and all original documents were photographed for us and the originals returned to the owners by the O.U.P. Of course these owners had to be thanked, and sometimes a rewarding correspondence recalled even more than had their first letters.

Ralph's manuscripts had been as much his private hoard as my drafts of verse were mine. Now we had to explore a part of his past that had been left, as silted over by years and by new works, as some lost city covered by newer streets and dwellings. We found a few treasures, but not many. There were early works withdrawn later (and properly, we agreed), and some unfinished sketches – through which we three shared the knowledge of his growth and development as a composer. In time they were all collected, collated, and given to the British Museum[89] with all the other manuscripts from his publishers. It took a long time to achieve but it seemed a sensible and practical project to give the Museum the whole mass of surviving manuscripts with a ban on performing those he had withdrawn. I also noted the fact in earlier versions that he had made alterations after performance, and that the revised version was the proper one. Hunters after *Ur*-texts seem ill advised in supposing that a working musician's first thoughts are what he really meant when the experience of sound and effectiveness has been reassessed after performance.

While all this was going on Imogen Holst and I did a short book together. I had found some long letters from Gustav to Ralph, just after a revised reprint of her biography of her father had been published. They were lively letters, so we set about editing all that remained of their early correspondence with other relevant writings by them both. It was a good run-in for the biography which I still had to write, and I learned a little of what I would have to do in the bigger book. I had never tackled any sort of prose writing before and I had no idea of how to research, deal with documents or other such matters. After a great deal of wakeful despair at the thought of what I had undertaken, I bought a filing cabinet, made a folder for each family, Vaughan Williams and Wedgwood, one for childhood

---

[89] Now the British Library

at Leith Hill Place, for Charterhouse and for Cambridge, and then one for each year of Ralph's subsequent life. I also made an alphabetical set of folders for all the undatable material, for many letters and papers were without dates or envelopes that would have given postmarks. Some were eventually translatable by internal evidence, but that came later as I battled through time. This method did give me some sort of structure to start with. Then I had to see many people. All of both Ralph's and Adeline's families were tremendously helpful, as were many friends. Little by little the work took shape. Michael and I shared all the material according to which book it seemed to suit, and kept lists of each other's problems – mostly of dating events – to answer if we could. It was strange, and sometimes desolating, to explore so much unknown territory, and to re-live the parts of Ralph's life I had not known. To see him as a child, a young man, a soldier, a struggling composer and to be unable to ask him about those days or to be with him while he lived through them. Time was quite changed, for I lived as much in his past as in my own present.

Indeed, there were many questions I had never asked. Elsa and Lohengrin, Bluebeard and his last wife are well known examples of doing the wrong thing, which one takes to heart. It is no good anyway to ask: "Were you happy?", for who can tell, when years have overlaid days. And would one really want to know if the answer was no? – and could one bear to say it of years of life? And if the answer was yes, as the best part of one would like it to be, would one be wise enough not to feel the anguishing tentacles of jealousy? And what, in the end, does it matter when the certainty of one's own shared happiness is filling the present and all the past has led one to it? Biographers must try to find answers to such questions, but at the same time behave to the dead as to the living, with good manners, modesty and respect. About other things, though, there were many questions I should have asked Ralph if he'd been there. Some could be answered more or less factually by people who'd known him far longer than I. Maud Karpeles knew about his song collecting activities, and she had been at most of the earlier as well as the later first performances of his works. Steuart Wilson had been his friend since early in the century. Bobby Longman had been at many Leith Hill Festivals and had known about London amateur music making. Herbert Howells, Adrian Boult, Arthur Bliss and Paddy Hadley were friends of long standing and each of them made it their business to find any information I needed and told me of events and of music making they had shared.

While all this was going on I got in a state about leaving Hanover Terrace. The house was ridiculously big for me, though Frank Hollins, still living in the mews house, asked if he could use some of it as spare bedrooms for his friends, and although Gil was still there and I still had friends to stay, often the LeFanus, and the Hornsteins, or Frances Cornford. But once, when I found myself cooking breakfast for nine people, I knew that I could easily find myself turning into an amateur caravanserai, so I started looking for a small house. I'd persuaded our cook, Edna, to adventure to America, and though the housework was looked after by an ex-daily who now lived in, it was not a sensible permanent arrangement. In a frenzy I found two houses I thought I liked, and a flat over the RAM which was then empty, and I paid deposits on them all. Then sense prevailed and I stayed on till I'd finished my work with Imogen, cleared up all the music and assembled much of the biography material.

Meanwhile, I wanted something for myself, a proof perhaps of my own continued existence as I was so deeply committed to living through Ralph's life. All my books of verse were out of print except the last 1950s pamphlet and I had quite a number of unpublished poems. Through the good offices of Veronica Wedgwood, Hutchinsons had seen my typed collection and were prepared to publish it. I was unhappy though when they made it a condition that I should use my married name rather than the name of Wood, which I had used always for all my published work. I explained that I had never wished to use Ralph's name for my work, and that I was, mildly, established as a writer in my earlier name. But nothing I could say made any difference. It was too soon after Ralph's death for me to be able to be as tough about it as I should have been later, and though I knew it was a mistake, I allowed it to happen. They sold some five hundred copies in the first year, then no more. When I enquired why, I discovered that they'd moved their stocks to a new warehouse, damaged the remaining volumes of mine in the process, and without telling me, had pulped them. I felt terrible about this, being totally out of print and having had to change my identity in the process.

Imogen and I finished our work on the book of letters which we called *Heirs and Rebels*[90]. It came out in the autumn of 1959 and had a lot of cheeringly good notices. That winter the New Opera Company staged Elizabeth Maconchy's *The Sofa* at Sadler's Wells in a double bill with *The Drought* by John Joubert. Betty and I spent a number of evenings at rehearsals in a chapel off Lisson Grove. I think it was once Benjamin Haydon's[91] studio, in which he gave parties after Hazlitt's lectures. In our day it was a dreary place but we enjoyed ourselves and despaired, in about equal amounts, as I had long learned that one does at rehearsals. The producer, Michael Geliot, was very young, and we had to explain the procedure at balls, for instance, that chaperones sat around the room, and did not dance (there were some extra women in the chorus for this production) and that everyone, men and women, wore gloves. We felt that we were, probably, the last survivors of an age that had gone to such festivities, but we were startled when we discovered that word had got round that we had both been at the Eve of Waterloo Ball in Brussels. As it was a workshop production I found myself much involved in helping with wardrobe problems, for the choice was limited to a collection of hireable old clothes

---

[90] *Letters between RVW and Gustav Holst*, ed. Ursula Vaughan Williams and Imogen Holst (OUP 1959)
[91] Benjamin Haydon (1786-1846): painter and author

from a sub-department of the Wardrobe of Sadler's Wells kept in a house a few doors up the road from the theatre. Michael Geliot and I blundered about in the confined spaces between dress racks, clutching lists of measurements of the cast, and later I spent a good deal of time inventing decorations for hair, based on old fashion plates. This was an amusing occupation involving combs, feathers, flowers, sequins and glue, and I eventually helped with the disguise of the all-important sofa. I disposed of some flat-heeled soft shoes I'd had to descend to when recovering from an immobilising sprained ankle. Decorated with buckles they achieved an honourable end on the stage.

I had thought that I might have no further involvement with the musical profession. Being a non-musician myself it seemed more than likely that I should not go to any more rehearsals, and to concerts only as audience. But it turned out quite differently. Ralph had been President of the Composers' Guild, and I'd gone with him whenever he went to the Guild's annual lunch. Very charmingly they invited me the winter after his death, and continued to do so. The secretary of the Guild, Topsy Levan, became a friend, and as the Guild's premises were in some sort of pantry at the Arts Council's headquarters in St. James's Square, they had nowhere to entertain. So when Kodály[92] came to England they asked if they could use my house for a party for him. He was asked whether he would prefer it to be six to eight or at eight thirty. He said firmly seven o'clock, as he always went to bed at nine. We groaned as this obviously meant food. So Topsy, the composers Betty Maconchy and Thea Musgrave and I spent a hard day concocting rather a lot of supper, with a garden lunch picnic for ourselves. It was a warm evening, so we arranged a little group of chairs on the balcony where Kodály could give audience to one or two musicians at a time. This worked well, food and drink held out, for we realised before long that 'bed at nine' was a device to protect from boredom. Eventually Kodály left about midnight, and

---

[92] Zoltan Kodály (1882-1967): Hungarian composer and teacher

the party had obviously been fun for him, and everyone seemed to have had a chance to talk to him as well as to each other. My session was enlivened by his rather surprising demand "Tell me, now, are all English composers boggars?" He swivelled his chair round to look at the cheerful groups whose chatter drifted through the open windows. "Well?" he said. "Not that one – not that one, not that one," I said waving my hand dismissively at various well known heterosexuals. "Oh," he said, "So. Not all?" He had remarried very recently but the Hungarian Government had not allowed his wife a visa to come to London with him, though she was allowed to go with him on later visits.

Steuart and Mary Wilson continued to come to stay with me when they were in London, and I sometimes stayed with them in Birmingham[93] for concerts. We all enjoyed each other's company, and it was good to be with someone who had known and loved Ralph as Steuart had for so long. When they went to India in 1960 they suggested that I should come out to spend Christmas with them in Goa, "the only place where you can drink", said Steuart. I'd never been to the East at all, and although I was not far on with the biography, I thought that it was time for a proper holiday, and it was settled that I should go out in early December. But, sadly, Mary got polio and died at the end of November. Steuart went on with his examination tour and did not return to England until much later.

At this time Adeline's nephew, Adam Curle, and his wife Anne, who was a friend of my friend Kanty, were at the University of Ghana, just outside Accra. His mother, Cordelia, was living with them. They invited me to stay, as exciting a prospect as Goa had been. The dates fell out very happily for me, as I started the holiday with two days in Rotterdam where the Russian pianists Victor Babin and Vitya Vronsky were to play Ralph's piano

---

[93] where Steuart Wilson was Principal of Birmingham School of Music (1957-60)

concerto. I'd met them at the Edinburgh Festival (where they had played the work a year earlier), to which I'd been with Simona Pakenham. They were a totally congenial couple, and we'd seen each other in London where I'd caused them to meet the Hornsteins. The ensuing chatter in Russian, with occasional asides to me such as: "Darling, why do you not speak Russian?", and a lot of English as well, made a sort of honorary Russian of me when I was with them. For this journey I went with Yanya Hornstein who had business in Holland. We whipped round Amsterdam on a boat trip and went to Rembrandt's house between arriving by plane and catching a train to Rotterdam.

I had not been to Holland before, and the little landscapes of windmills and fields of bulbs were astonishing. The flowers looked awful as crops. Paintbox stripes of tulips or bright pink acres of hyacinths were hideous. But at the hotel I found them in a delectable, welcoming bunch from the orchestra. The concert was splendid, and after there was a supper party, then a long talking session in the Babins' room at the hotel – literature, music and the soul, the expected Russian mixture. Next morning I flew to Rome, where I was lucky enough to be lent a British Council car for sightseeing. I did not want to go to the places I had been with Ralph so I went to look at old Ostia. The first purple stocks were out, growing on the ruins, and long summer grasses where lizards were enjoying the sun. Dinner was in a Roman Palazzo, with Mr. White of the British Council as host, and I caught a midnight plane for Accra. I woke just as the first dawn light showed endless-seeming desert. But it did end, and it was like seeing the beginning of history, a ridge of hills, a road, scrub, forests, and with clear daylight I could see the tall silk-cotton trees and the gothic anthills. We stepped into the hot lovely air of Africa and there were the Curles, all welcome, and the strangeness of Ghana.

I had never thought about Africa at all in terms of sight, and I was very soon aware that everything was different from any place I had ever seen. I did not know the names of any tree or bird, while flowers such as frangipani had been only names to me before. The afternoon of my arrival we went to a wedding in a Methodist church. The bridegroom was the Curles' gardener's brother. He was, like many of the congregation, dressed in a dark European suit. The bride, almost too pregnant to be out and about, wore trailing white lace, her child bridesmaids were in blue and pink, and a whole lot of relations arrived dressed in gorgeous tribal clothes, one carrying a spear. It was a good beginning to my stay.

The University was new, spacious and grandly situated, the staff international and everyone was easily friendly. There were also mysteries. How had it come about that when an artificial lake was made in the new botanical gardens a pair of crocodiles arrived the day after it was filled with water?

There were pleasures everywhere. The nests of tailor birds like little parcels hung on trees, village street markets with a vulture perched above each stall to tidy up after the selling was done, then taking off into the sky with a purposeful and noble flight.

Though I enjoyed shopping in Accra, the most exciting times were when we spent weekends in rest houses. One was on the borders of Togoland, in woods and hills, with new sounds of birds and new smells at night, one at Cape Coast. There we stayed in a dramatically beautiful Portuguese slave castle. It was above the town and a little outside it. We swam from a sheltered sandy beach in the warm sea, and then sat on the terrace drinking. Adam and Anne had a very sound feeling for drink and managed supplies of ice with competent ingenuity. We watched the fishing-boats come in at dusk, and then women carrying baskets of fish on their heads, walking through the streets, hi-life (the local pop music) sang from every house, the light grew rosy over the sea and the inland marsh, while little lights shone between trees beyond it. Then, from the other castle, right on the headland, which was a police barracks, there came the unexpected sound of the Last Post.

Later, I stayed in a hill village some miles out of Accra with David Brockensha. He taught in the university but had taken a house in Larteh where he had made friends with the people who lived there. I had become interested in all I had read about the shrines and the priests and priestesses who worked in them, and the healing and the magic that still prevailed. So, as there was a particularly famous shrine in Larteh, David invited me to stay. The house in which he lived had been built fifty years or more, and was stone. The lower floor was haunted, and locked. The top floor which he had rented was cool and had a view over the plain below to the sea. I heard the ghost one night. We had been sitting out on the porch looking at the stars till late, and I went to sleep directly I was in bed. I was woken by a great deal of noise from the room below mine. It sounded as if people were blundering about and falling over furniture, not at all frightening but – I was glad that I was not alone in the house. No Africans would come near the place after dark. David told me that he had often heard these noises and had been downstairs with a torch to look for intruders but he'd never found anyone there.

He was much liked in the village and while I was there we were invited to breakfast with the widow and brother of the late chief, as well as for drinks with the present chief. He invited us to come at 9am and gave us gin and tonic to drink and told us a lot of splendid stories; one was about a tune played for the Durbars held every year, when the Governor General would bow grandly to the cheering crowds. "Only," said the Chief, "he never discovered that the tune was one played after a great victory, and was about the defeat of the enemy, and everyone else there, all the band and the crowd and the army, of course, knew this, and cheered loudly while the poor man sat in his carriage bowing and beaming at the applause." He showed us his regalia; he was a friendly, but immensely grand and impressive man. Another village character I visited several times was the goldsmith. He was very tall and thin and wore glasses. His assistant was a boy of twelve or so. They lived in a very plain hut where all his work was done with the simplest of equipment, a charcoal fire, two or three little saucepans, and cuttlefish which he used as moulds, carving in them beautiful elaborate designs, some traditional, some original, with a sharp knife, and little scraping tools of which he had, and needed, very few. He made me a pair of earrings in a few days, and it gave me great pleasure to see the pure gold of the fishes swallowing their tails, brilliantly golden on the back of his dark hand as he held them out for me to look at. That bright gold, like the brilliant clothes men and women wore, looked so much more beautiful against the glowing African skins than against European pinkness. It was a continual pleasure to the eye to watch the inventive dresses, the beauty of the walk and the general nobility of appearance of almost all the people in Ghana.

My only regret in Ghana was that I was not a painter. If I could have chosen, I would have liked, for that time, to be Rubens. The beautiful exuberance of flesh, the glow and the movement, the colours of fruit and cloths, all people walking like princes, was intoxicating to see. It was terrible to remember the bits of chain, the manacles and leg irons left as chastening reminders in the slave castles of what had been done to these proud and delightful people, and into what exile they had been driven. Not that they did not find problems enough in Western ways, as they adapted from pastoral life to the mechanised and un-seasonal life of the commercial present. I cannot be grateful enough to Adam and Anne for showing me such an unfamiliar world, such an enlargement of experience.

I went home by way of Malta, staying there for a few days. As the plane flew low over the sea and circled towards the island, I recognised the square fortress of Verdala, then the Dragonara

Palace, then the Grand Harbour. Though many years lay between my twelve-year-old departure and this return, memory was clear enough to recall names and places most vividly. I walked about Valletta remembering the streets whose names had been changed from Italian to English at the beginning of the war. My birthplace, the Auberge de France, was a hole in the rock, having suffered a direct hit, but the little row of houses in Windmill Street was there still. The opera house had gone, but the kiosk where we bought flowers remained. Later I looked at our old quarter in Tigné and saw that the present inhabitant, the O.C., was someone I had known slightly when he was on one of the young officers' courses while we lived at Porton.

I came back to London to the house I had bought the summer before, and into which I had moved on my fiftieth birthday. It is in Gloucester Crescent, which was in those days a bit down at heel. The house had been fun to do up, having the ravages of many years' neglect put right, and it was with the feeling of making a new start in life that I plunged into more work on Ralph's biography. Michael Kennedy and I, with Roy Douglas to advise, were in frequent consultation, and at a party given by the Oxford Press to celebrate William Walton's 60th birthday we, aglow with champagne, gave a date on which we promised to deliver the books. When that day came we took our bulky manuscripts down to the publisher at Amen House. There was a queer patch of time waiting for our scripts to be read, then a final session for each of us with a few revisions and, in my case, making some fairly substantial cuts, then another hiatus till the first proofs came for correction. The most awful task followed with the page proofs, namely compiling the index. Michael's was a far more serious horror than mine, for he had to compile a complete and fully detailed list of works, an index which is a model of thoroughness and gives the information that answers all questions researcher or performer could need, and for which I have been immeasurable grateful. My own job seemed bad enough, but I was helped by Gil Jenkins, and finally we completed a set of cards with names and page numbers in alphabetical order, and handed it over with great relief.

I found life very empty then. It had been my first prose book, and it was the only time I had lived with a work in progress as the background of my life for several years.

By now my first tenant, who had lived in the basement flat, the Hornsteins' second daughter Renata, had married and had been succeeded by a young composer, Jeremy Dale Roberts. Jeremy had been a great encourager when I'd had black times with the biography and now he dared me to write a novel.

For this I linked two episodes, the film John Schlesinger had made in Cornwall and a long holiday I had shared with a party of friends in a little caique sailing round the Greek islands. I had been invited to join in this pleasure by the Day Lewises when we were all at Coventry for the Festival[94]. I had gone there with Steuart Wilson, not long home from India, and though he hadn't been when we planned the jaunt, happily about to be settled with Margaret Stewart who became his wife soon after. It was an exciting Festival, with first performances of Michael Tippett's *King Priam* and Benjamin Britten's *War Requiem*. It was lovely to see how warmly Steuart was welcomed by all the musicians there. He'd left Birmingham rather sadly, but he had not been, as he over-modestly supposed, forgotten, and that, and the promise of a new chapter with Margaret made him blossom. He and I were dining with Michael and Eslyn Kennedy, and Jill and Cecil joined us. They were very soon going to Greece with this party and they suggested that I might like to come too. It was all arranged very briskly, and for three weeks we lived a blissful life, in a most uncomfortable little boat. The company was stimulating, the weather mostly good, though we had one memorable storm, and the places magical. We were lucky, too, in having a brilliant cook, a fat, smiling little man who produced

---

[94] Held for the consecration of the new Coventry Cathedral

imaginative meals for the seventeen of us from a galley about four feet square.

In 1964, while I was already working on this novel, my biography and Michael's book were published[95]; the Oxford Press had a party on the publication day and I had one of a less official kind the next day. We had very good notices, though I was a little saddened that they were all written by musicians so my book was never reviewed as a biography, but as a life of a musician, and so read only by people interested in music.

The novel, *Metamorphoses*, was published by Duckworth two years later. By then I had done some more work for composers and started another novel, *Set to Partners*, which was published, again by Duckworth, two years later.

With Jeremy Dale Roberts in the house, it was pleasantly familiar to hear the sounds of a composer at work. Ralph's piano was in my sitting-room, and when I was out he had the use of it. Sometimes he played for Morag Beaton, a singer who had drifted into my life first when I was about to go to Italy and I had no one to look after the cats, and later she used it as a base between tours and engagements. She is as bad a correspondent as one can find, so it did not surprise me very much when she turned up after months in Australia in Joan Sutherland's company with three fur coats and no taxi fare, and at other times with delightful friends. One was the tenor Joseph Ward, of whom we all saw a great deal when the American composer Bernard Herrmann[96] cast Morag for Cathie in his opera *Wuthering Heights*. Bennie was a most extraordinary man. He had written the music for a great number of distinguished

---

[95] Ursula Vaughan Williams: *R.V.W. A Biography of Ralph Vaughan Williams*, OUP, 1964; and Michael Kennedy: *The Works of Ralph Vaughan Williams*, OUP, 1964

[96] Bernard Herrmann (1911-75): composer and conductor. Wrote 49 film scores, many of them for Hitchcock

films. *Citizen Kane* and *Psycho* are perhaps the most famous, but beyond that he seemed to have known and have known well almost every composer from Charles Ives onwards, to be knowledgeable about their work, as he was about painters and writers. He was, at first sight, a tough-looking, broad-shouldered and rather heavy man, given to wearing an improbable pale blue beret. But when he was listening to music, or to talk, his face showed grave beauty, and one became aware not only of his erudition but of his sensitivity as one got to know him. But he could be tough. He awarded me the rehearsals for the opera, because he was staying near, because he hadn't got a piano, and because Jeremy could play for him and his singers. Donald Bell was his Heathcliff, Joe Ward, Edgar, so with Morag as well as Jeremy in the house it was a practical arrangement. Donald seemed to grow taller and taller and paler and paler, Morag cried a great deal while Joe and Jeremy grew thinner and thinner and Bennie hotter and hotter, mopping his face in anguish and rage. I found it diplomatic to bring in whisky at regular and rather frequent intervals and when it came to the first recording session at Barking Town Hall I found many people I knew assembled to form the orchestra. One asked me what I was doing there. I heard my voice say "Prisoner's friend". After days of tempest and desperation a very good record emerged. It was sad that there was no stage performance to follow. Quite soon after this Bennie married Norma Shepherd and they came to live close to the Park, so we saw each other frequently. Both were devoted to their animals, a dog and some cats who they'd brought over from California, and who accommodated themselves to a house full of the most beautiful furniture, pictures, books and china. Benny asked me to write the libretto for an opera for him, but films kept coming to him and the necessary time for such a long undertaking kept receding. So, though we talked about it, and my first draft was long finished, it was one of the many things he was still planning when he died.

Working for and with composers is an exciting and an exacting business. It is one I have much enjoyed, partly because of the involvement with performance, I suspect; an immediate excitement and stress that books do not allow, for once the proofs are done it has all gone beyond recall, and the finished job is silent on the shelf. Words for music are of two kinds – those already written, chosen by the musician because they start a tune for him, and those written to meet a specific need.

In 1950 when Ralph and Bernard Shore asked for a cantata for schools they left the subject to me and accepted my idea, based on a Jewish legend told me by Canetti, that the angels of creation were the letters of the alphabet. Of course this was not enough material for a work[97] that had to last for about half an hour, so a bundle of other legends went in, starting with light and darkness, the horses of the sun suggested by those of the Parthenon pediment, the rearing heads of those drawing Apollo's chariot at morning and the tired horse at the further end whose bent head arches down towards the rim of night. Next came my first lesson in construction. "Something with short lines, a contrast section," said Ralph. So that was easy, the stars and man's use of them to define the seasons and to navigate the seas, then the original idea, a poem about words, with a triumphant place for man who has named all things. Still more was needed, so another section had to be fitted in for this. We had a quatrain for each of the creatures of the Zodiac which gave scope for a lot of contrast in the line of both voices and instruments.

Ralph asked me for a text for his contribution to *A Garland for the Queen*, so for that I wrote *Silence and Music*, a subject about which I had thought a great deal. Music is, for me, a foreign language rather than a native tongue. I understand it to a degree, and love some of it, but I do not know the grammar. I can go with it to some distances, and I think I can perceive the differences between truths and banalities, but I am not on the same footing as I am with words.

---

[97] *The Sons of Light*

I am very bad at some composers. I have a total disability for Elgar and Brahms: after their music I feel an urgent need for something very clear, plainsong or madrigals. Also, I know that I am unduly affected by words set to music. If I can't take the words of songs I often miss the pleasure of the music to which they belong, as well as being offended when poems I love and cherish get settings I don't take to. But I try to learn as much as I can from every kind of word setting. Another problem, almost an infliction sometimes, is that having been married to Ralph it seems generally assumed that my likes and dislikes must be the same as his. I have met with a good deal of surprise and even disapproval, and "surely your husband did not feel / think / believe this or that?" and I have answered that I speak for myself not for him. To begin with, I don't enjoy organ music, nor a lot of piano music, and I detest hymns; even when they have fine tunes they rarely have acceptable sentiments. And I can't bear going to churches except for the pleasures of architecture or sometimes for concerts; so, tempering dislikes with as good manners as I can manage, I dodge the events I know I shall disenjoy as far as possible.

When Anthony Milner[98] asked me to write a piece for the opening of the re-built Great Hall at the University of Bristol he added a major obstacle. He wanted to end the work with the hymn "Now thank we all our God". So my part had to lead to a big vocal and unison climax in a hymn – not the easiest of tasks. I thought that as we were celebrating a rebuilding, it would be suitable to write about building materials, of stone broken from the quarries to change from the structure of a mountain to walls and pillars, of trees summoned from forests to make floors, and of the dyes and colours to make adornments for the rooms, linking it to the cities of the imagination of mankind as well as to actual architecture. All this fitted and suited Anthony's plan. On our way to Bristol by an early train we were enjoying a leisurely breakfast in the dining car when a horrid thought struck me. I must have turned pale for Anthony

---

[98] Anthony Milner (1925-): English composer and teacher

said: "What is the matter?" "Do you think they'll have used reinforced concrete and plastic?" "Oh," he said, "I hadn't thought of that either." We could hardly bear to wait to see. But all was well, stone and wood, curtains and colour were there. Another hazard had been recognised, and luck was on the librettist's side. But next time, I thought, if I ever have to do anything about a building I shall ask for the architect's address.

Next came Charles Camilleri[99], wanting a script for a one-act opera. I felt that we should have a Maltese story, he being Maltese and I Maltese born. This caused us a lot of hilarious research, and most of the stories involved very large and clanking sea serpents, bronze towers and other difficult scenic impedimenta, but eventually we found a plot, one with a touch of the Psyche story, *Melita*, or *A Cup Full of Tears*. A cup full of tears is what it turned out to be for Charles and for me, for we had been promised a theatre performance in the Belfast Festival of 1968, and what we got was a school hall, a producer who had, it seemed, never before produced an opera, singers who had insufficient rehearsal time, a designer who disregarded my pictures of Maltese costume, including the faldetta, and general despair over the whole thing. However, Ralph's cousin Peter Montgomery was at hand with comfort and reassurance, so were Ruth and Philip Cranmer, and Michael Whewell of the British Council and his wife Doreen, who all sustained, supported and comforted us through a disappointing week. I should have loved to produce it myself. Perhaps, one day, it may go home to Malta, or be done somewhere where we can have a suggestion of that magic world where the sea and the white villages have their secrets and their stories.

One day I answered the telephone and a completely strange voice said "Would you like to write an opera – about Heloïse and Abelard?". I said "I don't think it would work. Too static mostly and anyway, how long?" "Oh – one act", said the voice.

---

[99] Charles Camilleri (1931-): Maltese composer and conductor

"Impossible", I said, "that would be all tiny scenes, couldn't make a good shape." "Well then, what?" the voice asked. "David and Bathsheba?" I suggested. "Yes, that might do. Will you do that?" "But," I said, pulling myself together, "Who are you and where are you?" "David Barlow[100]," he said. "Can we meet and talk about it?" So we did, and we found it made a very good one-act story, with four main characters and the usual devices of a maid, a sentry and a soldier to suggest and define time and place and the world outside the passions and relationships of David and Uriah, Bathsheba and the dark-voiced prophet. I did not see the performance in Newcastle as it was on the day that a friend had a major and very dangerous operation and I was with his wife who is one of my oldest friends. But I was able to hear a piano rehearsal and the music seemed exciting though I longed to hear it with the orchestra. David and I had met several times to talk about the things he wanted, but never for long and usually in a Chinese restaurant, where we sat with exercise books among the little blue and pink dishes heaped with rice and delicious fragments.

I think that it was a good collaboration, though I never knew David well. He died a few years after this, and so far the opera has not been revived. This is of course one of the troubles about one act operas, for it is very difficult to fit them into any repertoire unless they are 'Cav. and Pag.'[101] even when they are as magnificent as my favourite of all one-act operas, Bartók's *Bluebeard's Castle*. Probably the best place for them will be on television, where an hour long opera, or even a shorter one, may be acceptable.

While I had been writing *David and Bathsheba* another and much longer work was in rehearsal. Two years earlier Malcolm Williamson[102] had been commissioned to write a work for the

[100]David Barlow (1927-75): composer and teacher. Senior Lecturer, Newcastle upon Tyne University, 1968-75
[101] *Cavalleria Rusticana* (Mascagni) and *I Pagliacci* (Leoncavallo)
[102] Malcom Williamson (1931-):Australian composer, Master of the Queen's Music from 1975

National Federation of Women's Institutes. He invited me to think of a subject and to write the words. This was an interesting and challenging task. Ralph had written his *Folk Songs of the Four Seasons* for the W.I. years before, with the sensible arrangement of numbers that were easy, more difficult and difficult, so that differently sized and differently talented choirs could take part, with some songs for the whole company. This seemed to me a good principle, and one Malcolm approved. We were to be allowed soloists, men too, if we liked. I felt, though, that it would be more sensible to write for women only. It seemed to me that the history of England seen from the women's point of view might be a possible idea. I wrote the first number, for chorus and soloist, for Malcolm's approval. This was about the Battle of Hastings – Senlac, when Harold's mistress, Edith Swan-neck had been allowed to search the field for his body. From this episode on it was interesting to explore the situation in which women had found themselves. The wives of crusaders, girls waiting for the sailors to come back from the New World, witches, nuns dispossessed at the Dissolution of Monasteries, storytellers, dancers after the Restoration, and on to the Victorians, and finally the war workers in the wars of our own lifetime.

The librettist, as Ralph had long ago pointed out to me, is the junior partner in any shared enterprise. Sometimes one finds one's best lines are disguised by counterpoint, drowned by the orchestra, or otherwise lost. And often one longs for a hand in production, but on the whole I've found the composers for whom I have worked sympathetic and amenable to suggestion, and no acrimonious letters have passed for the entertainment of posterity. I've worked with seventeen musicians so far[103], and in each case – from a short carol to a three-act opera – I've been faced with interesting and varied problems of texture, of variety of how many characters are wanted,

---

[103] These lines were written in 1972. There have been other collaborations since then; all are being catalogued for eventual publication

and of trying to keep the staging as simple as possible. The challenges are endless and stimulating, and each work provides a mixture of excitement and despair. Usually a lot of the worry is due to the difficulties and expenses of adequate rehearsal. I have in my time arranged Chaucer – *The Pardoner's Tale*, for a cantata written by Roy Teed – translated folk songs, written a one-act opera with acting parts for opera students,[104] an opera for a school[105] and words for set subjects – *St Cecilia* for Herbert Howells, *Compassion* for Phyllis Tate, and a long piece of verse, *The Icy Mirror*, for Malcolm Williamson's third, and choral, symphony. The latest excitement has been a three-act opera on a subject chosen for me – the death of Philip of Macedon and the accession of Alexander the Great, for Roger Steptoe, the first resident composer at Charterhouse. This was a marvellous commission for history provided an exciting story that falls neatly into three acts and an array of truly operatic characters.

About 1971 I found that I was on twelve committees of various kinds. This was obviously ridiculous, so I removed myself from those on which I felt the least useful. The busiest at that time was the Governing Body of the Royal Academy of Music which celebrated its 150th anniversary in the same year as Ralph's Centenary. This was a very odd affair for me. There were many commemorative concerts, and though I was immensely glad that so many people wanted to celebrate, and wanted me to share the celebrations, I did feel like a bit of the true cross being bandied about. Or perhaps, more realistically, the remainder biscuit after a long voyage.

I had once been to Berlin with John Barbirolli to hear him conduct Ralph's Fifth Symphony and for a very interesting week of sightseeing, with the terrible menace of the Wall bounding all conscious enjoyment with its despair, and I'd loved the two

---

[104] *Stars and Shadows*, music by Brian Hughes
[105] *Serenade*, music by Anthony Scott

concerts, the marvellous sound of the Berlin Philharmonic Orchestra, and John's well known and magical interpretation of Ralph's music. Now in 1972 the Saint Louis Choir and Orchestra invited me to come over for their performances of the *Sea Symphony* in New York and Washington, in March. This was an irresistible invitation, and adding to all their kindnesses they gave me a first class return ticket, and most lavish hospitality. It was fascinating to be wafted over the Atlantic in a haze of champagne, and lovely to find that I was met by Larry Taylor, a musician who, for a few months, had succeeded Jeremy Dale Roberts as my tenant when Jeremy married. With him was the orchestra's PRO, Richard Freed, and between them everything was made easy. I have a lot of friends in New York, and some of them were able to come to the concert. The Curles had gone to Harvard from Ghana, so Adam was able to be with me for the evening. Larry Taylor and I did a little sightseeing, the only free morning I had was spent happily at the Frick collection. There were lunches and dinner parties and in between visitings I was able to see Rebecca Friskin[106], a very particular friend, beautiful and amusing as few late octogenarians manage to be. She came to one of the lunch parties, and back to my hotel for a long gossip afterwards. Richard Freed went on to join the orchestra in Washington and I followed after four days in New York. I had supposed that I should spend all my time in Washington at the picture galleries as I knew only one inhabitant there, but it was quite otherwise. Malcolm and Dolly Williamson were staying in Washington, and had a host of friends. John Owen Ward of the Oxford University Press was there, and one thing led to another in the way of shopping, party going and general conviviality.

On the day of the concert Walter Susskind, who was then the St Louis conductor, and his wife, the chorus, orchestra and I were all asked to tea at the White House, at the curious hour of two thirty.

---

[106] Rebecca Clarke (1886-1979): British composer of chamber music and songs

This was a fascinating experience. We were allowed – or invited – to go early and we had a chance to look at the public rooms. They were full of lovely furniture and some interesting pictures. Most of the earlier Presidents' portraits had been painted after they had lost their teeth, and they looked forbiddingly nutcrackerish. Someone had arranged flowers superbly in all the rooms, not formal set pieces, but bowls of garden flowers that gave a touch of intimacy to the grand surroundings. A military band played and we formed in a long queue to shake Mrs. Nixon's hand. A photographer was in attendance but he missed the Susskinds and me, so we had to go round again to be immortalised. Then after a tea of the most deliciously greedy kind, the choirmaster, unadvisedly I thought, started some of his singers on the *Serenade to Music* which he accompanied on the grand piano. I was standing next to Mrs. Nixon, and with a look of – what was it? One woman to another? One art lover to another? – she took my hand. I was acutely embarrassed for I knew how long the *Serenade* is and she didn't, and 14 minutes is too long to hold hands. But we managed to detach, and the *Serenade* faded into the general chatter of thanks and departure.

Then there was time to go back to the hotel and to get ready for a long evening for there was a large reception given by the British Embassy before the concert, then the concert itself at the Kennedy Centre, with some sort of extra party in the interval, and finally another party somewhere else in the Centre with pop music and a huge supper followed by the distribution of very odd presents. I was given a baseball cap, which – added to the security check badge, given to us before we went to the White House, which said 'Home's Where the Heart is, if it's St Louis' – made amusing trophies to bring home.

Both performances of the *Sea Symphony* were good, and it was a pleasure to hear Whitman's words sung by an American choir who, I gathered from some of those I'd met at the party, had enjoyed studying the work. I had the same report from Darwin Apple, a friend of Larry's who played in the orchestra and had stayed with him in London. I was sorry when this wildly crowded week was over and Richard Freed drove me to Dulles airport. He had been a wonderful Cicerone all through my visit, and very good company. It was a night flight home, and I was met by my American friend and neighbour Jean West, which rounded off the jaunt delightfully.

I'd written the text 'The Icy Mirror' for Malcolm Williamson's Third Symphony, and that had its first performance at the Cheltenham Festival[107]. Not too happy a concert, for there had been the usual problems of under-rehearsal – the difficult score needed more than could be afforded. But it was, as always, a pleasure to be at Cheltenham for the Festival and to find so much good company there.

The City of London Choir gave a series of concerts of most of Ralph's choral works, well worked-out programmes for which they asked me to write the notes. I had been asked to do programme notes for many of Ralph's works, and to write little articles to do with gramophone record releases and so forth, as well as choosing the sleeve pictures for EMI recordings. This was an enjoyable job, for I was able to find pictures well related to the music and ones that looked decorative on the sleeve, for which the notes were frequently written by Michael Kennedy. When I was asked, as I frequently was, to talk about Ralph or about his music, I refused, except for a few music magazine programmes for the BBC on special subjects. For though I know his music well, and have been to most of the EMI recordings, and they cover almost all the work, I do not feel able as a non-musician to give a lecture that would be of any interest. And people, in their quest for knowledge, forget that it is quite a different matter to write a biography, which is to some extent an objective task, than it is to talk about a life that is close to one's own. There was one talk that I did give on the one subject I

---

[107] 1972

felt I could manage – the texts Ralph had set to music. This was for the Royal Musical Association, an august body of which I had for a very short time, at Cedric Glover's[108] instigation, been a member. But I was far too unlearned for their evenings and removed myself from membership pretty soon. I was full of apprehension as I worked on my script. I'd talked about this subject once before at one of Mabel Ritchie's summer schools, but then there had been few recordings for illustration, and now there were many, which made it easier. I felt very nervous as I saw the audience arrive, among them many friends and acquaintances. Then I overheard one amazed stranger-to-me say to another, "I've never seen them line up to kiss the lecturer before", and began to feel better, and in the end I enjoyed myself. Also, as the text of the lecture was later printed, I knew I should never have to give it again.

One more Ralph book remained to be done, a picture biography which I did with John Lunn. He is a doctor who had made a collection of photographs gathered from all sorts of sources I had not explored, local papers and photographers in towns where festivals are held. We put our collections together and worked on the pattern of the book in big scrap books; I wrote the captions and lists of works. When we told Alan Frank[109] about it and showed him the amount of material we had, he agreed that it was promising and the OUP published our picture book in the winter of 1971.

I did, too, an Apollo Society programme for which I was lucky enough to have a marvellous cast. John Westbrook read all the Ralph pieces – letters, and from his own writings; Gabriel Woolf all the other words. We were allowed two musicians, and I wanted a baritone. Benjamin Luxon was available, and he and Philip Ledger completed the group. Philip started with Ralph's first piece, the four-bars-long *The Robin's Nest*, written when he was six, and Ben

---

[108] Cedric Glover: an old friend of Ralph Vaughan Williams and amateur musician
[109] Alan Frank (1910-94): Head of OUP Music Department, 1954-75

Luxon ended with the unaccompanied setting written in 1958 of Blake's *Mercy, Pity, Peace and Love*. The first performance was at the Purcell Room, and later it was done at the Royal Academy of Music, at the King's Lynn Festival, at Stroud, and it was also broadcast, when John Noble was the singer.

There was a film in the making too, with many of Ralph's friends involved. The producer was Stanley Williamson, and it was made for Norman Swallow's *Omnibus* series. Stanley and I went to France to see where Ralph had been with his ambulance unit in the first war, and I was startled to find that his battlefields of the Somme country were not far from Crècy. Not only the war cemeteries but the acres of corn and orchard grew from the bones of history.

One nice episode of this film-making happened in the Director's Room at the RCM. Keith Falkner, Director of the RCM, was there, and so were Jean Stewart, the cameras and sound recording team, Stanley and I. Herbert Howells was being interviewed about the first performance of the *Tallis Fantasia* at Gloucester. "Yes", said Herbert, "I remember well talking about this work of which we had heard strange rumours, with my fellow students, Ivor Gurney and..." the beautifully calculated pause, then: "... Ivor Novello". The camera stopped, the sound recording stopped. "Did you *know* Ivor Novello?" the question came in awe-struck voices. "Yes," said Herbert coolly, "I used to do his counterpoint for him".

I spent several days in the cutting-room watching the work done there, and whenever, as must be the case often in such affairs, I felt depressed, Paul Jefferies would run the sequence shot at Charterhouse backwards, so that the boys would back briskly up the steps and vanish into the chapel. When that too, was completed, I felt that I had done all I could to be a bridge between Ralph and both present and future.

Now my life should be a leisurely one, but it never seems to be. I have, for about twelve years, been a member of the Musicians' Benevolent Fund Committee and involved with the acquisition of houses for retired musicians. This has been vastly interesting, and I've enjoyed the house part of the work enormously. The problems of those who live in them is quite another matter, a practical problem and a question about the end of life. To make living conditions easy and agreeable for people no longer able to sustain the wear and tear of managing room, flat or house is one thing, to make some sort of community from an agglomeration of separate solitudes is another. With generosity and good manners something of the kind can be managed, but living as a one-age group, a camp on the shores of death, is difficult, a difficulty that can be disregarded by day – but, one wonders – possibly not by night, when loneliness prevails? However, everyone does all each of them can to make life as happy as may be, and sometimes it can be very pleasant, when the weather is fair and the garden doors are open to summer, and though I'd love to see houses for old people combined with lodgings for students – something that would have much to offer both groups – this does not seem possible at present. It would certainly provide, naturally, the drama that is needed to make the even tenor of elderly days bearable – and is a natural condition in youth.

The Trust Ralph and I started in 1956 is more lively. For ploughing his performing rights back into the fabric of music we have a big mixed-age committee and between us we usually have some knowledge of each applicant. We have seen a number of successes, and have had a hand in many performances, and our meetings are pleasurable for we all enjoy each other's company. Gil Jenkins was our first chairman, and he was succeeded by Michael Kennedy.

Two other committees meet less often at Cecil Sharp House, where I used to dance; I served on the Library Committee and I became Chairman of the Trustees at the Music Information Centre. All these are interesting commitments. I have been a member of the Governing Body of the Royal Academy of Music for about eight years and that too has brought many interesting problems and pleasures, friendships and chances to hear performances by the beginners in the profession who become swans, it seems, as soon as they take wing, while people I remember as young performers are now among the venerable professors[110].

These are all the external happenings, the day to day interests and involvements that use what time and circumstances have taught me practically. But when it comes to wondering what time has taught me for myself, it's gossamer stuff – now you see it, now it's lost.

There is a square in Floriana in Malta, where there are round stone lids in a huge pattern like some sort of draughtsmen lying on the ground.   These are the covers of underground granaries of the Knights, and in them the corn could be hidden and preserved. It is an analogy for age, too; these are the many harvests, each year's gathering, much forgotten, much neglected until some sudden word, some look, colour, music, uncovers a treasury, brings back to vivid recreation a day, a feeling, a character or a place in which I can re-live what was once wholly engrossing. So again I can be young, as well as old, with long-dead friends as easily as with the living, idle in a summer place as I am busy with winter necessities, and always hovering on the edge of magic and of wonder because it is still all there, always aware that this is both true and untrue, for none of these memories is more than the mirage of reality. Like the actual granaries where there's a little dust, a few old husks of corn left to remind the historians of the harvests they held once as a safeguard against famine.

FINIS

---

[110] It should be recalled that these lines were written in the 1970s.

Index

Aberdeen, Marchioness of, *see* Gordon, June
Ackland, Valentine, 195
Africa, 204-7
America, United States of, 176; visits to, 177-9, 218-20
Armstrong, Sir Thomas, 191
Apple, Darwin, 220
Arnold-Baker, Mary (*née* Norris), 53, 57, 62, 63, 66, 83, 90, 93, 100-1, 116, 117-8, 130, 144, 169
Arnold-Baker, Richard, 92, 100-1, 130, 144, 169
Arundell, Dennis, 183
Ashcroft, Dame Peggy, 53
Austria, 88, 188-9

Babin, Victor, 203
Baillie, Dame Isobel, 167
Balcon, Jill, *see* Day Lewis, Jill
Barbirolli, Sir John, 169, 173, 181, 194, 196, 217-18
Barbirolli, Lady (Evelyn), 169, 181, 194
Barcroft, Prof., 35, 42
Barlow, David, 215
Bax, Sir Arnold, 181
Baylis, Lilian, 48-9, 55, 140
Beaton, Morag, 210, 211
Beerbohm, Sir Max, 98, 99, 134, 146
Bell, Donald, 211
Benjamin, Arthur, 190
Benson, Sir Frank, 18
Bettws-y-Coed, N. Wales, 51-2, 58
Bishop, Christopher, 184
Blackheath (Red House), Surrey, 13, 14, 15, 17, 24, 62
Blackwell, Sir Basil, 101, 106, 129
Bliss, Sir Arthur, 200
Blunden, Edmund, 134
Bottomley, Gordon, 129, 140
Boughton, Kathleen, 185
Boughton, Rutland, 185
Boulay, Veronica de (cousin), 21, 22
Boult, Sir Adrian, 161, 167, 175, 187, 195, 196, 200
Bowen, Kenneth, 184
Britten, Benjamin (Lord Britten of Aldeburgh), 209

Brockensha, David, 206
Brown, Sir John, 197
Browne, Harold, 184
Brussels, 22, 31, 33, 44

Camargo Society, 56
Camberley, 5, 6
Camilleri, Charles, 214
Canada, 93-5, 113, 130, 178
Canetti, Elias, 146, 212
Canetti, Veza (*née* Calderon), 146
Cecil Sharp House, 80-1, 83, 89, 90, 223
Clarke, Rebecca, 218
Clapp, Cleeva, 68
Clopstoun, Georgina, 41, 44
Cole, Dr. William, 167, 172, 187
Cole, Winifred, 172
Cooper, Francis, 65
Cooper, Joseph, 90
Cooper, Kanty, 65, 66, 108, 118, 125, 168, 203
Cooper, Mrs, 65
Cooper, Paul, 65
Cooper, Ursula, 65
Corfield, Frederick, 93, 143, 145
Cornford, Frances (*née* Darwin), 183, 200
Cornwall, 10-11, 31, 60-1, 100, 151-2, 180
Craig, Edward (Teddy), 54
Craig, Edward Gordon, 54
Cranmer, Arthur, 167
Cranmer, Philip, 214
Cranmer, Ruth, 214
Cullen, Margery, 160
Curle, Adam, 115, 116, 203, 204-5, 218
Curle, Anne, 203, 204-5, 218
Curle, Cordelia (*née* Fisher), 128, 136, 145-6, 162, 168, 203
Curle, Pamela, 115
Curtis-Raleigh, Nigel, 147

Dale Roberts, Jeremy, 209, 210, 211, 218
Darwin, Charles, 167
Davies, Meredith, 184
Day Lewis, Cecil, 168, 174, 209
Day Lewis, Jill, 168, 170, 209

de la Mare, Guilbert, 26, 27, 28
de la Mare, Kathy, 26
de la Mare, Miss, 26
de Ropp, Robert, 142
Devonport, 2, 3, 5
Dolin, Sir Anton, 56
Doniach, Shula, 158
Douglas, Roy, 191-2, 193, 197, 208
Dowling, Denis, 174
Dyson, Ruth, 160

Easebourne, Sussex, 7, 9, 12, 13, 14
Edinburgh Festival, 204
England, Mr & Mrs, 67
Epstein, Sir Jacob, 125, 158
Epstein, Lady (Kathleen), 158
Evans, John, 133

Falkner, Sir Keith, 176, 177, 222
Ferguson, Howard, 184, 185
Fermoy, Lady (Ruth), 167
Ferrier, Kathleen, 112
Field Reid, Mary (*née* Carter), 169
Field Reid, Jerry, 169
Finzi, Christopher (Kiffer), 151, 152, 171, 184, 191
Finzi, Gerald, 126, 134, 142, 143, 151, 171, 182, 184, 185, 186
Finzi, Joy, 126, 129, 143, 151, 152, 171, 172, 182, 184, 185, 190, 195
Finzi, Nigel, 151, 171, 184
Foss, Hubert, 174
Fox, William, 53
France, 68-72, 153-4, 165, 180-1
Frank, Alan, 221
Freed, Richard, 218, 220
Friskin, Rebecca, *see* Clarke, Rebecca

Galliver, David, 164
Geliot, Michael, 201, 202
Gibbs, Evelyn, 92, 112, 155-6
Glanville-Hicks, Peggy, 186
Glover, Cedric, 146, 169, 221
Goddard, Scott, 167
Gordon, June, Marchioness of Aberdeen, 187
Goring, Marius, 53, 54

Graham, Morland, 53-4
Graves, Beryl, 186
Graves, Robert, 186
Greece, 180, 209-10
Greene, Eric, 184, 185
Griller Quartet, 132
Grinke, Frederick, 176
Grout, Prof. Donald, 177, 178, 179
Groves, Sir Charles, 171

Hadley, Dr. George, 148, 163, 190
Hadley, Jean, *see* Stewart, Jean
Hadley, Margaret, 191
Hadley, Nicola, 191
Hadley, Prof. Dr. Patrick (Paddy), 166-7, 184, 200
Hallinan, Victor, 46-7, 48
Hanover Terrace, London, 169, 173-5, 183, 189, 193, 200
Harrison, Tom, 164
Hemmings, Peter, 184
Hermann, Bernard, 210-11
Hermann (*née* Shepherd), Norma, 211
Hess, Dame Myra, 126
Hicks, William (Bill), 10, 11, 31, 143, 180
Hicks, Alice, 10, 11, 31, 180
Hicks, Roddy, 31
Hollins, Frank, 172, 175, 180, 195, 201
Holst, Gustav, 186-7, 198
Holst, Imogen, 45, 198, 200
Hornstein, Genia, 152, 165, 167, 189, 195, 200, 204
Hornstein, Renata, 209
Hornstein, Yanya, 152, 165, 200, 204
Howden, Clare, 125, 133, 147, 148, 155, 163, 166
Howells, Dr. Herbert, 185, 200, 217, 222
Hughes-Hallett, Miss, 22
Huxley, Sir Julian, 179

Ireland, 181
Isle of Wight, 74-9, 83-6, 87, 93-4, 95-8, 99, 112, 182
Italy, 22, 175-6, 180, 192-3; honeymoon in, 169-70

Jacques, Reginald, 112
Jefferies, Paul, 222

Jenkins, Sir Gilmour, 142, 155, 162, 163, 168, 169, 172, 181, 186, 189, 195, 196, 200, 208, 223
Joubert, John, 201

Karpeles, Dr. Maud, 88-9, 90, 98, 107, 108, 112, 126, 150, 199-200
Keen, Malcolm, 53, 54
Kelly, Sir Gerald, 192
Kennedy, Douglas, 80, 81, 88, 89, 90, 93
Kennedy, Eslyn, 181, 184, 194, 209
Kennedy, Helen (*née* Karpeles), 93
Kennedy, John, 93
Kennedy, Michael, 173, 181, 184, 194, 197, 199, 208, 209, 210, 220, 223
Kenny, Richard (Dick), 83
Kidd, Joe, 132
Kisch, Eve, 90
Kittermaster, Meriel, 164
Kittermaster, Ronald, 164
Kodály, Zoltán, 202-3

Laurie, John, 54
Ledger, Sir Philip, 221
Leeds, W. Yorkshire, 9, 10, 163
LeFanu, Elizabeth, *see* Maconchy, Elizabeth
LeFanu, William, 188, 200
Leith Hill Musical Festival, Dorking, 90, 159-60, 169, 187, 191, 200
Levan, Topsy, 202
Lewis, Sir Anthony, 164
Lindsell, Wilfred, 3
Livesey, Roger, 53, 54
Lock, Lady (Beryl) (mother), 1, 5, 6, 11, 12, 13, 14, 16, 18, 22, 29, 30-4, 35, 39, 43, 48, 49, 60, 64, 80, 93, 94, 130, 144-5, 169, 181-2, 189
Lock, Frederick (uncle), 16, 136
Lock, Alice Elizabeth (Grandmother), 3, 6, 7, 8, 9, 17, 156; death, 14
Lock, Henry (uncle), 17
Lock, John (brother), 4-5, 8, 11, 12, 13, 14, 18, 19, 22, 24, 28, 29, 38, 39, 57-8, 63, 64, 83, 93, 94, 117, 143, 145, 167; death, 131-2
Lock, Lily (aunt), 16-17
Lock, Mary (aunt), 17
Lock, Muriel (aunt), 17
Lock, Perceval (uncle), 17, 51
Lock, Peter (cousin), 17

Lock, Maj.-Gen. Sir Robert Ferguson (father), 1, 3, 4, 5, 6, 11, 16, 18, 21, 25, 29, 30, 31, 33, 34, 35, 37, 39, 42, 43, 47, 48, 49, 57, 59, 60, 64, 80, 87, 93, 94, 108, 130, 131, 144-5, 169, 181-2; death, 189

Lock, Rosemary (sister), 13, 19, 22, 39, 46, 58, 92, 93, 94, 113, 115, 144-5, 182, 189, 190

Lock, Vera (cousin), 51

Lock, Walter (uncle), 17

Long, Kathleen, 125, 142, 153, 173

Longman, Robert G. (Bobby), 200

Lovett, Leon, 184

Lund, Engel, 92, 113, 124, 130, 162

Lunn, Dr. John, 221

Luxon, Benjamin, 222

MacCarthy, Sir Desmond, 140, 165-6

MacLeod, Eileen, 124

Macaulay, Rose, 124-5, 140

Maconchy, Elizabeth, 188, 200, 201, 202

Mahoney, Hettie, 149

McKie, Sir William, 170, 196

Maitland, Florence (*née* Fisher, later Darwin), 183

Maitland, Prof. Frederic, 183

Malta, 1, 3, 18-21, 22, 72, 207-8

Marriot-Smith, Col., 30

Miller, Hugh, 124

Miller, Olga, 124

Milner, Anthony, 213-4

Montgomery, Peter, 214

Montgomery-Massingberd, Gen. Sir Archibald, 36

Montgomery-Massingberd, Lady (Diana) 36, 193

Moore, Enid, 177

Moore, G. E., 146

Moore, Gerald, 170, 177

Moore, Sturges, 140

Morison, Stanley, 141

Morris, Emmie, 135, 159

Morris, R. O., 119, 120, 127, 133, 135, 145; death, 159

Morrison, Angus, 166

Mukle, May, 113

Müller-Hartmann, Robert, 113

Mulliner, Michael, 176

Musgrave, Thea, 202

Nathan, Nora, 113, 124, 130, 141
Nathan, Dr. Paul, 113, 122-4, 129, 130, 133, 139, 154, 166; death, 141
National Gallery Concerts, 108, 122, 126, 130, 132
Nevinson, Evelyn (*née* Sharp), 92, 106, 107, 188
Nevinson, Henry, 89, 92, 106-7, 188
Noble, John, 184, 222
Norris, Mary, *see* Arnold-Baker, Mary
Novello, Ivor, 222
Noyes, Alfred, 93

Old Vic, 48, 49, 52, 53-5, 59, 66, 140, 164
Olivier, Sir Laurence (Lord Olivier), 194
Ord, Boris, 183
Oved, Moshe, 118, 172

Pakenham, Simona (Mrs Noel Iliff), 194, 204
Painswick, Glos., 24, 39, 65, 94, 110, 150
Pearsall Smith, Logan, 140
Penton, Arthur (grandfather), 1, 2, 4, 9, 11, 111; death, 14
Penton, Emilia Matilda (Mittie) (grandmother), 2, 3, 6, 9, 10, 11, 13, 15, 21, 22, 24, 25, 39, 44, 50, 65, 94, 121, 149; death, 110-11
Pollock, Ann, 73
Pollock, Jocelyn, 73
Portland, I-o-W, 74-9, 83-7, 112
Porton, Wilts, 30, 31, 33-50, 51, 57, 59, 61-2, 87, 143, 144
Potter, Beatrix, 52
Potter, Stephen, 128
Propper, Erica, 194
Purscher, Alfons, 112
Purscher, Nora (*née* Wydenbruck), 112

Quayle, Anthony, 53, 164

Rainier, Priaulx, 112
Rauter, Ferdinand, 113, 124
Raverat, Gwen, 56, 183
Redgrave, Sir Michael, 164
Renault, Mary, 45
Rhys, Ernest, 89, 92, 93, 101, 118
Richmond, Sir Bruce, 181
Richmond, Lady (Elena), 181
Ritchie, Mabel (Margaret), 221

Ritchie, Pegs (Meredith), *see* Spring Rice, Pegs
Roach, Helen, 96, 97, 99, 112
Rome, 22, 169, 176, 204
Rosé Quartet, 112
Rouira, Jane, 103
Rowntree, Dr. Ray, 189, 195
Rubbra, Edmund, 171
RVW Trust, 186-7, 223

Sackville-West, Edward, 129
Sadler's Wells, 55, 92, 201
Salkield, Dr. John, 189
Sargent, Sir Malcolm, 191
Schlesinger, John, 151, 153, 209
Scott, Anthony, 195, 217*n*
Scott, Ruth, 195
Shakespeare, Col., 18, 23
Sharp, Cecil, 188
Sharp, Evelyn, *see* Nevinson, Evelyn
Shore, Bernard, 161, 212
Short, Mea, 61-2
Short, Walter, 61
Sim, Alastair, 53, 54
Spring-Rice, Pegs, 163
Squire, Sir John C., 44
Steptoe, Roger, 217
Stewart, Jean, 90, 91-2, 101, 102, 108, 110, 114, 125, 127, 142, 143, 145, 147, 148, 163, 169, 190, 222
Stewart, Marjorie, 56, 113
Stone, Dr., 39
Strong, Leonard, 112
Sturgess, A. B. (Bert), 186-7
Susskind, Walter, 218-19
Sutherland, Dame Joan, 210
Sutton Veny, Wilts, 5, 10, 150
Swallow, Norman, 222

Tate, Phyllis, 217
Taylor, Larry, 218
Taylor, Noel, 191
Teed, Roy, 217
Thayer Street 7.5, London, 90, 92, 93, 94, 101-2, 107, 108, 115, 122, 125, 133, 142, 145, 163, 167, 173

Thistleton, Frank, 186
Tippett, Sir Michael, 194, 209
Toscanini, Arturo, 91
Trevelyan, Robert (Bob), 112, 126, 129-30, 134, 139-40, 140-1, 146, 148, 166
Trowell, Brian, 184

van Oye, Mlle, 31-2
van Wyk, Arnold (Nols), 142
Vaughan Williams, Adeline (*née* Fisher) (RVW's 1st wife), 82, 92, 99, 115, 119, 120, 127, 128, 129, 133, 135-6, 137, 145-6, 149, 150, 159, 161-2, 183, 199; death, 162
Vaughan Williams, Hervey (RVW's brother), 116-17; death, 137
Vaughan Williams, Dr. Ralph, 23, 36, 56, 80, 88, 89, 90, 91, 92, 108, 112, 113, 115, 116-17, 120, 123, 125-8, 133, 134, 135, 137-8, 143, 145-6, 147, 148, 149, 150, 158-9, 161-2, 163, 164-9, *et passim*; first meets Ursula Wood, 82-3; operation, 190; death, 195-6; works discussed: Symphonies, No.5, 127-8, 158, 217, No.6, 158, *Sinfonia Antartica*, 169, 190, No.8, 179, 181, No.9, 191-2, 195; *Hugh the Drover*, 92, 99, 170, *Sir John in Love*, 164, 183, *The Pilgrim's Progress*, 127, 158, 161, 162, 163, 183-4, *The Poisoned Kiss*, 188, *Thomas the Rhymer*, 193; *49th Parallel*, 127, *Coastal Command*, 127, *Scott of the Antarctic*, 158; *Job*, 56, 80; *Hodie*, 171, 176-7; *Valiant for Truth*, 119; *The Old 100th*, 170, 171; *Silence and Music*, 171, 212; *The Bridal Day (Epithalamion)*, 80, 89-91, 93, 128, 174; *An Oxford Elegy*, 165, 168; *The Sons of Light*, 212
Vaughan Williams, Ursula (previously Wood, *née* Lock), birth, 1; schooling, 21-2, 22-3; mastoid operation, 15-16; Girl Guides, 20; riding lessons, 20, 28, 34; 1st boarding school (Bussage), 25-6; St Margaret's Folkstone, 26-9; confirmation, 27-8; finishing school in Brussels, 31-3; life at Porton, 33-50; submits work to *London Mercury*, 44; meets Michael Wood, 43, 45; meets his mother, 47-8; Old Vic audition, 48-9; engagement to Michael, 49-50; 1st acting job at Old Vic, 53-5; marriage, 59-61, 62-79; German measles, 64-5; holiday in Provence, 68-72; 7.5 Thayer St., 90, 92, 93, 94, 101-2, 107, 108, 115, 122, 125, 133, 142, 145, 163, 167, 173; 1st letter to RVW, 80; 1st meeting with RVW, 82-3; meets Adeline, 98-9; Michael's death, 114-15; and funeral, 116; at White Gates, 98-9, 115, 119, 120-1, 127, 133, 135-6, 143, 145-6, 162, 172; working with Dr Nathan, 122-4; fire-watching, 111-2, 122, 127, 133; meets Finzis, 126; brother's death, 131-2; reviewing for TLS, 134-5, 140-1, 158; 1st performance of *Peter Grimes*, 143; Hiroshima, 143-4; Three Choirs Festival, 149-50, 163, 164, 171, 176; Paris Visits, 153-4, 165; Care Committee work, 154-5; death of Adeline, 162; marriage to RVW, 169; move to Hanover Terrace, 169; formation of RVW Trust, 186-7; 1953

Coronation, 170-1; visiting Italy, 169-70, 175-6, 180, 192-3; USA and Canada, 177-9; Majorca, 185-6; father's death, 189; RVW's 85th birthday, 190-1; RVW's death, 195-6; Abbey service, 195-6; visit to Africa, 204-7; Gloucester Crescent, 208; writes RVW biography, 197-200, 208-9; biography published, 210; USA again, 218-20; life after RVW, *passim*
Vernon Harcourt, Bernard, 75, 96-7
Vernon Harcourt, Gerd, 97
Vernon Harcourt, Mrs, 75, 96-7
Vernon, Stephen, 4
Vronsky, Vitya, 203

Waley, Arthur, 29, 129
Walton, Lady (Susana), 192-3
Walton, Sir William, 192-3, 208
Ward, John Owen, 218
Ward, Joseph, 210, 211
Warner, Sylvia Townsend, 195
Webber, Margaret, 152
Webster, Sir David, 163
Wedgwood, Lady (Iris), 137, 146, 163, 168, 169, 185
Wedgwood, Dr. C. Veronica, 23, 26, 56, 146, 147, 200
Wedgwood, Sir Randolph (known as Ralph), 137, 146, 163, 168, 169, 185
West, Jean, 220
Westbrook, John, 221
Westerham, Kent, 64, 72, 80
Whewell, Doreen, 214
Whewell, Michael, 214
White Gates, Dorking, 98-9, 115, 119, 120-1, 127, 133, 135-6, 137, 145-6, 149, 159, 162-3, 165
Willcocks, Sir David, 184
Williams, Harcourt, 49
Williamson, Dolly, 218
Williamson, Malcolm, 215-216, 217, 218, 220
Williamson, Stanley, 222
Wilmott, Betty, 102, 190
Wilson, Lady (Mary, 2nd wife of Sir Steuart), 163, 203
Wilson, Lady (Margaret, 3rd wife of Sir Steuart), 209
Wilson, Sir Steuart, 150, 163, 165, 168, 200, 203, 209
Wood, Christopher (brother-in-law), 58, 87, 109, 116, 137
Wood, Lt.-Col. (John) Michael (James Forrester) (first husband), 45, 46, 47, 48-9, 50-2, 56, 57, 58-9, 60-79, 83-4, 87-8, 90, 92, 94, 95-6, 98, 100, 101, 106, 107, 108, 109, 111, 114-15, 118, 119, 121, 135, 137, 159; first

meeting, 43; wedding, 59-61; father's death, 47; death, 114-15; funeral, 116

Wood, Mabel (mother-in-law), 47, 50, 51, 52, 58-9, 87, 92, 108-9, 111; death, 110

Wood, Rodney (brother-in-law), 58, 59, 87, 108-9, 114, 116, 119

Wood, Ursula (*née* Lock), *see* Vaughan Williams, Ursula,

Woolf, Gabriel, 221

Woolwich, London, 5, 13, 22, 24, 25, 30, 51, 57-8, 63, 64, 87